Program Evaluation

Program Evaluation

Alcohol, Drug Abuse, and Mental Health Services

Edited by

Jack Zusman
Gateways Hospital, Los Angeles
Cecil R. Wurster
National Institute of Mental Health

Lexington Books

D.C. Heath and Company
Lexington, Massachusetts
Toronto   London

Library of Congress Cataloging in Publication Data

Main entry under title:

Program evaluation: alcohol, drug abuse, and mental health services.

Includes papers presented at the Conference on Evaluation of Alcohol, Drug Abuse and Mental Health Service Programs held in Washington in 1974.
   Includes index.
   1. Drug abuse—Treatment—Evaluation—Congresses. 2. Alcoholics—Rehabilitation—Evaluation—Congresses. 3. Mental health services—Evaluation—Congresses. I. Zusman, Jack, 1934-   II. Wurster, Cecil R. III. Conference on Evaluation of Alcohol, Drug Abuse and Mental Health Service Programs, Washington, D.C., 1974. [DNLM: 1. Evaluation studies. 2. Alcoholism—Rehabilitation. 3. Drug abuse—Rehabilitation.   4. Community mental health services. WM30 E923]
HV5825.E93   362.2   75-6276
ISBN 0-669-99929-6

Published simultaneously in Canada

Printed in the United States of America

International Standard Book Number: 0-669-99929-6

Library of Congress Catalog Card Number: 75-6276

Contents

List of Figures

List of Tables

Foreword

This is the eve of a revolution in the provision of human services. The forces that are changing services for the mentally ill and for drug and alcohol abusers include the prospect of national health insurance, peer review, and quality control; the impact of legal guarantees of the right to treatment and confidentiality; the many different service models now available; and the taxpayers' insistence that their money truly provide service to those in need.

The power propelling all of these trends is the push toward accountability. For administrators and frontline helping professionals, this call for accountability comes as a welcome opportunity for demonstrating a job well done, and it carries with it the threat of exposing a job poorly done. For legislators and policymakers, it offers the prospect of establishing or dismantling social programs on the basis of merit rather than politics or other considerations. For private citizens, the new demands on administrators, together with renewed attention to civil rights and human dignity, promise that their concerns—the citizens' needs and the citizens' taxes—are treated with respect.

Somewhat utopian as these expectations seem now, they are nevertheless sensible. They are the ends we all seek. They are the goals that have brought about significant progress in evaluating human service programs.

This book reflects that progress. Based on a conference that was planned under the auspices of the National Institute of Mental Health, the book is a source of pride to those of us who sit on the accountability firing line. It seems only yesterday that we started our first evaluations of the "bold new approach" to care of the mentally ill. Unexpected snares and traps lay in the way. More experienced now, we know some of the difficulties—technological and political— that confront evaluation. We know, for example, that two kinds of evaluation may be necessary—one an economic and political analysis of the services offered, the other an evaluation of the success in meeting goals set for each individual who has received service. Both types are considered in these pages. So, too, are the problems and rewards awaiting those who conscientiously try to evaluate human service programs.

The conference itself also reflected the progress made in the past decade in evaluation. It covered philosophical issues, but it also confronted the practical, methodological problems in doing everyday evaluation. Although some 200 prospective participants had to be turned down before the conference began, more than 750 did take part—program directors, administrators, clinicians, planners, evaluators, researchers, and biomedical experts. This intense interest in evaluation was also evident when, during preparation for the conference, about 200 abstracts describing ongoing evaluation projects were submitted for presentation.

The authors who contributed the papers that make up *Program Evaluation: Alcohol, Drug Abuse, and Mental Health Services* are drawn from the ranks of the best evaluation experts. Their combined efforts represent the first true state-of-the-art report on mental health service program evaluation; they go a long way toward doing the same for evaluation of drug and alcohol abuse services. But the book is more than that; it provides a tool for refining the evaluation of all human service programs.

Bertram S. Brown
Director, National Institute of Mental Health

Introduction

Jack Zusman and *Cecil R. Wurster*

This book has been prepared in an effort to bring together reports, comments, and impressions from leading authorities in the areas of evaluation of alcohol, drug abuse, and mental health service programs. Although a number of specialized monographs dealing with segments of these fields are available, we felt, as changes were coming so rapidly and the literature was so widely scattered and difficult to locate, that we could be of great help to those concerned with evaluation if we brought together summaries of the latest information in one place.

The idea for the book grew out of a conference on Evaluation of Alcohol, Drug Abuse, and Mental Health Service Programs, sponsored by the federal Alcohol, Drug Abuse, and Mental Health Administration. This conference, held in the Spring of 1974 at Washington, D.C., was planned by a number of advisory groups whose members were drawn both from inside and outside the federal government and from individuals working in all of the related fields. The advisory groups had the mandate to select as speakers at the conference the leading experts then currently active in the various subject areas to be covered. Following selection, each of the experts was invited to prepare a paper on a carefully defined topic. In almost every case the initially selected experts agreed to participate and, therefore, we can say without hesitation that the conference speakers consisted of the very best group obtainable in the United States and elsewhere at that time.

Papers presented by the conference speakers became the nucleus for this book; they were revised by their authors and then edited for publication. In addition, a number of other individuals were asked to prepare chapters for the book either as a result of their participation in the proceedings of the conference or because of their well-known expertise in an area of importance that had not been adequately covered at the conference.

The subject of evaluation is very fashionable at present. For years a great variety of governmentally supported programs have required evaluation efforts and a number of agencies at various levels of government are devoted exclusively to evaluation of one sort or another. Increasingly, evaluation is becoming a subject taught in graduate programs relating to human services and it is not uncommon for local, even minimally funded, service agencies to expend a significant fraction of their scarce resources on employment of an evaluator. As proponents of the importance and usefulness of evaluation, we view these developments with mixed feelings. We are pleased at the great interest in a field that has been our own major interest for a number of years and that for a good part of this time seemed to be sadly neglected. On the other hand, we are concerned that evaluation should not be viewed as the answer to all of the problems service agencies currently face and that the high hopes — many of them unrealistic — currently being expressed for evaluation efforts should not lead shortly to an equally unrealistic discouragement.

Evaluation, like many of the key words of the health and mental health fields, is a term widely used and apparently universally understood but rarely, if ever, defined precisely. (Words in a similar situation include "illness," "treatment," "psychotherapy," "acute," "chronic," and the terms "health" and "mental health" themselves.) E.A. Suchman pointed out in 1967 that the looseness of definition leads to wide disagreement within the evaluation field, general interchangeability with other terms, and lack of a clear understanding of the basic requirements of evaluative research.[1] The situation has not improved markedly since then. Slightly differing definitions of evaluation or evaluation research can be found in a number of the major publications of the field.[2] The definition offered by E. M. Gruenberg[3] seems general enough to encompass all of the others while still specific enough to offer some guidance. *Evaluation research* is "analysis of program effectiveness, the use of scientific method in appraising the success of community health programs."

Beyond the issue of definition of evaluation and evaluation research is the categorization of the various types of studies. Among the leading systems proposed in the literature are those of G. James[4] and A. Donabedian.[5] (See J. Zusman[6] for a discussion of similarities and differences among approaches to categorization.)

Regardless of the particular definition used and the way in which categories are organized, there does seem to be a good deal of agreement among all of the experts as to what type of work is included and what the underlying theories and methods of the research include.

In principal, evaluation is rather simple and easily understood. A service of some sort is offered by an agency or practitioner to a patient, client, or community group. To carry out an evaluation, a set of goals for the service is established. The goals may be simply to provide some elements of a service in a particular way or to produce some change over a period. A method is decided upon to measure the accomplishments of the service toward the stated goals, and measurement then takes place. Finally, a comparison is made between the goals and the service accomplishments as determined through measurement. The closer the two are, the better the service has performed.

It is important to note that this model of evaluation is not restricted to what some feel is the essential or even the only question of evaluation: "Has the service done any good?" This — *outcome* — is indeed a central question for evaluation, but need not be the only one. In many cases, for one reason or another, it must be assumed that the service, when properly offered, is effective, and evaluation study is focused upon whether or not the service is properly offered — *process.*

We are aware of the introduction of the concept of "goal free evaluation" by M. Scriven.[7] However, this seems to us not to be a basically different approach, but simply to be a slightly modified form of outcome evaluation in which goals are not set by the agency but by some external authority.

Many of the benefits of evaluation are obvious. Indeed, they are so obvious that one must wonder why, in spite of its professed popularity, evaluation is performed so infrequently, relatively speaking. It would seem that problems in doing successful evaluation may be large and pervasive.

For the consumer of any sort of service, as well as for the purchaser (if consumer and purchaser are different, for example, in the case of third party payment), the most obvious point to evaluation is that it facilitates comparison among the offerings of a number of similar agencies and practitioners and a choice of the one that is best. Were evaluation studies widely carried out and publicized, it would be possible to prepare *Consumer Reports* types of listings of agencies. Consumers could then make informed choices and those responsible for funding could have information very useful for making their appropriate decisions. Without this type of information, selection of a service is essentially a blind process, relying mostly upon the impressions of individuals who have neither the expertise nor the information necessary to make decisions and upon the testimonials of agency employees who have a vested interest in supporting and protecting their agencies.

Evaluation makes it possible to go even a step beyond comparison among the services of similar agencies or practitioners to compare the services in relation to the costs. Cost-benefit or cost-effectiveness studies are essential in a situation where resources are limited and concern is not to determine the best possible work an agency can do, but with the work it does in ordinary circumstances under its usual constraints.

From the perspective of those inside the agency, evaluation studies provide both the impetus and the information to facilitate improvement. Without the systematic, specific, and presumably unbiased criticism resulting from an evaluation study, improvement is difficult, if not impossible, even with the best of intentions. For the agency or practitioner basically uninterested in improvement (if such exists), the knowledge that the nature and quality of service will not be a secret but will be exposed to the scrutiny of others or of the public is likely to be a strong stimulus to raise the interest in improvement.

The need to specify agency or practitioner goals — which is the first step in an evaluation study — is of benefit to all concerned. Without this specificity, it is all too easy — particularly in the mental health field — to fall into a pattern of carrying out treatment without first agreeing upon the problem at which the treatment is aimed, or the degree of improvement that will be considered success. Through specifying objectives, the client or patient is able to know what he will get and when his desires have been satisfied. The worker is able to know precisely what he is aiming for and when to terminate treatment. Occasionally the process of specification of goals serves to make it clear that there is no need for service or that the need cannot be met by the agency in question. This, too, is a major contribution to treatment.

Evaluation is a process — a service, and like any other service it requires expenditure of resources. Evaluation does not come free but has its costs, which sometimes are very high. One of the reasons evaluation work is not done more often by service agencies is that it requires the diversion of resources that otherwise could go into serving the public. When faced with the alternative of taking care of more clients or turning applicants away in order to evaluate the service, most agency administrators will choose to accept the clients and forego the study. This is particularly so in the absence of any external pressure to carry out evaluation.

The costs of evaluation, however, are not only in terms of expended resources. Evaluation can distort the work of an agency by requiring the agency to focus on overly specific goals and usually a small number at that. The evaluation process may lead to the slighting of important elements of service that are either not easily specified or left out of the list of goals. The temptation for agency workers may be to "treat the case record" rather than to treat the client, to be certain that examination of the record leads to a positive evaluation.

Finally, there are a myriad of minor but significant costs to agencies and clients that must be taken into account. These include, for example, the interference in agency work that results from the evaluator's presence; the risk of breach of confidentiality from the need of evaluators to examine agency records; the frequent need for agency staff to complete forms and procedures required by the evaluators but not by the agency's work; and the risk to the agency's reputation when evaluation study results are released inappropriately or interpreted incorrectly.

In addition to the costs of evaluation, there are significant difficulties.

Goals of most agencies and practitioners are numerous, subtle, and sometimes impossible to specify. For example, even where the goal of an agency devoted to treatment of alcoholics appears to be simply to reduce or eliminate clients' drinking, the agency is also very concerned with the clients' quality of life once drinking ceases. It would be of little use to produce a high rate of abstention among the client group, which then led, for example, to an equally high rate of suicide or drug addiction. Further, the agency's objective may be to have its clients stop drinking completely or to have them drink in limited quantities under approved circumstances. Quite possibly the former is an appropriate goal for some clients, while the latter for other clients. In that case, how does one determine which clients fall into which group. The problem is even more complex in an agency where the primary objective is not as clear-cut as in an alcoholism treatment agency, for example, an agency devoted to improving the quality of child rearing among its clients.

The choice of goals for an agency is a difficult task and the particular set of goals selected depends in large part upon who is designated to choose the goals.

Agency employees, professionals, are likely to be concerned with certain goals and aspects of service. Clients and/or members of the general public are likely to be concerned with others. Higher level public administrators are likely to be concerned with still others. If the goal-setting group contains representatives of all three segments and the resulting goals are compromised, professionals may well wind up feeling that the goals against which their work is being measured are professionally inappropriate and ones toward which they cannot work. Even when a set of goals can be agreed upon, in most cases the number and disparity of individual goals will require some weighting of means of comparison among them. This is another area where the various groups will differ widely.

Once done, the evaluation study is likely to produce a mass of statistics that then require interpretation. If, in spite of all of the obstacles and temptations, the study has been objective — "scientific" — up to this point, it cannot remain so during the interpretation. Particularly in the early stages of the development of evaluation as a field — the point at which we are now — evaluations are planned and carried out in relative isolation. There is little basis upon which to compare the evaluation of one agency with any other. What does it mean that an agency is somewhat effective with 50 percent of its clients for example, and has no effect on the other 50 percent? Does this mean that the agency is doing a poor job and its funds are being wasted, or does it mean that the agency is doing the very best that can be expected with a difficult group of clients who would be far worse off without the agency's intervention? How much prominence should be given to the fact that some of the agency's clients grow worse as a result of agency intervention in comparison with the fraction who improve? When an agency administrator and his staff are brave enough to permit an outside evaluation of their work and the report seems to cast a negative light upon them, should the results be kept confidential, or be made available publicly? If the results are publicized, will this not discourage other agencies from permitting evaluations? Might not the apparently poor rates of success still be better than other similar and unevaluated agencies would get? These are knotty questions that require careful consideration not only to avoid unfairness to any of the parties concerned, but also because inappropriate or unfair use of evaluation reports will discourage use of evaluation generally by community agencies. (In many communities the traditional first step in reducing the budget of an agency or in wiping it out has been to have "an evaluation.")

A final problem with evaluation, perhaps the most important one, is that most evaluation studies have negative results, that is, they are unable to demonstrate the effectiveness of the program under study. In spite of the professional and public consensus that an agency is having some impact on its clients, often the study shows none. P.H. Rossi, in discussing the work of J.S. Wholey and his group in evaluating maternal and child health programs, describes how data is likely to be fragmentary; estimates have to be made without the necessary foundations for appropriate estimates; only a small fraction of the individuals assumed to receive the service have actually done so; and the maximum possible effectiveness of the service is less than had been thought.[8] Each of these factors is enough to bury the evidence of effectiveness of the service without a trace and thereby unfairly and inaccurately label the agency as ineffective.

It seems no wonder then that evaluation studies are so rare and when carried out, so freely disregarded. The field is in its infancy and every evaluation study must be looked upon as an experiment, a unique situation that can be generalized from only with great caution if at all.

Yet, in some circles evaluation is being offered as the answer to many of the difficulties that presently beset social welfare services. Evaluation is seen as the panacea that will control or even wipe out such pervasive and unpleasant aspects of services as rapidly increasing costs, stable or diminishing worker productivity, low success rates and increasing numbers of applicants. But evaluation cannot solve these problems. A brief consideration of past experience and present conditions reveals why.

As has already been discussed, evaluation is not an objective process – it is a sociopolitical one. Even when it is possible to design a clean experiment that ought to provide valid, clear-cut results, interpretation of these results is almost always a matter of opinion. More commonly, it is not possible to carry out the study design as scientific standards dictate. Shortcuts, approximations, and estimates must be used. In this way opinion, judgment (or misjudgment), and chance factors can become as strong or stronger elements in determining the study outcome than the factors under study. Under these conditions it is understandable that those whose interests are threatened by a negative evaluation study attack the study and refuse to respond to its implications.

Evaluation studies properly done are very costly and often interfere with the service they are studying. It is a rare situation when the service administrator can afford to undertake to pay the cost of a study large enough to evaluate his service properly. Most often, a small inexpensive study is supported – one that cannot possibly yield meaningful results.

Many programs are not amenable to the effects of evaluation regardless of any lip service given by administrators and agency workers. The agency is not prepared to change its ways much less to go out of business in response to a negative evaluation study. In fact, it requires either a good deal of professional self-confidence or a serious threat of disaster before most agencies will take seriously the results of an evaluation study. These conditions are rarely obtained.

In carrying out a study, the difficulty in obtaining suitable control groups of patients or clients to compare with those receiving the program under study is a particularly serious one. It is not ethically acceptable to allow service applicants in distress to go without treatment unless there is no treatment that has been demonstrated effective. In most cases, therefore, the evaluation study must compare groups receiving different forms of presumably effective treatment. Assignment of applicants to these differing groups often is beyond the control of the investigator and all sorts of extraneous influences are introduced through the treatment assignment process. Comparisons then become difficult if not impossible.

Finally, there is the issue of time. Administrative decisions must usually be made rapidly and cannot wait for the results of an evaluation study. The administrator must know where his money is to go well before the experimenter can tell him what is likely to pay off. By the time experimental results are in, the administrator and the programs may be so heavily committed and so actively engaged that a negative study is bound to be disregarded.

What then is the appropriate place of evaluation? Evaluation is a powerful and effective tool when those who employ it are prepared to follow the recommendations evaluation studies suggest. Usually this occurs in the early stages of a program before a major commitment of resources has been made. This also occurs when a program is controversial. A program under heavy attack for reasons other than effectiveness can often be saved by a demonstration that the program is indeed effective.

Evaluation is useful to demonstrate the general utility and effectiveness of a class of programs. Because evaluation studies are so expensive, time-consuming, and require highly trained personnel, it is unrealistic to expect that every program or every service agency will undertake to evaluate. (Evaluation in this case must be distinguished from a management information system that operates to provide the program administrator with detailed information about the costs, quality, magnitude, and operating characteristics of his program. This is an essential part of every program.) Evaluation can be carried out properly only in selected situations, which means that a systematic search must be made for the best location to evaluate each class of program.

Completion of this book was aided by a great many individuals and organizations. We wish to acknowledge their help and express our thanks. The staff for the conference included Elmer Bertsch, Berna Koren, and Rebekah Czamanske. Staff of Division of Community Psychiatry, State University of New York at Buffalo — including Robert Joss, Diana Windsor, and Marie Speder — were also of help. The members of the various advisory committees established to assist in planning of the conference provided crucial help in suggesting topics and speakers. Dr. Morton Kramer and the staff of the Division of Biometry, National Institute of Mental Health, were of service in many ways.

Notes

1. Suchman, E.A. *Evaluative Research: Principles in Practice in Public Service and Social Action Programs*, New York, Russell Sage Foundation, page 27, 1967.

2. Wholey, J.S. et al. *Federal Evaluation Policy: Analyzing the Effects of Public Programs*, Washington, D.C., The Urban Institute, page 23, 1970; Weiss, C.H. *Evaluating Action Programs: Readings and Social Action on Education*, Boston, Allyn and Bacon, Inc., page 6, 1972; Bloom, B. The Evaluation of Primary Prevention Programs in Roberts, L.M., Greenfield, N.S., and Miller,

M.H. (Eds.) *Comprehensive Mental Health: The Challenge of Evaluation*, Madison, The University of Wisconsin Press, page 119, 1968; Wing, J.K., and Hailey, A. *Evaluating the Community Psychiatric Service: The Camberwell Register, 1964-1971*, London, Oxford University Press, page 15, 1972; Gruenberg, E.M. (Ed.) *Evaluating the Effectiveness of Community Mental Health Services*, New York, Milbank Memorial Fund, page 11, 1966; Zusman, J. Program Evaluation and Quality Control in Mental Health Services in Bellak, L., and Barten, H.H. (Eds.) *Progress in Community Mental Health*, New York, Brunner/Mazel, vol. 3, in press, 1975.

3.   Gruenberg, E.M. (Ed.) *Evaluating the Effectiveness of Community Mental Health Services.*

4.   James, G. Evaluation in Public Health Practice, *American Journal of Public Health 52:* 1145-1154, 1962.

5.   Donabedian, A. Evaluating the Quality of Medical Care, *Milbank Memorial Fund Quarterly 44:* 166-203, 1966.

6.   Zusman, J. Program Evaluation and Quality Control in Mental Health Services in Bellak, L., and Barten, H.H. (Eds.) *Progress in Community Mental Health*, New York, Brunner/Mazel, vol. 3, in press, 1975.

7.   Scriven, M. quoted in Anderson, S.B. et al. *Encyclopedia of Educational Evaluation*, San Francisco, Jossey-Bass, pages 178-179, 1975.

8.   Rossi, P.H., Testing for Success and Failure in Social Action, in Rossi, P.H., and Williams, W. (Eds.) *Evaluating Social Programs: Theory Practice and Politics*, New York, Seminar Press, page 27, 1972.

Part I

Theory and Overview

1

Evaluation in Alcohol, Drug Abuse, and Mental Health Programs: Problems and Prospects

David Mechanic

It takes none of the great virtues to proclaim the importance of evaluation and the necessity to assess the impacts of expensive social programs that compete for scarce resources. Posing questions in a fashion that allows them to be addressed effectively and that facilitates appropriate research designs requires somewhat more sophistication, but certainly these are skills that can be taught and learned without too much difficulty. The slow pace of evaluation efforts, thus, results less from failures to proclaim their importance or to initiate studies than from the political context of social programming, the vested interests of administrators and program personnel, and the perceived threat implicit in the development of evaluation efforts. These same considerations have much to do, ultimately, with the flawed quality of many evaluations. If we do not attack these issues frankly and realistically, our methodological and analytic skills will come to naught.

My charge is to begin the discussion of the prospects for evaluation in the areas of alcohol, drug abuse, and mental health. I take it that those who organized the 1974 conference focusing on this subject purposefully used the term "evaluation" in contrast to "evaluation research." Increasingly, the concept of evaluation is being narrowed to describe the assessment of the effectiveness of programs targeted toward specific social goals by means of the more sophisticated social methodologies used to study such interventions.[1] I prefer to retain the wider meaning of the concept to designate the broad range of efforts that administrators and others engage in to assess what it is that they are doing and what their effectiveness is in reaching their goals. Evaluation thus spans a range of activities, from the qualitative assessment of how adequately an agency balances its commitments in respect to a variety of competing goals to large-scale social experiments designed to ascertain the relative impacts of differing policy interventions on a variety of critical indicators. We may be able to learn what we want to know through feedback from personnel, recipients, and other interested persons, or our questions may require formal collection of statistical information and special investigations. In this regard, Edward A. Suchman's distinction between evaluation and evaluation research is pertinent:

> [Evaluation] will be used in a general way as referring to the social
> process of making judgments of worth. This process is basic to almost
> all forms of social behavior, whether that of a single individual or a
> complex organization. While it implies some logical or rational basis

3

for making such judgments, it does not require any systematic procedures for marshaling and presenting objective evidence to support the judgment. Thus, we retain the term "evaluation" in its more common-sense usage as referring to the general process of assessment or appraisal of value.

"Evaluation research," on the other hand, will be restricted to the utilization of scientific research methods and techniques for the purpose of making an evaluation. In this sense, "evaluative" becomes an adjective specifying a type of research. The major emphasis is upon the noun "research" and evaluative research refers to those procedures for collecting and analyzing data which increase the possibility for "proving" rather than "asserting" the worth of some social activity.[2]

My discussion is also based on certain additional assumptions: I firmly believe that it is necessary to make the process of evaluation as rigorous and scientific as possible. Thus, given a choice, evaluation *research* is always preferable to other methods of evaluation. There are, however, circumstances that lead a skilled administrator to resist evaluation research in order to protect his program from political attack or budgetary reductions. In these contexts it is essential to stimulate alternative approaches to evaluation and to develop incentives that achieve this.

The discussion begins with some general considerations concerning evaluation and the sociopolitical context within which it takes place. This is followed by an examination of the formulation of the evaluation task and its various aspects. The discussion then focuses on particular types of evaluation, such as social experiments, monitoring, and social indicators. This is followed by a more specific discussion of evaluation and monitoring in the areas of alcohol, drug abuse, and mental health. The chapter concludes by addressing such issues as the appropriate criteria for assessing the value and potential of evaluation research, the implementation of evaluation, evaluation as education, and possible incentives for improving efforts in the evaluation field. My conclusion, which I will amplify in a variety of ways, is that the potential for evaluation is very much enhanced when it builds on the common desire among professionals and administrators to do their jobs more effectively and when it is implemented in a manner that minimizes threat and uncertainty. In short, I maintain that evaluation is more properly viewed as part of a process of continuing education rather than as a regulatory function.

General Considerations

Since the goals of evaluation—as well as the resources that can be devoted to it—are so diverse, the tools of evaluation are quite varied. They range from simple monitoring or self-assessment to sophisticated multivariate analysis and social experiments to measure the intended and unintended effects of particular policy interventions. Evaluation may be carried out intramurally as part of a service program where personnel wish information about how to allocate their efforts better, or it may be imposed from above and implemented by an independent research agency. The evaluation may reflect internal needs of a particular agency or requirements for self-justification, or it may be for the purpose of policy planning and budgetary allocations at a higher administrative level. There are, of course, better and poorer methods of evaluation—those that are confounded and self-serving, and those that are more rigorous and disinterested. While we strive to implement the most valid methods to fit the circumstances, we appreciate that the choice of methods and the approach to evaluation may come into conflict with personal and organizational needs, political factors, and professional pride and insecurities. If we insist on being purists, oblivious to the practicalities of existing situations, we serve the goal of evaluation badly in the long run. By stimulating evaluation efforts, even those with imperfections, we contribute to upgrading the standards applied to policy decisions. As higher standards of evidence develop, it is likely that social agencies will come to see that more serious evaluation built into programs from the beginning is important to their own survival as well as to a more effective response to social problems.

Evaluation is an inclusive concept encompassing such activities as organizational intelligence, monitoring, the use of social indicators, demonstration projects, applied social research, and the like. The concern may be with the practical and administrative problems of program implementation, as in many demonstration efforts, or with the impact of changes when successfully executed. Evaluation research is somewhat more restrictive than applied social research in that the latter concerns itself with a wider range of influences than those generally characteristic of policy formulation or social intervention. Although evaluation efforts are very broad, they are concerned with variables that are believed to be within the range of control of social policy and social programs. Thus, in the health field, evaluation research is more likely to focus on the study of specific therapeutic interventions, varying forms of financial incentives, and different manpower arrangements rather than on such issues as sociocultural differences among populations, varying social values and orientations, or dominant patterns of power or influence in the community.

In considering varying social policies, the more rigorous evaluation researcher tends to focus on behavioral outcomes and, thus, assumes a relatively conservative stance. For example, it is typical for such persons to maintain that if a particular social intervention has not been proven effective, then public programs should not extend such services. In contrast, both administrators of intervention programs and the interested public may value a service—not because it has with some degree of frequency objectively altered behavior in the desired direction—but because it has been deemed valuable in the society more generally and provides a sense of security or reduces a subjective sense of discomfort. Whatever the uncertain effects of psychotherapeutic intervention (and I, for one, believe that they are uncertain), the fact that those who are more affluent value such services makes it likely that those with lesser means will aspire to more equal access; and thus unions bargaining for health benefits for their employees increasingly seek such coverage. In the political context it is not scientific demonstration that often carries the day, but rather what the public defines as the reality; and this requires the evaluator who focuses primarily on more objective behavioral outcomes to pause for thought. The public's views may reflect ignorance, as scientists have argued from time to time, but they may also reflect the fact that the indicators valued by the researcher are not identical to those valued by the public. The tenacity of chiropractic—and the recent history of its extension under various forms of social insurance—should alert us, I think, to the fact that what people seek from help sources in the community may not be the services that help providers believe they are there to give.

From the administrator's perspective evaluation efforts themselves have costs as well as benefits. First, they require time, manpower, and funds. Serious evaluation is frequently expensive, and when there is a failure to understand how such expenditures will result in more efficient or effective performance, or will enhance the organization in other ways, the feeling frequently emerges that such resources might better be spent more directly for organizational activities. To the extent that funds are explicitly earmarked for evaluation and cannot be converted to other uses, evaluation may still be resented but does not pose the same trade-off problems that exist when administrators have an option. Second, there are frequently pressures from evaluators to modify organizational behavior in some fashion to meet the needs for a more rigorous methodological design, or at the very least evaluation research may require efforts on the part of program personnel to provide information, to complete forms or keep special records, or to allow their work to be observed. While much research emphasizes the importance of assessing the consequences of one or another clear intervention over time, practitioners tend to be highly eclectic in their efforts, may change their practices with new information, and thus are frequently resentful of limits imposed by a research design. To the extent that the types of data demanded by the evaluation depart substantially from those routinely recorded, to the extent that the research demands that practitioners adhere to some artificial routine, and to the extent that the purposes of the research are not well understood or perceived as threatening in some fashion, resistance is likely to be encountered. Increasingly, those in evaluation research are developing approaches that are less likely to impose artificial limits on an agency and that do not demand that the agency adhere to a particular time sequence before modifying its operations.

One important source of resistance to evaluation results from the fact that organizational personnel are often professionally and psychologically committed to the interventions they promote. It is proper and desirable that they have such commitment, and fortunate that they do not remain detached and solely engaged in the bureaucratic game. Without a sense of commitment and the conviction that one's activities count, much of the enthusiasm and the possible impact of program interventions are lost. To the hard-nosed researcher, intervention effects may be merely "Hawthorne effects"; but from the point of view of the people served, "Hawthorne effects" may be as important as any others. Particularly in the human services, it is necessary to convey to clients a sense of optimism and hope;[3] and when professionals doubt their own efforts, they are likely to communicate these doubts to their clients and create a climate of despair. This commitment to one's programs creates a certain protectiveness and suspicion of evaluation research.

Beyond simple self-protection, evaluation can also be a tool used by administrators to support and enhance their own position in the competition for continued and new funding. Such data, however, are frequently not collected for the purpose of objectively and fairly appraising performance and need, but rather to make the case that the agency's programs are of vital importance and deserve priority and resources. Given the general administrative structure of programs—particularly within government—an administrator who failed to buttress his claims with whatever supporting data he could muster would be delinquent in his responsibilities to his goals and would soon lose ground in the battle of maintaining resources. The process thus encourages cycles of exaggeration and justification that conform to few of the canons of serious assessment.[4] In this context evaluation becomes the chips with which various parties play political poker, but the currency is frequently counterfeit. But in a context where decision makers have difficulty differentiating the counterfeit from the real, the incentive is to trade in bad currency.

It is commonly advocated that the more stringent methods of evaluation useful in one type of setting be applied to others. In recent years one of the most pervasive evaluation techniques—cost-benefit analysis, which was a valuable tool in military planning—was inappropriately urged on administrators who worked with problems and outcomes that were more intangible, and where it was impossible to specify in any quantitative sense the various costs and benefits.[5] Although the implementation of such analysis was farcical from one viewpoint, it was useful in directing administrators to consider more consciously the costs and benefits of various alternatives that might be appropriately applied in their areas. It fostered a useful style of thinking about social programs. Particularly in professional agencies, which have an orientation toward using whatever technology is in vogue regardless of the absorption of resources,[6] cost-benefit consideration was a valuable corrective even if it could not provide any precise answer to the conceptual issues. It is important to address ourselves to frameworks for program planning and evaluation that help make salient those issues important for administrators to consider.

In developing approaches to encourage more widespread evaluation efforts, we must do so with full understanding that social policies are the culmination of a political process in which objective information is only one of many elements— a fact often not genuinely appreciated by academic researchers. But even in the political arena feedback from the environment is essential to shape goals and future efforts. There are issues of social intervention, such as welfare policy or national health insurance, that are highly visible in the public arena and, therefore, highly politicized. Although research is relevant to the resolution of such problems, decisions, because of their public visibility, are likely to be dominated by political considerations. But a good many important issues affecting administrative policy, incentives, and implementation of programs are neither visible nor of particular interest to politicians or to a very large public; and it is in such areas that good evaluation probably has its greatest potential and impact.[7]

One of the greatest difficulties in implementing evaluation efforts is inherent in the threat they pose under conditions where program support and survival are substantially part of a political process. An unfavorable evaluation can potentially threaten and weaken further claims for resources and support, particularly if the sponsoring legislature or bureaucracy is not seen as supportive of the agency's goals, or understanding of the difficulties of the problems they are trying to cope with, or sympathetic with the fragmentary state of knowledge of what works. Administrators also know that there is a political rhetoric that encompasses the slogan "evaluation," which may mean anything from, "We don't care much for your kind of program," to "Provide us with some justification," to "Let's seriously evaluate the best use of our dollars to deal with these problems."

Yet, all in all, although there are many bureaucratic and professional resistances to evaluation, I am firmly convinced that most agency personnel want to be effective. Their resistance stems, thus, not from lack of interest in self-improvement, but from the fear of uncertainty and the sense of threat. Introduced in a nonthreatening way, evaluation can become a positive force toward self-improvement.

Rather than bemoan the anti-intellectualism or the ignorance of the self-protective maneuvers of the administrator, the proponents of evaluation research would do well to give more attention to the environmental contexts in which serious evaluation is nurtured and to the incentives that might be developed to promote the conditions for its success in improving practice.

Formulating the Evaluation Task

The first requirement for evaluation is that the goals and expected impact of program interventions be formulated as explicitly as possible. While seemingly simple, agreement on intended effects is frequently exceedingly difficult to achieve.

Many major programs are enacted without clear specification of goals or expected impact. Indeed, the political process may require sufficiently complex and ambiguous goals, so that varying interests support the program for different reasons. Some may support methadone treatment programs because they regard them as a humane alternative to no program regardless of its objective impact; others may provide support not because they believe it will necessarily assist the addict, but because they believe it may result in a reduction of crime and lessen the possibility of social disturbances; others may believe that it improves the functioning of persons addicted to heroin and increases the probability that they will work; and still others may see it as a way of alleviating the anxieties of an aroused public opinion. Many social programs are shaped in a process of compromise among groups having different values and preferences and who may support a program for different and even contradictory reasons. Evaluating methadone treatment is relatively easy compared with many other social programs, but even here the assessment of both short-run and long-range effects on a variety of dimensions is no simple task.

To take a somewhat more difficult example, evaluators are increasingly asking what effect the extension of medical services has on health outcomes, and it has become commonplace to assert that increased use of medical services has only marginal influence on health. The broad statement, however, is frequently misleading because it begs the question of the appropriate measures of health or the functions of much of medical practice. In the case of particular interventions, one can clearly inquire as to the outcomes in respect to specific conditions and populations. Similarly, one can inquire as to whether a particular modality is applied properly, consistent with knowledge of its effects and adverse consequences. Medical practice consists of many interventions, varying in effectiveness and in their correct application to appropriate populations. But in each case the question must be addressed in a specific sense. Much of medical practice has greater relevance to relieving pain and discomfort, minimizing disability, and providing a sense of security and relief of worry, than to modifying physical conditions. Much of ambulatory medical care is sought by persons who require support and caring services, and to measure the effect of such services by indexes of mortality misses the point. This is not to assert, however, that the current conceptualization and practice of medicine maximizes those outcome measures we value, whether they be longevity, lesser disability, relief from discomfort, or whatever. But if evaluation is to be really useful, it must give attention to the entire range of functions of multipurpose organizations and must address the more intangible impacts as well as those that are readily measurable. Even if we knew that medicine and psychiatry had zero impact on disease outcomes, I think we would find that the population would continue to seek assistance for problems that are frightening or with which they could not cope.

It has become fashionable in health and in other areas to inquire whether limited social programs have impact on global characteristics of persons and populations that are in reality a product of a vast number of influences. It is not difficult to demonstrate that social programs tend not to have major impact on these global indicators whether they be overall health status, academic achievement, or whatever. Using a multiple regression approach and such indicators of impact, most programs could be shown to explain only a very small amount of variation in the dependent measure. Selma Mushkin has stated this problem extremely well.

> If a study attempting to determine whether diphtheria immunization makes a difference in national health were to use a familiar regression technique, a superficial finding would be "no go." Diphtheria immunization would be quantified as having little explanatory power in the variance of health status.
>
> The reasoning behind such a finding would go something like this. Before the development of the toxoid, diphtheria had an incidence rate reaching 3 per 1,000 persons of all ages. It occurred, on the average, in 9 of each 1,000 children. Of those who suffered from the disease, some fraction had no long-range consequences, 5-10 per cent died, and impairment of varying severities continued for the remaining number of cases. At the present time, all but 2.5 per cent of children receive some diphtheria toxoid doses. In 1971, no diphtheria deaths were reported for the over 200 cases of the disease. Obviously, immunization has removed the hazard of the one specific disease, diphtheria. But in a static regression analysis limited to a single recent year, such as 1971, the difference in diphtheria immunization and incidence is small and the figures would be interpreted as having little power to explain difference in the general health status of the population.
>
> Given a finding of little or no explanatory power of diphtheria toxoid on general health status, would we conclude that immunization doesn't matter? Would findings suggest that one could press for reallocation of resources away from diphtheria vaccination? Is it wasteful to ask the local health departments, or the states and the Congress, to finance diphtheria immunization? Should parents spend their income on things other than diphtheria immunization for their children? In brief, the analyses based on data for a single period (after diphtheria is no longer a hazard) say little about policy conclusions based on such analyses.
>
> In a multiple regression analysis in which the dependent variable that is being explained is a fairly general factor (such as crime rates, death rates, rates of recidivism, stays in mental hospitals, or educational achievements) each of the many independent variables that may be included in an analytic model is likely to have small power to explain variation. Further, analysis of variance in regression does not

methodologically produce the causal connections required to examine any hypothesis made regarding the programs. Yet the results of regression analyses are being applied as if they in fact examined those causal relationships and concluded in the negative.[8]

In evaluating a program, one attempts to specify as carefully as he can the various goals—both immediate and long term. He also attempts to anticipate unintended or possibly adverse effects that must be taken into consideration in balancing the advantages and costs. Although every evaluation must limit its concerns to selected variables, it is prudent to begin with an inventory of possible effects that is quite extensive and then perhaps limit the measures used on the basis of methodological and practical considerations. By reviewing relevant literature, examining the issues that were raised when the program was implemented, and by discussions with administrators and operational personnel, it is possible to obtain a fairly extensive sense of possible intended and unintended effects. Since evaluation results are usually contrary to someone's interests—and therefore likely to be attacked, however well executed—the best recourse for the evaluator is a strong offense, that is, careful specification and measurement of as many of the dimensions of impact as is feasible. If funding constraints or other practicalities make it important to limit the study considerably — and thus only a small subset of indicators can be included — these should be selected so as to represent the most important contrasting views of the impact that the program might be having. This selection may be undertaken at a sacrifice, and it might be maintained that it is more prudent to assess one type of impact well through a variety of proxy measures rather than to scatter one's efforts too widely. This is a matter of judgment, but in general I doubt the usefulness of evaluating the typical multipurpose program on a single dimension.

In the mental health arena the problems of specifying and measuring the impact of interventions are particularly difficult. Intervention programs claim to do everything from maintaining mental health and preventing mental disorder to providing community supports and reeducating important decision makers. Although controlled trials are a powerful methodology for considering specific interventions for particular kinds of patients, they are more difficult to apply to the overall organization of services in mental health agencies. It is particularly difficult to get therapists to define their goals, and such goals are often expressed vaguely as in the concepts of "maturity," "self-realization," "reeducation," and the like. The problem is further compounded by the introduction of concepts like "symptom-substitution," which tend to deprecate alleviation of specific disturbing symptoms or behavior because a more fundamental "reorganization of personality" has not been demonstrated. Thus, not infrequently, tangible measures of impact are dismissed as irrelevant or superficial, while vague and unmeasurable concepts continue to justify existing practice. The evaluator—by selecting a range of measures of outcome, including proxy measures for some of

the more vague psychological terms—is in a stronger position than one who dis-
misses the vaguer concepts as therapist resistance and makes no effort to examine
their basis. Although it is often difficult to develop adequate indicators of symptom substitution and other current psychological concepts, with some attention
to the issue it is possible to develop credible measures. Thus, for example, while
one cannot prove that symptom substitution does not occur, one can measure a
wide range of symptoms and behavior, and demonstrate to what extent the
patterning of other symptoms has undergone change. Research, after all, is a
matter of plausibility and credibility. It the researcher makes a serious effort to
understand the concepts and goals of therapists—and to include consideration of
these in his study—he carries greater credibility. Also, by including a variety of
measures of both objective and subjective outcomes, the researcher is in a better
position not only to consider a variety of outcome dimensions, but also to
examine to what extent they present a consistent pattern.

Controlled Trials and Social Experiments

The evaluation of most social programs involves several different questions.
First, there is the specific issue as to whether a particular intervention does or does
not lead to intended changes in specified populations, by whatever indicators are
used to measure impact. At this level evaluation is logically the same as in the
assessment of any therapeutic modality, such as particular drugs or surgical interventions. Although careful clinical observation of responses to new therapeutic
agents may be extremely valuable in assessing impact, such evaluation is frequently associated with wishful thinking, the confusion of suggestion effects
with effects attributable to an active therapeutic agent, and to unconscious biases
introduced by the clinician. The methodology of controlled double-blind clinical
trials has been well developed, and it is fully appropriate to many evaluation
questions in the health services areas. There are, of course, serious resistances to
the application of controlled trials to health services delivery problems; but as
A.L. Cochrane has so beautifully illustrated—as much by his own example as
through his advocacy—we often have opportunities for controlled clinical trials
in health services research that are not inconsistent with ethical standards or the
needs of practitioners.[9]

To the researcher there is nothing more elegant and convincing than an
experiment, one that successfully randomizes recipients and exposes them to
varying interventions or no interventions at all. A successful experiment eliminates the difficulty of selection that is a pervasive bias in much social research
and that interferes with making clear inferences. The elegance of the experimental methodology has led some to the short-sighted conclusion that nothing
less than an experiment is acceptable and has infrequently resulted in a certain
arrogance as expressed in the statement by one researcher that " . . . the fault

lies not in the model, but in those who out of ignorance prevent the random assignment of units to programs of control groups."[10] Whatever the advantages of randomization and experimentation—and there are many advantages—they may be significantly eroded by the real difficulties and constraints characteristic of carrying out complex experiments in uncontrolled social settings. Outside the experimental laboratory, the researcher has little control over the multitude of variables that may change the meaning of the experimental manipulations as occurred in the New Jersey Negative Income Tax Experiment when the state changed its welfare payment structure and disrupted the ongoing experimental manipulations.[11] In situations where we require informed consent and where there are significant resistances to particular social treatments, the problems of nonparticipation and attrition of subjects become difficult. We have not as yet learned how to cope with the attrition problem in long-term experiments; and to the extent that it is large and nonrandom, we no longer have an experiment at all. Social experimentation can be extremely expensive in time and resources and, frequently for both practical and methodological reasons, quasi-experimental methods[12] or other types of evaluation approaches are more prudent.

Experiments are most feasible when the issue concerns the impact of a specified intervention within a relatively narrow time period in contrast to a complex set of interventions directed toward a variety of goals. In the areas under consideration here, randomized controlled trials are much more useful to study approaches to treatment of specific problems than they are to an overall evaluation of government policy. Thus, an experiment is the optimum way of evaluating methadone treatment or a program that offers a community alternative to hospitalization for schizophrenic patients. However, an experiment is not a particularly good approach to evaluating the impact of such multipurpose institutions as mental health centers or to assess the impact of training programs on the mental health sector. Of course there are significant resistances to experimentation that are both feasible and appropriate, but there is a growing tendency to urge very expensive experiments that are not appropriate for answering the social policy questions at issue.

Social Monitoring and Social Indicators

In situations where programs have multiple goals—and where the bulk of agency effort is given to no single goal—the agency requires some feedback as to how well it is dealing with responsibilities within its orbit. In order to obtain feedback, monitoring is a useful device. Monitoring refers to the continuing effort to assess the occurrence of various events, including unexpected changes, in the environment. Through experience we have developed a variety of social indicators such as those that yield some assessment of the state of the economy. In the health field the most common indicators include birth and death rates, occurrence of morbidity and use of health care services, and disability and impairment. These indicators sensitize administrators to emerging problems, to unanticipated changes, and to significant differences among subgroups in the population that require social action. Such information is useful for the agency in carrying out its programs, but it does not clearly delineate what impact agency programs have. For example, a public health department may monitor the rate of infant mortality since this might be one of their program responsibilities. But positive changes in such indicators may be indicative of a wide variety of possible influences and cannot be attributed to program efforts. Such information does, however, alert agency personnel to geographic areas or social groups that require special attention and perhaps special studies as well.

Public agencies frequently cannot monitor important indicators themselves, and thus depend on the availability of vital statistics from local and state authorities and from the National Center for Health Statistics. If these data are to be most useful, they must be as current as possible, they must be relevant to public policy issues, they must provide estimates for important subgroups in the population, and they must be compiled in a fashion that not only provides an estimate of morbidity but information as to the extent to which these problems are being dealt with or corrected. For example, a report on visual acuity in the population is more useful for public policy if it also includes information on the extent to which problems of acuity have been adequately corrected.[13] Furthermore, the data systems should be organized to facilitate obtaining further analyses of particular importance for a given program than those published. The Committee to Evaluate the National Center for Health Statistics has made a variety of useful suggestions that, if implemented, would contribute importantly to the improving health monitoring at the present time.[14]

Monitoring and Social Indicators: Mental Health

In the health field, as in many other noneconomic areas, the available indicators are highly inadequate for assessing the existing social trends and the most salient needs. In recent years there has been a great flurry of efforts to develop new indicators or to improve existing ones, and a number of attempts to collect new types of data on health and health services have been initiated by the National Center for Health Statistics. In the areas of alcohol, drug abuse, and mental health our indicators are less adequate than in many other areas of health. We have yet to develop reliable and valid measures of conditions and events of relevance to administrative and operational decisions, and the available data are frequently too outdated or confounded to gauge the existing problems reliably on the basis of them.

The existing state of indicators in the health field brings into sharp focus the importance of basic methodological and substantive research in improving evaluative efforts. Without a better concept of what constitutes disorder and a clearer understanding of the natural history of symptoms or impairment, we will have great difficulty in developing indicators in which we can have very much faith. Presently, most available indicators include such items as mortality due to suicide, resident mental patients, and admissions and number of visits to various psychiatric facilities. Suicide is a poor proxy for mental health problems in general, and the other indicators reflect the availability of services and administrative decisions more than existing morbidity in the population. Thus, almost everything we know in our area of concern comes from special surveys initiated from time to time on limited population groups.

We do know that psychiatric impairment is extremely common in the population, and that alcoholism and drug abuse are very significant problems. The prevalence of high rates of psychological distress found in most investigations[15] is consistent with studies of medical practice that suggest that a significant proportion of all patients seeking the assistance of physicians are primarily motivated in seeking help by psychosocial and psychiatric difficulties.[16] But when we examine the surveys from special community studies we find that estimates of incidence and prevalence have an extraordinary range depending on the definition of a case or concepts of problems and impairment. Over the years a common pool of items to measure psychological distress has been used, based on items from the Army Neuropsychiatric Screening Adjunct and related studies. In 1970 the National Center for Health Statistics reported data from a national sample in 1960-62 on a subset of these items, also finding a high prevalence of reports of such distress.[17] But there are many problems with such indicators that suggest that we have much basic work to do before we can depend on them to any extent.

In the Graduated Work Incentive Experiment, Russell Middleton and Vernon Allen[18] used 12 items of psychological impairment taken from the pool of items generally used in most epidemiological studies, and these were administered to the primarily lower class sample at intervals of one, two, and three years. The correlations of the items across time periods were uniformly very low (around 0.20), and this is not inconsistent with the findings of other studies that have examined the stability of such indicators. Given the frequent use of such indicators, it is remarkable how little we know about their reliability, validity, and how they behave over time. Similarly, the great dependence on psychophysiological indicators of distress tends to result in confounding psychological and organic disorders, particularly in older populations suffering from greater physical morbidity.[19] To the extent that comparisons cover a wide age range, it is unclear to what extent the index is comparable from one age group to another. Finally, most studies indicate that women report higher rates of psychophysiological distress than men,[20] and it is not clear to what extent this reflects real differences in experienced distress, differences in expressing distress, or the fact that male forms of expression of distress—as perhaps expressed in acting out behavior, drug abuse, drunkenness, and the like—are not reflected in these indicators.

The basic issue we face—and which we have not resolved adequately in the mental health field—concerns the appropriate definition of a meaningful case. A monitoring system for some purposes might wish only to track the incidence and prevalence of specific known entities that involve considerable impairment such as schizophrenia and manic-depressive illnesses. Such estimates, of course, would be pertinent to only a very small proportion of the population and would not give much indication of what the state of mental health or impairment is in the population at large. The complexity of the issue is suggested by the observation that diagnosed manic-depressive psychoses appear to be more common in higher status groups,[21] while reports of depressive affect are inversely related to social class.[22] If this difference is a true one, which case definition is the more relevant concept for public policy formulation?

Since we know very little with certainty in the mental health field, we have no alternative but to depend on very gross indicators of feeling and performance in evaluating our efforts. At the most global level we might even wish to focus on happiness as an indicator—on the assumption that one of the roles of public policy is to assist citizens to have a more fulfilling and satisfying life. Happiness is an interesting indicator in that it appears to be a product of two independent dimensions: the absence of psychological distress (as measured by such items as those from the Army Neuropsychiatric Screening Adjunct) and the occurrence of positive and satisfying events.[23] The measure shares part of the domain encompassed by most existing measures of distress and impairment, but also takes into account the extent to which people have reinforcing and satisfying experiences in life. One of the major disadvantages of the measure is that it may not be particularly stable over time, and it is sensitive to uncontrolled environmental events that may have nothing to do with social programs. Thus, if we use it as an indicator, we are at the mercy of transitory fluctuations in the environment that affect values on the indicator for short periods. Significant fluctuations have been observed in this indicator among panels in response to the Cuban missile crisis and to the assassination of President Kennedy.[24] In some respects this indicator is akin to popular ratings of how well the president is doing his job. Long-term trends are of considerable interest, but the indicator itself is highly responsive to dramatic events. Existing measures of distress used in community surveys are similarly responsive.

Areas where adequate indicators do not exist—but where there is considerable agreement that they are important—include behavior problems, successful performance of social roles, disabling psychological symptoms, and positive mental health. In each of these areas it is exceedingly difficult to develop appropriate social norms for evaluating the state of mental health because the prevalence of the behaviors themselves may be dependent on social values that differ from one subgroup to another. As long as we speak in rather vague terms, we might agree that aggression is undesirable, but when we actually face the issue of developing indicators, we will find quite diverse attitudes about conditions justifying aggressive behavior. Similarly, expectations about social functioning may vary from one context to another, and patterns of behavior may reflect subcultural expectations as much as any other factor.[25] Even when we deal with rather primitive concepts of functioning, such as the ability to meet basic responsibilities in work and family life, it becomes clear that such behaviors may reflect situational contingencies and social expectations, and these may differ significantly from one setting to another. We presently lack adequate knowledge of the usefulness of existing indicators, particularly in respect to the anticipated effects of specific program interventions. Moreover we are usually lacking information on the stability and natural history of these behaviors, thus leaving it unclear as to what impact we can reasonably expect from a particular type of intervention. To use such indicators unrealistically— on the naive assumption that they should be responsive to public intervention— can result in a nihilistic attitude harmful to mental health efforts. In short, existing indicators are ambiguous for public policy formulation and evaluation, and presently have limited usefulness. If they are to be useful eventually in program appraisal, a good deal of basic effort is necessary in social epidemiology.

One of the great difficulties in using mental health indicators successfully is our ignorance of the etiology and natural history of most psychological disorders. Lacking clear models of causal links and thus having no clear concept of targeted intervention, most of our efforts are stabs in the dark. We generally proceed not with specific knowledge but with the hope that by providing services, support, empathy, and understanding we will somehow alleviate the course of impairment. Because we have such an unclear idea of what we are doing, evaluation is more important than ever, for it is only through the greater specification of intervention efforts that it becomes possible to develop more effective programs of care.

In the areas of alcohol and drug abuse we have had some periodic national surveys but no continuing monitoring of changes in the incidence or prevalance of problems. Collecting adequate data in these areas involves a variety of problems: the highly stigmatic aspects of some of these problems and resulting underreporting; conceptual difficulties in defining concepts adequately so that they are comparable to the behaviors that alarm the community and are of greatest concern; practical difficulties in monitoring behaviors that are illegal and where full protection of confidentiality of such data by law is lacking; and the obvious difficulty of finding and successfully interviewing persons who are likely to have the most substantial difficulties with alcohol and drugs.

In spite of these problems existing surveys reflect very high levels of alcohol and drug abuse. Once again, however, the artificial norms that are developed for the purpose of reporting rates of problem drinkers or drug abusers are not really consistent with the complexities of the phenomena themselves. Heavy consumption of alcohol is not synonymous with the problem of alcoholism as seen by affected families or the community, and the use of heroin does not make a heroin addict. It is only through the more careful study of the natural history of alcohol and drug use that we can begin to develop the kinds of distinctions that more accurately separate the problem cases requiring special attention in contrast to the larger populations that use drugs and alcohol. Existing data suggest that we have a problem of massive proportions; but we lack a sophisticated ability to characterize cases in a way that allows more specific application of therapeutic and other approaches to change.

One of the most ambitious attempts to monitor the occurrence of psychiatric disorders and the use of services occurred with the development of service registers in particular communities.[26] In addition to providing an overview of the transactions between patients and the mental health services system, psychiatric registers also offered a population from which to select more adequate samples of patients with particular diagnoses that could be used in more focused studies. This venture was not only very expensive, but was more complex operationally than advocates had appreciated. Most of the registers that were developed lacked the necessary skilled personnel to maintain the register and at the same time to retrieve data for administrative evaluation and program planning. Most of the registers had difficulty enough in continuing to operate, much less in using the collected data productively. The concept of registers was not faulty in itself. The failure was to anticipate realistically what skills and funds were required by such monitoring, the difficulties in attracting persons with the necessary talents and interest to develop and utilize them effectively, and the enormous problems in maintaining the quality and completeness of reports from participating institutions. Furthermore—more frequently than not—a clear concept of how to organize and retrieve data useful in the development of service policies was absent. Although there are examples of the effective use of register data for program planning, for the most part this effort at monitoring must be viewed as a failure.

The growing complexity of administrative decisions, the need for information, and the requirements for evaluation will lead to renewed efforts to develop mental health monitoring systems. In considering broad needs and problems, however, we often fail to improve data sources that are within our capacities to change more readily. Simple improvement in existing record sources and standardization of collection of modest information that is routinely available can be of great utility in evaluating what we are doing. Yet, few publicly supported programs in mental health collect uniform data that provide even simple descriptive information on recipients and services. A well-organized internal data system often offers innumerable opportunities for simple studies that are revealing not only about program components but also about basic issues relevant to mental health.[27] We are too often captured by the fancy technology of mass data processing and too rarely give sufficient conceptual thought to what it is important to obtain data about or how to intelligently use simple data sets more readily available.

Assessing the Value and Potential of
Evaluation Research

Because of the sociopolitical factors already discussed it is unreasonable to evaluate the effectiveness of evaluation research on the basis of whether there is an immediate implementation of the research findings. An immediate response may be impossible because of political factors or because of the very long time lag between the formulation of the research conclusions and the diffusion of this information to the multiple decision makers who have responsibility for social programming. Moreover, few evaluations are sufficiently clear-cut or unequivocal to avoid criticism or conflicting interpretations of their relevance or implications. Thus, it seems that we require more modest and more realistic criteria to assess the value and significance of the evaluation process.

One important dimension for assessing the significance of evaluation research is the extent to which it contributes to growing sophistication about the appropriate questions to ask and how to evaluate information about social programs. Even when its results are not directly implemented, evaluation affects the climate of thinking and may affect the direction of future efforts if done carefully and in communication with the personnel involved. It may contribute to an active and analytic perspective that stimulates program personnel to be more involved in their work and thoughtful about it, and indirectly may contribute to morale and intellectual ferment. Evaluation can have adverse effects as well if it undermines commitment to goals or induces despair. But if properly performed, evaluation contributes to a sense of direction and development of mastery, and becomes an important component of excellence.

Perhaps the most common form of evaluation in social agencies is to monitor program efforts. Its popularity stems from the ease with which it is performed. Moreover, in the bureaucratic game it provides a device that one can always use to make claims for success. But of all the possible forms of evaluation, program monitoring is perhaps the least effective and least informative. It might be far more valuable for social agencies to devote attention to a sample of their most important programs, using more powerful evaluation devices, than to dilute their efforts and resources in routine program monitoring.

Many social agencies lack the trained manpower to do anything more than program monitoring. Thus, such agencies have a great need to develop a social science capacity to anticipate future issues, to obtain information relevant to policy options, and to carry out analysis and evaluation of ongoing efforts. One of the great difficulties of implementing a capacity for evaluation is that social agencies are under great pressures to keep up with the day-to-day operations, and available talented personnel are likely to be mobilized when the agency faces problems that require immediate operational decisions. We have not as yet found the proper organizational formula in social agencies for developing analytic groups who are sufficiently close to the work to be useful in resolving policy issues, but insulated enough from day-to-day demands to be able to carry out serious and long-range evaluation.

With patience and persistence it is possible to make some progress. The extent of evaluation and the approach followed, however, will need to take the context into account. Of course, there are many circumstances where successful evaluation depends on only minimal cooperation of the agency being studied, as in surveys of recipients of human services. In still other circumstances, cooperation is mandated by the administrative program of which an agency may be part.[28] But I hope that our view of the evaluation process is much broader than this, and that we seek ways to make most administrators and professionals receptive and committed to seeing evaluation as an important instrument to increase their potential. However, I would not deny that the presence of a mandate assists the development of both receptivity and commitment.

Implementation of Evaluation of Social Programs

Much of this discussion has addressed the issue of whether a particular intervention significantly affects outcome. A related but somewhat different issue, which too often receives inadequate attention, concerns the effective implementation of a successful intervention. Health programs are highly decentralized with innumerable points of decision concerning implementation. Much ineffective care results not from the lack of knowledge and experience but rather from the difficulty of diffusing experience and knowledge to the various decision makers who administer and carry out health programs. Many interventions, appropriate in particular circumstances, are applied in a fashion that induces iatrogenic illness and disability, while others that should be used are frequently not understood or implemented. The diffusion of appropriate practice patterns is an enormous problem for even the more straightforward therapies, such as use of antibiotics and simple general surgery. In the case of more complex intervention approaches that are more difficult to understand and apply, error is further compounded. Evaluation must not only be concerned with what effect programs have, but also with the failures to use established interventions appropriately and the misapplication of those that are used. There has been an enormous expansion of drug use, and the psychoactive drugs are those most commonly prescribed. Careful control and supervision of drug regimen is one of the more problematic aspects of medical and psychiatric practice, and deserves much more attention than it has received to date.

Many social programs are not administered and executed by a single administrative entity, but rather by a variety of programs and agencies at the local level. The actual operational units may be state and local health departments, universities, hospitals or other nonprofit corporations, profit firms, individual practitioners, or a conglomeration of individual programs. Even when the intent of a program is clearly specified at the highest administrative levels, the translations at the local units can be quite bizarre; and the operational units tend to have their own agendas and priorities and often quite diverse goals. To some extent the diversity might result from the fact that agencies and programs may solicit funds for a project as a means of sustaining other activities to which there may be greater commitment. It also results from the fact that agencies deal with different populations each with its own profile of problems, and the availability of other community resources may also differ substantially from one context to another. In addition, the skills and leadership available may make concentration of effort on particular areas a reasonable and effective way of using resources. All of this is very untidy to the evaluator, but it is the reality with which evaluation must cope.

In many if not most circumstances we do not have a developed strategy for evaluating the efforts of social agencies. Too frequently, policy makers and administrators have not determined explicitly what might indicate reasonable progress and whether the efforts of the organization might be better applied in some other way. All social organizations take on a life of their own with their own particular dynamics and priorities; and without an unequivocally clear mandate the goals and practices tend to drift toward those that are most enjoyable, comfortable, and that confer the greatest prestige. The emphasis on evaluation will have made an enormous contribution if it did nothing more than encourage administrators to think through clearly what their options are and how they are expending their effort, and if it stimulated a more active and searching perspective among those who deliver social and medical services to the population.

Evaluation as Education

The evaluator must always be clear as to the purpose of his efforts. There are many circumstances where a valid study is impossible, and the concern in any case is improvement of the quality of work among relevant practitioners. Here it may be more useful to develop tools that facilitate practitioners' abilities to assess their own efforts without threat and defensiveness. If we are honest with ourselves, we know that few of us really enjoy being subjected to outside evaluation, and particularly by parties we feel are not sympathetic to the problems of our work and the difficulty of our tasks. The fact that we might resist such evaluations does not mean that we are not interested in self-improvement or in developing skills to do our jobs better. How to use this commonly shared desire for self-improvement in improving performance is a major challenge.

I am impressed by the extent to which some of the medical specialty societies appreciate these concerns and by the programs they have developed that allow physicians to anonymously evaluate their strengths and weaknesses with feedback on how to improve performance in areas requiring remedial efforts. No doubt the complaint—that persons who participate in such programs are frequently those who need them the least—is often true; yet, it is possible to provide incentives to many professional workers for continued self-improvement without threatening them or making them defensive. In the areas of mental health, drug addiction, and alcoholism, much effort must be given to improving postgraduate professional education. Most of these problems are managed by physicians and other professionals with very limited understanding and preparation for such work. Rudolph Moos[29] has developed relatively simple measures of treatment environments, which can be applied to various treatment contexts and which can be used to measure the outcome of directed change, providing relatively simple feedback to treatment personnel. In England the Royal College of General Practitioners has developed means to encourage practitioners to investigate their own practices so as to have a better appreciation of what they really do and how they can better organize their efforts. They have developed various materials that allow general practitioners with little research training to carry out investigations in their practices. Since the goal of evaluation is improved practice, I believe that we must give great attention to the issue of how to assist professionals and others to make their own assessments and to improve their own performance.

Incentives for Evaluation

In urging evaluation and critical self-awareness, we must face the dilemma noted earlier. Much of helping works because the therapist has confidence in himself, and the patient has confidence in the helper. By inducing doubts and self-criticism, and making consumers aware that at least objectively the emperor has no clothes, do we produce human betterment? By making therapists skeptical of their own efforts, do we so dampen enthusiasm and commitment that we lose rather than gain ground? The physician still remains somewhat of a priest and magician, and part of the effectiveness of medicine is the mystique of medicine.

This is no easy or trivial question, and where one stands depends in part on one's values and life perspectives. Thus, I provide no resolution but only some considerations relevant to the larger question. Secular values generally support demystification on the assumption that—all things considered—it is best for people to come to terms with their real options, and that the scientific aspects of helping can only be developed through a critical and searching perspective. Much of the problem is inherent in the fact that medicine, which had its early origins in religious concerns, has been translated and conceptualized in technical and scientific terms so as to make scientific effectiveness synonymous with what is worthwhile. Thus, the caring function of medical practice has come to be seen as the province of the romantic or the theologian. There are, however, things to be done because they are right and humane, regardless of their demonstrated effectiveness in altering "objective outcomes." Practitioners must come to accept that some functions of medicine are too important, too central to our sense of ethics and humanity, to judge them solely by utilitarian criteria. Hopefully, these considerations are not so romantic that evaluators cannot apply them as criteria in evaluating how helping institutions enhance the quality of life. To the extent that the caring function is accepted as an important part of medical practice, it is more possible to remain optimistic and enthusiastic in the face of discouraging evaluations on the ability to alter "objective outcomes." Also, to the extent that commitment is built around the idea of searching for the best techniques for managing patients in contrast to being developed around particular forms of treatment or schools of thought, it is more possible to maintain momentum than if egos are tied up in particular treatment philosophies or modalities. Organizations must search for ways to build commitment around tasks and goals in contrast to specific interventions. I am not naive about the professional and other barriers to achieving such changes in values and commitments, but the fact that they are difficult to achieve makes them no less important.

In examining the outcomes of health services, somewhat different criteria must be applied to techniques of caring as compared with techniques of cure. All treatment involves some balance between benefits and risks. Treatments that carry the greatest risks to life and health and those that involve the most expensive modalities must meet the most rigorous of evaluation criteria. Those that are less expensive or involve few potential adverse consequences should be judged not only by the extent to which they bring about demonstrable change in the course of illness and disability, but also by the degree to which they make patients feel more comfortable, more hopeful, and more optimistic. Evaluation must inquire not only whether things work and to what degree, but the possible dangers and costs of using particular treatment options relative to others that offer comparable management at less risk and less cost.

In short, evaluation is a complex and multifaceted process. Its definition and elaboration are very much influenced not only by scientific method, but also by social values and political processes. It can be used as a political tool or a means of self-assessment and improvement. And depending on how the effort is organized, it can be seen as a threat or a valuable adjunct to one's efforts. Because of this complexity and the political and professional sensitivity of evaluation, it is often talked about but less frequently implemented. In considering both the costs and benefits of evaluation as a tool for government and professional practice, I am convinced that its effects are likely to be influential if evaluation is viewed as part of a process of education and continuing education as opposed to a policing or regulatory function. Evaluation methodologies can be developed to assist practitioners of all types in comprehending what they are doing, in sharpening their thinking and practice, and in using their energies and resources with greater effect. Like all tools, it can be used for noble or despicable purposes. But this is a matter as much for society as for the evaluator.

Notes

1. Rossi, Peter and Walter Williams (eds.), *Evaluating Social Programs: Theory, Practice, and Politics.* New York: Seminar Press, 1972.

2. Suchman, Edward A., *Evaluation Research: Principles and Practice in Public Service and Social Action Programs.* New York: Russel Sage Foundation, 1967, pp. 7-8. © 1967 by Russell Sage Foundation.

3. Frank, Jerome, *Persuasion and Healing.* Baltimore: Johns Hopkins Press, 1961.

4. Wildavsky, Aaron, *The Politics of the Budgetary Process.* Boston: Little, Brown, 1964.

5. Hoos, Ida, *Systems Analysis in Public Policy: A Critique.* Berkeley: University of California Press, 1972.

6. Fuchs, Victor, "The Growing Demand for Medical Care," *New England Journal of Medicine*, 279:190-195, 1968.

7. Mechanic, David, *Politics, Medicine, and Social Science.* New York: Wiley-Interscience, 1974.

8. Mushkin, Selma, "Evaluations: Use with Caution," *Evaluation*, 1:30-35, 1973. Reprinted by permission. Copyright © 1973 by The Minneapolis Medical Research Foundation, Inc.

9. Cochrane, A.L., *Effectiveness and Efficiency.* London: Nuffield Provincial Hospitals Trust, 1972.

10. Houston, Tom R., Jr., "The Behavioral Sciences Impact-Effectiveness Model," in Rossi, P. and W. Williams (eds.), *Evaluating Social Programs*, p. 63.

11. Kershaw, D., "Issues in Income Maintenance Experiments," in Rossi, P. and W. Williams (eds.), *Evaluating Social Programs*; Kershaw, D. and J. Fair, *Report on the New Jersey Negative Income Tax Experiment*, Volume 3. Princeton, N.J.: Mathematica, 1973, Chapter 12.

12. Campbell, D.T. and J.C. Stanley, *Experimental and Quasi-Experimental Designs for Research.* Chicago: Rand McNally, 1963.

13. Institute of Medicine, National Academy of Sciences, *A Strategy for Evaluating Health Services.* Washington, D.C., 1973, pp. 3-5.

14. Report of the Committee to Evaluate the National Center for Health Statistics, *Health Statistics, Today and Tomorrow.* Washington, D.C.: U.S. Government Printing Office, Series 4, No. 15, 1973.

15. Dohrenwend, Bruce and Barbara Dohrenwend, *Social Status and Psychological Disorder.* New York: Wiley-Interscience, 1969.

16. Shepherd, Michael et al., *Psychiatric Illness in General Practice.* London: Oxford University Press, 1966.
17. National Center for Health Statistics, *Selected Symptoms of Psychological Distress—United States.* Washington, D.C.: U.S. Government Printing Office, Series 11, No. 37, 1970.
18. Middleton, Russell and Vernon Allen, "Social Psychological Consequences of the Graduated Work Incentive Experiment," mimeo, University of Wisconsin-Madison, 1973.
19. Dohrenwend, Bruce and D. Crandell, "Psychiatric Symptoms in Community, Clinic, and Mental Hospital Groups," *American Journal of Psychiatry*, 126: 1611-1621, 1970.
20. Gove, W.R. and J.F. Tudor, "Adult Sex Roles and Mental Illness," *American Journal of Sociology*, 78:812-835, 1973.
21. Hollingshead, A.B. and F.C. Redlich, *Social Class and Mental Illness.* New York: Wiley, 1958, p. 231.
22. Warheit, G. and J. Schwab, "An Analysis of Social Class and Racial Differences in Depressive Symptomatology: A Community Study," *Journal of Health and Social Behavior*, 14:291-299, 1973.
23. Bradburn, Norman, *The Structure of Psychological Well-being.* Chicago: Aldine, 1969.
24. Ibid., pp. 211-222; Caplovitz, David and Norman Bradburn, *Reports on Happiness.* Chicago: Aldine, 1965.
25. Freeman, H. and O. Simmons, *The Mental Patient Comes Home.* New York: Wiley, 1963.
26. Gardner, Elmer, "The Use of a Psychiatric Case Register in the Planning and Evaluation of a Mental Health Program," in Schulberg, H.C. et al. (eds.), *Program Evaluation in the Health Fields.* New York: Behavioral Publications, 1969, pp. 538-561.
27. See, for example, Mann, K.J. et al., *Visits to Doctors.* Jerusalem: Academic Press, 1970.
28. Wholey, Joseph et al., *Federal Evaluation Policy: Analyzing the Effects of Public Programs.* Washington, D.C.: The Urban Institute, 1970.
29. Moos, Rudolph, *Evaluating Treatment Environments: A Social Ecological Approach.* New York: Wiley-Interscience, 1974.

2 Evaluation: State of the Technical Art
Daniel M. Wilner

In the ideal situation all public programs to alleviate sociomedical and psychological pathology are based on sound understanding of causation; the resulting programs are thought out carefully and applied in sufficient extent and depth to effect favorable outcome; and program support (funding) is adequate and continuingly plentiful. Ideally, also, data needed to evaluate program effectiveness are simple and easily obtained; measures of behavior and ideation have relevance, high reliability, and validity; there is agreement on what constitutes meaningful gain or loss to client or patient, with the state of measurement of gain or loss being at a high level of performance; and resulting reports are uniformly presented and easy to comprehend. And, finally, ideally the feedback of results of all the foregoing are judiciously implemented: If programs are beneficial, they are expanded; but if not, there is willing adaptation to program modifications, drastic if need be, but with few or no sleepless nights, nor ego damage, nor — the ultimate threat — danger to job tenure.

With considerable regret it must be admitted that the ideal situation just described in no way resembles current reality, a conclusion reached by reading 25 recent books in the evaluation field,[1] by the preliminary results of a data bank of evaluations being assembled at UCLA,[2] and by 25 years of personal experience in the field of evaluation.[3] For the short run it may not really matter either way, because there seem to be secular trends in program support that are apparently independent of anything that evaluation activities uncover. It is the long run that holds some hope for the future. Innovative program breakthroughs, appropriately documented, will get their fair share of the program dollar when their outcomes are visible.

The present state of the art of evaluation is embodied in the 25 or so books already mentioned. These are the works that are recommended — in addition to technical and research textbooks — to students in evaluation curricula and to practitioners in actual evaluation efforts such as those assembled at this conference. These are interesting and valuable books, telling of big evaluations and little; describing various levels of interest, accomplishments and shortcomings; and offering specific instruction in the conduct of evaluation studies. The

Supported in part by a grant from the National Institute of Mental Health, Mental Health Services Development Branch (MH1R12-22761, "Mental Health Evaluations: Analysis and Dissemination"). The examples used in the chapter are taken from the resulting data bank of program evaluations.

27

28567

combined bibliographies within these 25 books number perhaps 1,000 to 2,000 additional references that surely describe the field in detail.

For the practical administrator these books are highly recommended but should by no means be considered the sole panacea for problems. There is a need to put what these books in one way or another attempt to say into each individual's perspective. It is possible to summarize the principal issues as those of (a) the several definitions of "evaluation," (b) the many motives and purposes of interested parties, (c) the variety of programs, (d) the variety of designs and data collection strategies, and (e) the many measures to be considered. The key words are "several," "variety," and "many." No sensible discussion of evaluation can avoid recognizing and dealing with the pluralism in the field.

Definitions and History

There are broad and narrow definitions of the term evaluation. The broad definitions do not normally deal with gain or loss to patient or client, but rather are in the category of program bookkeeping or monitoring. Broad evaluations are widely demanded by program funding agencies and are the object of much record keeping and necessary busywork. The broad definitions include counts of numbers of programs, as well as numbers of dollars spent in connection with various program elements. Thus, it is possible to talk about costs associated with various units of service. Such counts may be but are not always included in narrow definitions of evaluation, although they certainly evaluate something, namely, the volume of service activity generated by a program. Even these seemingly simple counts are not always easy to make. For example, is a single-name program that gives four separate street addresses four programs or one? How do we distinguish clinic visits from clients or patients in treatment? Every program in the ADAMHA (Alcohol, Drug Abuse and Mental Health Administration) range of interests makes such counts either as "mandated" reports or for internal purposes.

Somewhat more complex than head and dollar counting are program descriptions. Attempts are made to describe program components such as the elements of "day-night" hospitals, methadone treatment, or alcoholism halfway houses. Such classifications are also evaluative in nature, responding to the question, "On what treatment schemes is our money being spent?" It is very much harder to answer this question than to obtain the more simple counts, there being no wide acceptance of uniform terminology for identical elements of service, nor clear identification of "intensity" of service rendered. Program descriptions often include enumeration of professional staff of various disciplines, clinic hours, etc., but normally little of the content of program details. Even programs in which administration of pharmaceuticals is a key element, (e.g., antabuse, darvon N, tranquilizing drugs) can vary enormously in important program detail.

More complex still is the assessment of program quality. Quality of care in all health settings is currently of high concern in evaluation discussions. Measurement in this area is particularly complex, especially in programs requiring services of indigenous staff, staff derived from patient or client ranks, or staff with no particular qualifying characteristics other than "they are there." Judgments are also difficult to make regarding the "atmosphere" of a treatment setting and characteristics such as continuity or discontinuity of care.

From program descriptions and quality assessments much valuable information can be derived: how the money is being spent (even by component), the staff employed, the treatment modalities used (however globally described), and the state of the program art. One can also derive secondary measures: for example, costs per patient or client treated, even by treatment modality. But one thing such evaluative approaches cannot do is to show how the patient or client gained or lost as a result of the treatment program — and this, after all, is the heart of a cost-to-benefit analysis.

The gain or loss to the consumer of the service (the client or patient) and to his or her family, or, the gain or loss to the broad community in which the service is being rendered, is, of course, the narrowest definition of evaluation. Whereas counting and program descriptions are, or should be, administrative program-monitoring requirements, gain/loss is the payoff evaluative measure. It is the focus of the 25 books mentioned earlier, and it constitutes a topic that deserves some historical treatment.

Society has for centuries been interested in the consequences of its medical and social interventions, particularly those inspired by help-providing professionals. Perhaps the earliest confirmed perceptions of cause and effect in this context came in connection with communicable disease. There comes to mind the work of John Snow on cholera, and a succession of titans of the nineteenth century, including Pasteur, Ehrlich, and Koch, and in the twentieth century, Goldberger on pellagra, and Salk on poliomyelitis.

The Salk vaccine was used in a mammoth experimental trial and subsequent evaluation in 1954, twenty years ago. The method, which is by now standard, included analyzing and hypothesizing — interwoven with a protracted period of laboratory research by hundreds of investigators. Finally, there was a program of action — a vast trial of the vaccine involving several hundred thousand school children — and subsequent tracing or evaluating the results. The outcomes are known to us all. In 1973 there were in the United States fewer than 100 cases of polio and fewer than a dozen deaths from the disease.

In the mental health and social action fields, there was no such signal progress. Because of sheer complexity, analysis has not always led to testable hypotheses nor to replicable studies, and studies have not always led to broad and economical programs of action. Until recent years treatment itself was perceived organizationally as a solo operation, hard to effect by massive application of effort. Furthermore, as we know, tracing results of any action is difficult

when results are either secret (case-record confidentiality), or are not systematically maintained — if they are kept at all. Finally, the social action field has
lagged in intervention studies because there were, in earlier days, fewer professionally inspired interventions.

Nevertheless, as we know, there have been many efforts to communicate in
durable form the results of individual treatment and of broader social action
programs. Since the nineteenth century and continuing in many journals today
there have been individual reports by therapists about treatment success and
failures in their personal office practice ("one on one" reports).

There have been psychopharmacological studies — also continuing unabated
today — testing every conceivable compound and substance in an attempt to
understand "treatment outcomes." Since the 1950s many of these studies have
concentrated on the outcomes of narcoleptic drugs and have showed promise of
usefulness in the treatment of one mental illness or another, but pharmaco-
therapy has, unhappily, not yet fulfilled the promise of a decade ago, with increasing uneasiness regarding side effects of well-established drugs. Programs in
the fields of alcohol abuse and drug abuse have concentrated on antagonists and
legal substitutes for the substances that give rise to unwanted addictions. These
programs have also been the object of numerous outcome studies. In recent
years there has been a surge of reports of evaluation of behavior modification
efforts.

There have been a host of studies continuing to this day emanating from
hospitals and other settings caring for the mentally retarded. These are studies
reporting on efforts — therapies, milieus, instructional procedures, and pharmaco-
logical interventions — purportedly affecting intellectual functioning.

Some evaluative reports came out of the social work field, where the intervention sometimes had a helping/counselling quality and emphasis, and dealt
with "problem families": for example, in earlier days with white immigrants,
probationers or prison inmates, and other objects of social work concern. Re-
latedly, the field of housing was another setting calling forth evaluation work.
Here the professionally inspired intervention was not human contact with professionals, but rather variation in housing quality. The effects of housing on a
host of outcome measures were studied in several hundred published works.

The 1950s and particularly 1960s saw another element emerge — this one of
critical importance. The infusion through presidential and congressional action
of huge sums of money into the social and helping fabric of our times gave un-
precedented impetus to program development in several fields. Mental health,
addiction, and broad social intervention programs were developed and funded by
various elements of the Department of Health, Education, and Welfare — which
survived numerous reorganizations — as well as the Department of Labor and the
Department of Housing and Urban Development. At the center of much activity
was the Office of Economic Opportunity.

The scenario is a heady one — those were the days!

In addition to federal sources, state funding and sometimes, as in New York, California, and other states, local counterparts unleashed money like dogs of war to fight battles against poverty, racial and social injustice, school impactment, and the ravages and injustices of aging, as well as mental health impairment, alcoholism, and drug abuse.

With vastly increased sums of money came a new theme in evaluation work. It is fair to say that the earlier — pre-1950 — motivation to measure program outcomes lay mainly in curiosity — personal, professional, and scientific. Curiosity is not a bad motive if the costs are small and the activity can be worked into normal tasks, and if one's job is not at stake as one of the evaluation's outcomes. However, the social programs of the 1960s and those that continued into the 1970s carried the implicit promise of gainful outcome to the patient or client. Congressional testimony in the period is studded with forecasts of demonstrable positive outcomes as a result of mental health and social action programs. Recital of the very phrases would embarrass us all if tapes were to be found that played back — in their entirety — our comments at the time.

So it was that along with the newly increased funding came an urgency to understand what was being accomplished by the expanded social welfare and sociomedical programs. Early in the 1960s one began to hear — echoing phrases from the Pentagon — about the amount of "bang for the buck." The newer motivation for evaluation departed from curiosity and began to resemble the motivation of business accounting. Emphasis was on the "bottom line" — a term borrowed from corporate balance sheets — where the positive accomplishments (or if luck ran out, the failures) would be revealed. The hope was that evaluation would become the fulcrum on which program acceleration or attenuation could be decided. Programs shown to be "working" — normally, reducing the incidence of some social ailment, or showing a rise in desirable social reaction or behavior — could thus be reinforced. Programs shown "not to be working" — not showing such gains — could be reduced or substantially revamped if the program idea still seemed a good one.

Increased emphasis on evaluation activities gave rise to a cadre of professionals closely linked to developments in the various action areas. Before 1950 the low-key evaluation effort was peopled by a small number of statisticians and, depending on substantive area of interest, by psychiatrists, psychologists, social workers, and sociologists. Later, economists, planners, political scientists, and others interested in the budget process came on the scene, as well as persons knowledgeable about specific programs and problems of measurement. Every federal governmental agency had its Office of Program Planning and Evaluation (PPE), and any subordinate organization worth its salt also had an office so named or serving a kindred function. Today there are few state, county, and city agencies without planning and evaluation personnel.

During the expansion period there also developed an outside arm of evaluation activity. Universities, "think tanks," research institutes, and private R&D corporations or subsidiaries all got into the evaluation business. These "outside" organizations were often the conceptualizing and research-action troops of funding agencies, both in special social interventions (e.g., Westinghouse Learning Corporation in connection with Head Start,[4] and the University of Wisconsin and Mathematica, Inc., in connection with the New Jersey Graduated Work Incentive Experiment[5]) and in more routine program delivery (e.g., Stanford Research Institute in connection with programs of NIAAA [The National Institute on Alcohol Abuse and Alcoholism]).

All these efforts, both inside government and outside, sought some understanding of the principles of allocation of scarce resources (ideas and money are examples) and were entranced by the prospects of developing measurements between program benefits and associated costs, often with more or less complex speculation and mathematics, and always with the aid of the modern computer.

Motives and Purposes of Interested Parties

Much has been written about motivation in connection with evaluative research. Reference is to various processes in the *willingness* versus the *resistance* to gathering data and other information for evaluation, both in the broad and narrow senses. Motivation is of high importance, since attitudes, feelings, and pressures have their effects on the nature and quantity gathered, assembled, and channeled, in addition to having a role in the interpretation of findings.

Discussions in this section are devoted to the source of stimulation or *mandate* for data, the nature of the data to be collected, and the purposes to which the data are put. The reason for this interest is the very substantial demands made of ADAMHA line-action agencies to supply systematic evaluative information for various purposes. The imminent danger is the possible clogging of the pipelines of communication by the sheer quantity of the data thus generated. The impetus for collection of information about programs comes from federal agencies; from state, county, and certain city administrative agencies; and, of course, from direct service organizations. The governmental "mandates" for certain information arises not only because of the desire for supervisory neatness, but also because of the need for accountability for public funds.

Federal agencies (e.g., ADAMHA components) are at the top of the hierarchy and generate requests for information about programs that federal funds help to support. State alcoholism, drug abuse, and mental health agencies have similar requirements, partly because state public funds are involved, or if not, because states, in getting grants-in-aid, generally are funnels for federal data requirements. County and some city alcoholism, drug abuse, and mental health agencies are in the same boat, since they likewise either funnel information upwards or are responsible to local public funding sources for programs with local support. Direct service organizations (e.g., alcohol treatment centers, various drug abuse control programs, and community mental health centers) are at the bottom of the pyramid and normally initiate the information that is used stepwise in higher echelons.

There are gaps, of course. Data collection is sometimes beyond the resources and capacity of some publicly supported direct service agencies. Also, certain private nonprofit agencies (hospitals and clinics) do not accept public funds aside from Medicare or Medicaid — there are a number in California — and will not participate in some cadence-counting data collection schemes. Thus, for example, there are few really good estimates of all patients and clients served by private practitioners in ADAMHA's sphere of interests.

Program data and information gathered and funneled upward are of several varieties and are often to be found embodied in data forms (ranging from very modest formats to printed setups prepared for key punching or optical decoding), folders, and voluminous files maintained on each client or patient as part of treatment and management. The task is to record information about the client's personal background (demographic data about self and family); history of the pathology in question (e.g., history of addiction or of mental illness); past treatment or institutionalization (including various brushes with hospitals, clinics, and rest homes, as well as involvements with the law, correctional institutions, and probation systems); ideation and attitudes, since these are the undeniable precursors, accompaniments, and results of our interventions; details of the current treatment process; and, sometimes, evidence or judgments about the effects of the "treatment" on the client or patient, which might lead to some conclusions about gain or loss. Needless to say, when the patient returns for further treatment, or even in follow-up of a successful outcome, much of the information needs to be collected again — often to confirm history, or even to reinvent it. The upper bounds of amount of information collected seem to be limited by the magic "one hour," by client literacy or patience, and by professional or occupational capacity of the interviewer or intake person.

The purposes for collecting information about programs include routine reporting, management guidance, "research," and evaluation of outcome. Routine reports are aggregated to reveal volume of program efforts, and the various subcategories of information reveal pithy detail one welcomes in the more literate interim and annual reports. The volume of business thus enumerated also to some extent reinforces evidence about the extent of the problem that the program—federal, state, county, or private sector—was organized to combat.

The management guidance function of data collection is very important if initiated thoughtfully and handled carefully. It is sensible—and sometimes easy enough—to keep track of patient tenure and movement in and among elements of a mental health center as well as between the center and various inpatient and posthospitalization facilities. Good management also requires knowing how representative the clientele is of the surrounding community, which can be revealed by comparing patient characteristics with catchment area characteristics or to the characteristics of alcohol and drug-using populations. If, for example, a Community Mental Health Center (CMHC) in a catchment area half black in population has only a handful of black patients in its walk-in service, management needs in all likelihood to review center characteristics such as accessibility, staff composition, and general image.

The "research" motive in collection of data in ongoing clinical settings is laudable enough—who can be against research in substantive areas where systematic empiricism seems to be so badly needed? The truth is that most data collected through standard forms of various kinds are in actuality seldom processed adequately or analyzed thoroughly, and that "research" activity becomes mainly a kind of status symbol. Sometimes the research motive leads to a wild proliferation of questionnaire and interview schedules with little or no rationale for the individual questions or items, too few plans of analysis, and too little thinking ahead of how the information is to be used. In such cases the burden of asking, answering, and recording becomes simply enormous for the clinical staff and for the client.

Collection of information for routine reporting, program management, and for research, if brief and well done, can sometimes provide an exhilarating note to any clinical operation. It is widely observed that research elements, intelligently and sparingly applied, add interest and zest to day-to-day activities. But when information collection gets out of hand, the beneficial purposes are defeated and staff boredom and exasperation may result.

We come now to motives and purposes of data collected in order to evaluate outcome of the intervention—is the client or patient better off for having been in the program? Nothing tugs at the heartstrings like evaluation research. Nothing else makes clinical staff yearn so much for body-English that reveals successful impact of the program. Yet, nothing is so hard to demonstrate simply, with clarity, and decisively. There are pressures to justify program existence, to demonstrate theoretical and technical grasp of the issues involved in treatment, and, further, to demonstrate and justify personal professional competence. I have found over the years—widely documented—that clinical personnel in the mental health and addiction fields resent nothing so deeply as they do these various pressures.

Unhappily for clinicians, the situation probably will get worse in the short run rather than better. Helping professionals in *all* health and welfare fields are increasingly being asked to justify their therapeutic procedures. Professional Standards Review Organizations (PSRO) are now springing up in the 50 states, a first institutional − and as yet imperfect − step on the way to monitoring performance of physicians and related personnel in medical and health settings as applied to Medicare and Medicaid reimbursement. It is not difficult to see similar developments in the mental health and addictions fields, although the direct sums spent are as yet small in comparison to costs bracketed in under Titles XVIII and XIX of the Social Security Act.

A doctoral dissertation just completed by one of my students has documented how irrelevant evaluation research activity is to the local clinical goals of many community mental health centers.[6] In any case not every clinical center, whether dealing with alcohol or drug abuse or with general mental pathology, has the capacity for carrying out solid evaluative studies. There are simply not enough funds nor qualified personnel to conduct thorough gain/loss evaluative studies of programs in the several thousand appropriate ADAMHA settings. Such studies actually can be carried out best in only a small number of clinical programs, and the state of the best of program art should then fan out everywhere. This would be analogous to the research situation in large medical centers versus small hospitals: not every 50-bed hospital in the United States need necessarily confirm the goodness of techniques and procedures that are developed in a large medical center that has the best available research facilities.

Local installations and programs can only perform in accordance with the best ideas in the field. What is needed is a PSRO scheme for ADAMHA progams. It is a clinical facility or program performing as well as the state of the art suggests it could? Meanwhile, I can only counsel modesty for the staffs of mental health and addictive treatment programs. Some candid admissions about the tentative state of the program art would help promote credibility for the entire enterprise.

Programs

Programs, of course, are the heart of the matter. To a great extent program is everything; and evaluation is only parasitic. This section discusses several matters related to the content of programs and to the populations and individuals to whom the program is delivered. The first consideration is the theory, or at least, the principles underlying the program. Theory is always an important preconsideration for everyone concerned and gives evaluators clues regarding measurement possibilities. Second are the joint matters of program extent and program intensity. Most ADAMHA programs are in the familiar double bind: fixed, limited, or even shrinking resources on the one hand; and on the other, a broad population to whom to deliver services. If several subpopulations need but cannot all receive the service, who will be left out? And once the recipient subpopulation is settled on, how much service does each client or patient receive individually? The third consideration has to do with the description of the programs or the measurement of program content. Planners need to know, for example, whether two programs with the same or opposite outcome findings are the same or different programs.

Theory and Principles

Theories and principles underlying programs in the alcohol and drug abuse fields seem still to be fairly volatile, with substantial eclectic elements. Theories of substance abuse deal with an amalgam of personality elements (character defects), exposure to addicting substances, opportunity for repetition and social conditioning (the community), and various physiologic factors (metabolic, systemic, cellular). The consequent programs touch on almost all aspects of these principles: Alcohol and drug abusers need to be detoxified, dehabituated, and rehabilitated. The physiologic craving is blocked in various attempts with drugs like disulfuram (antabuse) or with methadone (which also has a legal "substitute" quality). Almost all alcoholism and drug abuse programs are linked with efforts at socialization. In addition, these programs need to be prepared to cope with practical problems such as job failure, family disruption, and possible illegal behavior associated with getting money to support the addictive habit.

There has been a certain clutching at straws in substance abuse programs— the search for unimodal, inexpensive, easy-to-administer magic bullets to quell the addiction. There are none, as yet. The truth lies in the word "multimodality," not easy to administer, requiring coordination, and being extremely expensive. The experience with methadone is instructive in this connection: pharmacologically soundly based (as far as we know, but what about long-run side effects?), effective with many drug users, but lending itself to black market usage and to simultaneous and dangerous use along with other drugs.

In the community mental health field there also exists a set of principles that underly the nature of services offered. One principle is to do away with the distant mental hospital and to offer a complete array of treatment in the patient's home community, although a grave disservice is done if a broad array of necessary community facilities and services are in fact not available. Another principle is continuity of care. This is ideally reflected in provisions for inpatient as well as ambulatory care and through partial hospitalization in the same CMHC or close by. A third principle recognizes the crisis nature of some emotional disturbances, with the result that emergency services ("walk in, no waiting") are included in CMHC programs. A fourth principle concerns the pathogenic quality of some contemporary social institutions in the etiology of emotional disorder or behavior pathology. This is reflected in the consultation and education facet of CMHC's concentrating on caretaking agencies and individuals, with a range of objectives from improvement of "early detection" of pathology to advice about how to improve human organizations.

All modalities of psychiatric treatment are used, with some abandonment of orthodox psychoanalysis, and substantial abandonment of the more violent therapies, although in a number of inpatient settings there is still a quiet room where electroshock therapy is administered. There is heavy use of psychoactive drugs. Conversational therapies tend to stress "here and now" ideas rather than deep-rooted historical ones.

Program Extent

Program evaluators frequently reflect on the mix of patient or client populations who are actually in touch with services in the alcohol abuse, drug abuse, and community mental health fields. All three ADAMHA services stress accessibility, with facilities close to the people needing them, located in formal buildings or store fronts, near public transportation, and with automobile parking where necessary or possible. The idea is, of course, to overcome barriers to service arising either from health care provider predilections (deliberate or inadvertent) or from disabilities of the client or patient.

The truth is that, although progress has clearly been made, there remain individuals who have as much difficulty obtaining service as in earlier times, even though their service needs are high and they are particularly good candidates for showing gain from the program. For example, community mental health centers normally must, among other requirements, show familiarity with their catchment area when obtaining staffing or construction grants. The idea is that with this knowledge programs might be forged to reach persons in the area who are otherwise underrepresented in ordinary psychiatric practice. Common experience is that with some notable exceptions, in the long run this good idea suffers erosion.

Community analysis is not an easy matter at best, and like consultation and education (as well as evaluation) is not an income-producing activity. Denominator data (census materials) quickly go out of date, and relevant numerator data (social indicators) are often not aggregated neatly by census tracts, are hard to obtain if they exist in usable form at all, and also have a tendency to be out of date. Besides, for any real relevance, there has to be someone around who is the community advocate as well as data analyst trained in the monitoring of the center's responsiveness to the community. The result is that in many instances there are pockets of neglect of service not easily reached because of the normative trends in any clinical setting.

The situation is sometimes not too different in alcoholism treatment centers and in drug abuse treatment settings, although in these connections, there is less concern with geographic responsibilities. All analysis of the "market" is difficult, particularly when there are natural financial limits on who can be served in any event, once the group is identified. In the alcohol and drug abuse settings a particularly vexing problem has to do with exclusions or exceptions to service. For instance, there are guidelines widely used in methadone treatment describing ideal patients for therapy and suggesting patient characteristics less amenable to treatment. The effect is the same as in community mental health centers. Some individuals or subgroups in need of therapy—and likely to be heavy beneficiaries—find difficulty getting themselves into treatment hands.

Program Intensity

Evaluators also worry about whether the program as delivered to the

individual patient or client is of sufficient intensity and continuity to make realistic the anticipation of measurable outcome. Are one to six visits (median three)
to an emergency psychiatric service really enough to explore patient problems
and to formulate lasting solutions? Do alcoholism halfway houses really offer
much more than just room and board? Are partial hospitalization arrangements
really anything more than baby-sitting operations or day rooms? Are there really
adjunctive services to methadone delivery? Are indigenous treatment personnel
(catchment area residents, or former mental patients, or former drug or alcohol
users) sufficiently *prepared* for their roles as treatment agents?

One might assert that these are the very questions that evaluation outcome
studies answer. But, not really. The difference is between the program as ad-
vertised and that actually delivered — similar to the difference between the
spending budget a householder plans at the start of a month and how it actually
works out 30 days later. There are a host of factors, financial, organizational, and
situational, that could reduce program intensity to a level that would interfere
with program delivery. And it is what the program actually *does* deliver — not
what it *should* deliver — that is the concern of evaluation outcome studies.

There is always a possibility that the treatment program under evaluation is
not being given a fair chance because of program "thinness." It is for this reason
that evaluators sometimes seek additional funding and support for program "fat-
tening" in order to provide a real test of the value of a given treatment mode.

Program Description

The description of program content is no easy task. A review, for example,
of several hundred published reports of evaluations often reveals gaps in the
description of a program as delivered. Details of conceivable importance are in-
advertantly left out, partly because there are no systematic, ongoing accounts
maintained that would reveal thoughts about treatment extent and intensity, and
thus, produce useful judgments about the input qualities of the program.

In particular settings some of these details may not matter very much. In
surgery or other varieties of nonpsychiatric medicine, the interaction of treater
(surgeon, anesthesiologist, nurse) and patient may be of less importance in outcome than the nature of the treatment. In the ADAMHA range of programs,
however, treater intentions, treatment characteristics, and the interaction of these
with patients' motives, anxieties, and social qualities are likely to be of considerable significance.

As we enlarge the ADAMHA evaluation scene and attempt to understand and
integrate replicable studies from treatment settings in different communities,
states, and sectors of the United States, it will become increasingly important to
know exactly what it is that has been evaluated. Maintenance of the requisite
ongoing accounts of program details might be made possible through a shorthand

scheme that describes briefly in standard format the significant details of program input, so that readers everywhere might know about important elements of the intervention. Such a shorthand system would require time and effort to develop. Application of such a scheme would require more than normal candor on the part of the individuals reporting the evaluation; but what else is an evaluation report than organized candor?[a] Accounts of program details based on a standard rotation system could very well be assembled into program description archives, with ADAMHA conceivably serving both as the repository and the disseminator of the material.[7]

A further thought related to program description has to do with the catchment areas served by CMHCs, or in which CMHCs are located. It should be possible for the reader of a report about a program serving a catchment area to have access to the important geodemographic details of that area. This raises the possibility of another kind of archive altogether, namely, a collection of catchment area descriptions that instantly pinpoint the community characteristics that are relevant to the program being delivered. This information would be extremely valuable in assessing the national relevance of a given evaluation, certainly for CMHC programs, but equally for alcohol and drug abuse evaluations where geographic boundaries are relevant.

Measurement

Measures of accomplishment in the fields of alcoholism, drug abuse, and mental health treatment programs are of two kinds: (a) *social indicators*, generally tied to locales (catchment areas, cities, counties, states, etc.) and not necessarily involving the patients or clients who have received treatment or other services; and (b) *individual measures* obtained from or about persons for whom the treatment program was designed, and sometimes including the effect of treatment on related persons (i.e., families). Both kinds of measures have been the subject of scholarly and applied activity for many years; social indicators have been of special interest recently, particularly in the light of attempts to measure the impact of the "great society" and "new federalism" programs of the past decade. For neither social indicators nor for individual measures has any great uniformity developed regarding what sort of information is most useful, nor where and how it is to be assembled, nor how it is to be used. Also, in neither

---

[a]One can take a leaf from other disciplines (e.g., comparative and experimental psychology) where it is customary even now in research writeups to give what was formerly considered extraneous detail, even in studies dealing with the behavior of laboratory animals. In such studies it became clear that *"surround variables"* (for example, amount of handling) were as important to understanding experimental results as were the express stimuli.

case is there broad consensus on what is to be considered social or individual gain or loss.

Social Indicators

Social indicators are modeled to some extent after health indicators, which are alleged to yield broad information about the health status of a community, state, or nation. Thus, everything else being equal, or at least taken into account, it is possible to compare governmental or geographic jurisdictions at one point in time, or the same jurisdiction at two points in time, in order to detect trends in health matters. A widely used health indicator is infant mortality, partly because it has intrinsic appeal and partly because it has achieved some statistical stability. And since the United States does *not* rank lowest in the world (actually 15th in 1971), this fact has sometimes been used to suggest speed-up of maternal and child health programs in this country and is regularly reported in expert testimony before congressional committees. There are, in fact, few really good health indicators that are not subject to flaws that resist interpretation; for example, the fact that diagnostic and vital and health statistics reporting procedures are extremely variable and may influence observed or reported differences.

Social indicators are particularly subject to such variation, which thus limits their usefulness in attempts to link outcome to social programs. For example, at first blush it is reasonable to expect that a particularly successful drug abuse control program in a community would result in a detectable reduction in incidence of selected crimes and attempts or in adult or juvenile arrests, in the known light of how drug users support their habits. There are several problems related to this expectation:

1. Rate of reported crimes and attempts, or of arrests, are affected by many causative events and the direct reduction due to the good program, per se, may be too small to be detected.
2. If concentration of the program is on a particular section of a city or county, social indicator data may not be available in reliable and/or usable form for that section where the greatest social indicator effect is anticipated.
3. Not all data are assembled and aggregated equally completely. For example, crime and arrest counts are made and automatically reported by the New York and Los Angeles police departments, but not all other cities or counties as yet have this capability. There may be similar variation among police reporting districts within the same city or county.
4. There are, in fact, a large number of reasons for variation in crime and arrest rates aside from their "true" occurrence. Rates are affected by differential reporting of crimes to police, by police investigation, and by arrest practices, as well as by a host of pressures and social and subgeographic factors of great variety.

Aside from crimes and arrests, it is possible to mention a host of items that are useful, potentially, as social (i.e., areawide) indicators in various ADAMHA contexts. Thus, good programs might possibly have "successful" effects on school performance of children (grades, achievement tests, dropouts); social dependency (welfare, OAS—old-age security), ADC (aid to dependent children), Medicaid status; probation and parole; illegitimacy; venereal disease; suicide; mental hospitalization or general level of mental health service utilization; and cirrhosis of the liver and infectious hepatitis as direct links to alcoholism and drug abuse, respectively.

Many of these indicators are, with other measures, potentially valuable in describing the "quality of life" in a community. But most are subject to the same kinds of flaws as in the crime and arrest data mentioned above. The problems include: loose definitions; files not always up to date; record-keeping clerks not always qualified or sufficiently trained; haphazard assembly, subject to "drives" and other pressures; irregular reporting; individual cases subject to status reports only, with reasons for status not given and changes in status often not noted; and no geocoding of address, thus making difficult census tract assignment.

Some of the flaws can be corrected, at considerable expense, by evaluation research staff (e.g., geocoding); others cannot. Even the best of agencies in this regard offer insuperable problems. Some agencies come nowhere near providing usable social indicator data, although potentially theirs is the most valuable of all; for example, welfare agencies, probation and parole departments, and mental hospitals.

Nevertheless, social indicator data are possible to assemble and to aggregate, and play some role in the attempt to understand outcomes. If such data are considered as actual events rather than as reports and records of events, care must be taken in interpreting the links to the ADAMHA program in question. The reason is that other causes may be implicated in the occurrence of the event *other* than the program. Finally, there is the meaning of the event itself. For example, even getting on welfare may be a step up for down-and-out alcoholics.

Individual Measures

A full discussion of the kinds and uses of individual measures in outcome studies may be found in treatises on research methods in various disciplines such as the behavioral and social sciences, psychology, sociology, psychiatry, and, where appropriate, in medicine and physiology.[8] Such discussion covers the important technical matters of reliability and validity. This section concentrates on the broad behavioral and social sciences context, with selected topics particularly germane to evaluation in the ADAMHA fields.

Individual measures may be taken at any of several points in time. They may be made prior to treatment participation (either for screening purposes or to establish baselines for later comparisons), in the early stage of treatment, in the middle of treatment (at any point well before treatment ends), and at the end (when a formal phase of client-program interaction concludes). A particularly important point of measurement comes in follow-up, since the object of most treatment is enduring gain from program participation.

Individual measures are either designed specially for the purposes of evaluation or are maintained routinely and thus would be made even in the absence of evaluation activity. Routine records look like great finds until, as has been suggested earlier, it becomes apparent often that there are gaps in recording, lack of precision in judgments, or loose principles of classification. Sometimes routine measures can be adapted to evaluation purposes by evaluation staff in a general tightening up of judgmental and recording approaches.

The most frequently used measures made or reported in ADAMHA evaluation studies include ideation, behavior, and various physiologic measures, and there are different ways to get at each. *Ideation* is what is inside the head and is valuable as a precursor, accompaniment, or consequence of behavior change; or is valuable for itself, and in helping to understand program events or resistance to change. Ideation is a broad term that includes measures of "feelings," "emotions," "attitudes," "mood," "depression," "worry," "self-esteem," and other concepts communicating state of mind. In this sense ideation also includes expressions of satisfaction or dissatisfaction with service rendered or particular elements of service found laudable or repugnant or insufficient by the patient or client. Sometimes the ideation measured is that of the family ("How do you feel now that— the patient – is home?"). And sometimes it is that of the treatment or administrative staff.

Behavior change is in some respects the high priority goal of all ADAMHA programs, and evidence of valued behavioral alteration is taken most seriously as indicative of program benefit. It is, however, the most elusive and most difficult to measure. "Behavior" can range from facial expressions (grimaces, smiles), to acts with the most serious personal and social consequence, including death. In the ADAMHA context, behavior sometimes refers to behavioral violence or passivity, which also have ideational qualities. Very often the reference is to a social situation that reflects summative behavior, for example, "the patient remained in the program for six months"; "has been abstinent (alcohol) for eighteen months"; "is now back with his family and doing well in his old job"; "is living at Bayview Halfway House and attending AA meetings regularly."

Physiologic measures (medical and laboratory workups) include those important in diagnosis of the physical accompaniment of mental stress (EEG, reflex tests, and the several tests of systemic functioning obtained through analysis of blood and urine) as well as those that reveal ("betray") unwanted behavior (e.g., traces of alcohol and heroin in blood and urine, respectively).

Data measuring ideation and behavior are obtained in a variety of ways, none completely satisfactory, and none as simple as a temperature reading on a clinical thermometer. In a large number of studies in the ADAMHA range of interests, clients or patients are sometimes interviewed or they are asked to fill out a questionnaire themselves.

In interviews there is customarily an interview schedule or at least an interview guide; in any event, an interviewer asks questions and obtains answers that are then recorded (check marks, narrative remarks). In interview schedules the questions are preset. The interview guide is looser, permitting variation in question ordering, the guide serving largely as a reminder not to omit questions. Skill is needed in the interview, and thought is given to which staff members should conduct interviews, conditions of interviewing, etc. The point is that not just anyone can ask questions unimpassionedly, nor elicit nor record answers properly. Consideration also needs to be given to where and when (busy intake desk in the middle of tumult?), language (is the interview in Spanish?), aura and rapport (is the interviewer perceived as hostile?).

The questionnaire resembles the formal interview schedule, but has the special quality of self-administration, although a common practice is to offer "help" in coping with difficult questions. Consideration must also be given to the when and where and how of questionnaire administration. There is, in addition, the matter of literacy of the client or patient, or even general ability to cope with a paper and pencil task.

The preparation of both interview schedules and questionnaires requires careful thought, and, done properly, is a demanding and time-consuming job. Questionnaires and schedules are often "thrown together"; they tend thus to be overlong and repetitive, and to borrow vastly from established or older instruments (the Taylor, Zung, MMPI, etc.) sometimes inappropriately. Careful preparation of instruments should, on the other hand, consider purpose, length (the shorter the better), the use of single items versus scales and indexes (single questions are subject to irrelevant fluctuation in response whereas scales and indexes are more stable but are longer and sometimes boring). Additional considerations include question wording, question order, opening questions, closing questions, and many other nuances of instrument construction.

Interview schedules and questionnaires are sometimes used not only with client or patient, but also with family (spouse, parent), employer, caretaking personnel (caseworker), fellow patients, and treatment staff. These instruments are used to capture background and history, various elements of ideation as already discussed, reports of behavior (by no means the same as the behavior itself), and reactions to medication and other physiologic responses.

One special variety of measurement of outcome has to do with judgments of client or patient improvement as reported by clinical personnel (psychiatrists and other physicians, psychologists, social workers, and related therapeutic staff). These judgments have been under a fair amount of question since, to the outsider, they sometimes appear to be subjective appraisals unsupported by objective "visible" evidence. At the least (aside, say, from confirmed objective evidence of abstinence from alcohol or addictive drugs), the judgment of expert clinicians should be no more suspect than expressions of client or patient feelings and attitudes obtained from interviews and questionnaires. Clinical judgments received a bad press in early evaluation work in psychiatric clinics where the available evidence showed that the general run of psychiatric outpatients seemed to benefit equally *whatever* the treatment afforded, or if none was afforded at all. The culprit was really the treatment success or lack of it and its underlying theory (psychoanalysis), and not the judgment about it, although the issues are intermixed.

In the discussion of social indicators, mention has already been made of public records as a source of group or population data regarding program outcome. It is often thought appropriate, also, to check a public record to see if an individual client or patient has been arrested, sentenced, or recommitted; has shown up on welfare rolls; is enrolled and doing well in school; has been divorced, etc. Warnings about "flaws" in such public data (from police, courts, social welfare agencies, or school systems) apply to the individual case as well. There are several problems for the ardent evaluator to be aware of. The first is that of gaining cooperation from the public agency. Many are sticky about bandying individual names about, in spite of the high-mindedness of the purpose. The second, more basic problem is the valuation placed on data themselves. "Divorce" and "dropping out of school" need not be bad outcomes for patient or client. In any event, ideally, the public record event must be understood in the individual's context, without preconception of good or bad.

In spite of the fact that evaluation measurement is "for the client's own good," there is growing distrust of individual and social measurement, including interviews, questionnaires, and public records. The matter has a general societal echo in present resentments against storage, use, and misuse of personal information in various computerized databanks and registries. There are feelings about unwarranted, to say nothing of unconstitutional, invasions of privacy, connoting prying, spying, and "big brother" surveillance.

In research and clinical settings these suspicions have been translated into concerns for "human subjects" in research in the broad health and mental health fields and the requirement for informed consent from subjects and patients about their participation. It takes no great swami to forecast that we will meet more of this issue in years to come, as part of a package of patients' rights. Clearly this is a warning to overeager evaluators.

Recently there have developed procedures for the assessment of individual patient change in programs of community mental health centers, based on the setting of treatment goals and subsequent success in meeting them. Goal attainment scaling[9] (and several similar varients) attempt to make public the explicit treatment objectives agreed upon at the outset between patient and goal setters at the mental health center. For best use, clearly, goals that are set need to be pertinent, important in the life of the patient, and realistic of attainment although not trivial. Thus, there can be forecasts of the patients' involvement with drugs, other social functioning such as probation performance, alcohol intake, dependency on mother, and performance (scores) on personality tests. Goal attainment follow-up (were the goals reached?) depends on some combination of measures of ideation, behavior, and physiology obtained in ways already mentioned in this section. Its main novelty and gain is the effect on treatment ideology and the involvement of both patient and program staff in setting treatment goals.

The idea of goal attainment is appealing because of its forthright quality. Questions to be attacked include: Is the patient steamrollered into accepting goals? How many goals? How realistic? Do behavioral and ideational goals go beyond symptoms and get to the heart of the problem?

Most evaluators attempt to hedge their bets by using and reporting a number of measures of outcome rather than only one or two. The objective is to seine several facets of ideation, behavior, and physiological functioning as evidence of gain or loss to client or patient as program outcomes. While often theoretically justified as a scanning of outcome possibilities ("leave no stone unturned") the procedure almost certainly results in mixed affects as a consequence of sheer volume of measures. Evaluations need to stipulate clearly a rank ordering of importance of measures used.

Evaluative Research Designs

Attention is increasingly being called to the need for tight study designs in evaluating outcomes of program interventions. Without a suitable research design, it may be impossible to conclude that study results – however gratifying they appear to be – are attributable to the professionally inspired treatment program under scrutiny.

As with measurement, the *design* of studies to throw light on outcome is not a simple matter, and is deserving of the best thought and reflection. Elements in design include the manner in which patients or clients are chosen for inclusion in the study, the point or points in time at which measurement is made, and the use of comparison groups.

The design of an evaluative study may call for the inclusion of the entire group of patients or clients in the program, or more customarily, some sample. For example, there could be interest in the effect of a drug abuse control program on all patients during a specified period (e.g., from the clinic's opening to a given point in time). Data for this group are, therefore, being studied while the clinic is still accepting and treating new patients or clients. Or, there may be interest in special subgroups – women, teenage, black youth, older addicts. In any case, the total number of persons involved in a program may be too large, the work generated may be beyond the capacity of the research group, and it may statistically not be necessary to test everybody anyway. The solution in such situations is a sample.

There are various sampling procedures, random or systematic. Care must, in any event, be taken to avoid conscious or unconscious sampling biases that would interfere with generalizing findings to a larger group. Thus, it is clear that findings about treatment effects of a peer-control drug abuse program on women may be inapplicable to men patients or clients in the same treatment setting. However, if there are findings about treatment outcomes for "100 consecutive cases," generalizability may depend on which consecutive cases they were, and a more sophisticated time-connected sampling scheme with randomizing features may be preferable. The exact numbers of cases needed in a particular test sample may also be of concern. Sampling advice needs to be sought regarding sample size in given cases, since the interpretability of outcome data for samples of a given size depends to some extent on the magnitude of the responses or "differences" expected on various measures.

When and how often to measure effect is also an important matter. Many ADAMHA studies have a single point of measurement, namely, after the treatment is concluded for the patients or clients ("All of our patients have been in the group therapy program for at least six months"). This is "after only" measurement and in selected characteristic instances can be powerfully persuasive (e.g., survival after kidney transplant). But in most ADAMHA contexts one either relies on retrospective judgment ("I think I feel better"), which is notoriously unreliable and subject to variation, or on a single time statement of current behavior ("I have not had a drink in a month"). In either case a principal difficulty is that of assigning cause of the ideation or behavior to the program in question, since many events aside from program events are taking place at the same time. Further, the amount of gain or loss is difficult to judge since only one point in time is really observed.

Some ADAMHA studies show better design in that they provide for several points in time for measurement ("before and after"); for example, scores on a "depression" scale prior to the time treatment began, at termination of treatment, and six months later than that. This design feature eliminates retrospective unreliability and permits concentration on current status. With the proper instruments individual gain or loss can be calculated (by subtraction) and considerable precision obtained. In this method there is always the possibility of showing loss as well as gain. In any event, the proper statistical analysis must be settled on to detect gains or losses beyond acceptable chance variation. Special problems also arise in before-and-after studies, particularly if the identical instruments are used at two or more points in time. These problems include "practice effects" (familiarity with instruments), and statistical "regression effects" (extreme "before" scores tend, because of imperfect instruments, to be less extreme in "after" measurements). The principal flaw remains concurrent external events, and before-and-after measurement does not overcome this difficulty. Since many events are taking place at the same time as the treatment itself, these events rather than the treatment might account for all the gains or losses detected.

The answer to many problems in the interpretation of outcomes of interventions lies in the judicious identification of comparison groups, and more ADAMHA studies than formerly — but still only a small proportion — show use of this design feature. Thus, a "control" group is identified and is compared to a test group. The control group is not exposed to the treatment in question ("no treatment") or, in modified situations, is "treated" in some other way than the test group. To some extent this rules out the effects of external events, since the same relevant nontreatment events are presumably happening to the tests and controls alike.

Well-managed evaluation studies with a test group and one or more control groups, both subject to the same before-and-after measures certainly go a long way towards reducing ambiguity in interpretation of outcomes. The key elements here are the extent and surety of initial comparability of the test and control groups, and the maintenance of test and control conditions throughout the evaluation study period.

Initial comparability deals with the manner of selection of the various groups. Control groups can bear many relationships to the test group; in an evaluation study both groups should suffer from the same disability, to the same intensity and extent and with the same pathological features that need treatment, and they should be similar demographically. Initial comparability of test and control groups is, within chance limits, assured by random assignment, a mode to which there has recently been directed considerable attention. The alternative is some other scheme in which there is matching of test and control individuals — one pair at a time or in groups, but *not* through random assignment.

The basic problem — giving rise to frustration and wrangling — is the hidden differences that may occur in two matched groups that have not been determined through random procedures. There might, for example, be important but invisible differences in personal history, outlook, motivation, and aspiration between nonrandomly determined comparison groups. Suppose there are discovered differences in treatment outcome, "tests" (exposed to treatment) doing much better than "controls" (not exposed to treatment or exposed to different treatment). What is this difference due to? The treatment? Or, to some pretreatment difference not uncovered — in spite of close scrutiny — that determined the later differences in outcome?

Perhaps as important as initial comparability is maintaining test and control conditions for the duration of the evaluation study. Ideally, "test" cases should be in treatment for the study duration and "controls" in nontreatment for the same period. In actual settings controls may "wander" over into test conditions (are accepted into treatment somewhere) and "test" individuals may drop out. In both instances sample sizes shrink, and case attrition may be selective.

There are serious misgivings about the ethics and morality of withholding treatment in an arbitrary ("random") way from patients or clients who seek it, and it is sometimes also against the law to withhold treatment in this way. Many program personnel applaud these social and legal constraints, but others advocate a more moderate position on the issue of randomization. This view holds that randomization and other tight study design features are needed in order to thoroughly evaluate a program's effectiveness, particularly when there is agreement that the program itself is only tenuously understood.

Undeniably, in an increasing number of life and death settings in recent years there have been "clinical trials," with controls (often randomly assigned), and with before-and-after measures. A classic case is cancer chemotherapy, with many substances being tried out experimentally — after obtaining signed permissions (informed consent). There is currently underway a nationwide clinical trial of another sort, nonetheless dramatic in its use of controls. The disease involved is diabetic retinopathy, which frequently results in damage to the eye, and for which a sophisticated repair technique has been developed. The design of the clinical trial provides that one eye of each patient will be selected randomly for treatment, while the other eye will be observed without treatment unless and until there is convincing evidence that treatment is beneficial.

We have not heard the last of the pressures for systematic test-control, perhaps randomly assigned before-and-after measurement for patients and clients in selected ADAMHA programs. There have been expressions to this effect from top administrators of health and welfare agencies at federal and state levels, from legislators and politicians, from influential science policy agencies (e.g., Social Science Research Council in the context of large-scale social experiments), and from observers of and participants in ADAMHA efforts at the universities.

In addition to individual case controls, there is also the possibility of utilizing "geographic" controls. Assuming that treatment programs have community impact, then beneficial outcome might be visible if the "treated" community is compared with a community in which a comparable program is not present. Thus, a program is delivered in one state, county, city, or catchment area and since there are, for example, 3,000 counties in the United States, and at least 2,000 catchment areas of size, it might not be difficult to locate and identify counties, cities, or catchment areas similar in most or all significant respects to the geographic unit in which the program "under test" is operating. This requires social analysis of communities as well as analysis of relevant social institutions, social landmarks, and epidemiologic data. A suggestion has been made earlier about the "banking" of catchment area characteristics that would permit identification of catchment areas similar in important respects, only some of which have ADAMHA programs in force.

Conclusion

The evaluation field is now in ferment, and some probable directions are clear. Insofar as federal, state, and county health and welfare agencies are concerned as well as fiscal officers everywhere, there will be continued pressure to describe how tax-derived funds have been spent and with what medical and social gain, as well as pressures originating from scientific curiosity. Wise administrators will get with it where possible and where evaluation studies can sensibly be carried out.

But before a tidal wave of evaluation studies overwhelms us, we must ask: How many evaluations are really needed and where ought they be done? It is manifestly not possible to evaluate, in the narrow sense, every single treatment and rehabilitation facility. There are at least 400 federally supported community mental health centers, and several thousand alcohol and drug abuse treatment and rehabilitation facilities and programs. To launch and carry out credible evaluations in such an array is clearly not manageable. All programs, hopefully, are, or should maintain management data systems of some sort to understand patient flow, but outcome evaluations clearly exceed capacity. There is needed the identification of a small set of ADAMHA facilities representative of those serving various patient and client populations with the capacity, credibility, and *funding support* to initiate systematic evaluations of a full array of treatment options in the ADAMHA sector. In this way it may be possible to make faster inroads in the solution of problems that give rise to untold anguish to millions of Americans.

Notes

1. See Recent Evaluation Literature, page 50.
2. Wilner, D.M., Hetherington, R.W., Gold, E.B. Ershoff, D.H., and Garagliano, C.F. "Inside DOPE: Databank of Program Evaluation," *Evaluation, 1* (3): 3-6, 1973.
3. See Supplementary Bibliography, page 51.
4. Westinghouse Learning Corporation-Ohio University. *The Impact of Head Start on Children's Cognitive and Affective Development.* Springfield, Virginia: Clearinghouse for Federal Scientific and Technical Information, July 1969.
5. University of Wisconsin, Institute for Research on Poverty and Mathematica, Inc. *Summary Report: The New Jersey Graduated Work Incentive Experiment.* Washington, D.C.: U.S. Department of Health, Education and Welfare, December, 1973; Orr, Larry L., Hollister, Robinson G., and Lefcowitz, Myron J. *Income Maintenance, Interdisciplinary Approaches to Research.* Institute for Research. Chicago: Markham Publishing Company, 1971.

6. Garagliano, C.F. *Mental Health Program Evaluation: Attitudes, Culture, and Performance.* Doctoral dissertation. Los Angeles: University of California, 1974.
7. Through such agencies as the National Clearinghouse for Drug Abuse Information, National Clearinghouse for Alcohol Information, and National Clearinghouse for Mental Health Information — all in Rockville, Maryland.
8. See Selected Outcome Measures, pages 53-54.
9. Kiresuk, Thomas J. and Sherman, Robert E. "Goal Attainment Scaling: A General Method for Evaluating Comprehensive Community Mental Health Programs," *Community Mental Health Journal, 4:* 443-453, 1968.

Bibliography

Recent Evaluation Literature

American Institutes for Research. *Evaluative Research, Strategies, and Methods.* Pittsburgh: American Institutes for Research, 1970.

Bauer, Raymond A. (Ed.) *Social Indicators.* Cambridge, Massachusetts: The M.I.T. Press, 1966.

Bergin, Allen E. and Garfield, Sol L. *Handbook of Psychotherapy and Behavior Change: An Empirical Analysis.* New York: John Wiley and Sons, 1971.

Campbell, Donald T. and Stanley, Julian C. *Experimental and Quasi-Experimental Designs for Research.* Chicago: Rand McNally, 1963.

Caro, Francis (Ed.) *Readings in Evaluation Research.* New York: Russell Sage Foundation, 1971.

Dorfman, Robert (Ed.) *Measuring Benefits of Government Investments.* Washington, D.C.: The Brookings Institution, 1965.

Etzioni, Amitai and Eva. *Social Change.* New York: Basic Books, Inc., 1964.

Evaluation, Volume 1, Numbers 1, 2, and 3, 1972 and 1973.

Ferman, Louis A. (Ed.) "Evaluating the War on Poverty." *The Annals of the American Academy of Political and Social Science*, Volume 385, September 1969 (entire issue).

Freeman, Howard E. and Sherwood, Clarence E. *Social Research and Social Policy.* Englewood Cliffs, New Jersey: Prentice-Hall, 1970.

Ginzberg, Eli and Solow, Robert M. (Eds.) "The Great Society: Lessons for the Future." *The Public Interest*, Number 34, Winter 1974 (entire issue).

Grundy, F. and Reinke, W.A. *Health Practice Research and Formalized Managerial Methods.* Geneva: World Health Organization, 1973.

Herzog, Elizabeth. *Some Guide Lines for Evaluative Research.* Children's Bureau Publication Number 375-1959. Washington, D.C.: U.S. Department of Health, Education, and Welfare, Welfare Administration, Children's Bureau, 1959.

Mullen, Edward J. and Dumpson, James R., and Associates. *Evaluation of Social Intervention.* San Francisco: Jossey-Bass Inc., 1972.

Rossi, Peter and Williams, Walter. *Evaluating Social Programs.* New York: Seminar Press, 1972.

Schulberg, Herbert; Sheldon, Alan; and Baker, Frank. *Program Evaluation in the Health Fields.* New York: Behavioral Publications, 1969.

Suchman, Edward A. *Evaluative Research.* New York: Russell Sage Foundation, 1967.

Tripodi, Tony; Fellin, Phillip; and Epstein, Irwin. *Social Program Evaluation.* Itasca, Illinois: F.E. Peacock, 1971.

Tripodi, Tony; Fellin, Phillip; and Meyer, Henry J. *The Assessment of Social Research.* Itasca, Illinois: F.E. Peacock, 1969.

Tufte, Edward R. (Ed.) *The Quantitative Analysis of Social Problems.* Reading, Massachusetts: Addison-Wesley Publishing Company, 1970.

U.S., Department of Health, Education, and Welfare, National Institute of Mental Health. *Planning for Creative Change in Mental Health Services: Use of Program Evaluation.* Publication Number (HSM) 71-9057. Washington, D.C.: U.S. Department of Health, Education, and Welfare, National Institute of Mental Health, 1972.

U.S., House of Representatives, Committee on Government Operations. *The Use of Social Research in Federal Domestic Programs*, Parts II and III. Washington, D.C.: U.S. Government Printing Office, April 1967.

Weiss, Carol H. *Evaluating Action Programs: Readings in Social Action and Education.* Boston: Allyn and Bacon, Inc., 1972.

Weiss, Carol H. *Evaluation Research: Methods for Assessing Program Effectiveness.* Englewood Cliffs, New Jersey: Prentice-Hall, 1972.

Wholey, Joseph S.; Scanlon, John W.; Duffy, Hugh G.; Fukumoto, James S., and Vogt, Leona M. *Federal Evaluation Policy: Analyzing the Effects of Public Programs.* Washington, D.C.: The Urban Institute, 1971.

Williams, Walter. *Social Policy Research and Analysis: The Experience in the Federal Social Agencies.* New York: Elsevier, 1971.

Supplementary Bibliography

Chein, I.; Gerard, D.; Lee, R.S.; Rosenfeld, E. with the collaboration of Wilner, D.M. *The Road to H: Narcotics, Delinquency and Social Policy.* New York: Basic Books, Inc., 1964.

Eisenberg, L.; Landowne, E.J.; Wilner, D.M.; and Imber, S.I. "The Use of Teacher Ratings in a Mental Health Study," *American Journal of Public Health, 52:* 18-28, 1962.

Hopkins, C.E.; Walkley, R.P.; Wilner, D.M.; and Gold, E.T. "Intra-Family Correlation and Its Significance in the Interpretation of Sample Surveys," *American Journal of Public Health, 53:* 1112-1120, 1963.

Jacobson, G.; Wilner, D.M.; Morley, W.E.; Strickler, M.; and Sommer, G. "The Scope and Practice of an Early-Access Brief Treatment Center," *American Journal of Psychiatry, 121:* 1176-1182, 1965.

Kassebaum, G.G.; Ward, D.A.; and Wilner, D.M. *Prison Treatment and Parole Survival: An Empirical Assessment.* New York: John Wiley and Sons, Inc., 1971.

Sherman, S.R.; Mangum, W.P., Jr.; Dodds, S.; Walkley, R.P.; and Wilner, D.M. "Psychological Effects of Retirement Housing," *The Gerontologist, 8:* 170-178, 1968.

Wilner, D.M. "Interracial Contact and Attitude Change," *Transactions, New York Academy of Science, 16:* 354-365, 1954.

Wilner, D.M.; Walkley, R.P.; and Cook, S. *Human Relations in Interracial Housing.* Minneapolis: University of Minnesota Press, 1955.

Wilner, D.M.; Rosenfeld, E.; Lee, R.S.; Gerard, D.L.; and Chein, I. "Heroin Use and Street Gangs," *Journal of Criminal Law, Criminology, and Police Science, 48:* 399-409, 1957.

Wilner, D.M.; Walkley, R.P.; Glasser, M.; and Tayback, M. "The Effect of Housing Quality on Morbidity – Preliminary Findings," *American Journal of Public Health, 48:* 1607-1615, 1958.

Wilner, D.M.; Walkley, R.P.; and Tayback, M. "The Housing Environment and Mental Health," in: Pasamanick, B. (Ed.) *Epidemiology of Mental Disorder,* Washington, D.C.: American Association for the Advancement of Science, pages 143-147, 1959.

Wilner, D.M.; Walkley, R.P.; Pinkerton, T.C.; and Tayback, M. *The Housing Environment and Family Life: A Longitudinal Study of the Effects of Housing on Morbidity and Mental Health.* Baltimore: The Johns Hopkins Press, 1962.

Wilner, D.M. and Kassebaum, G.G. (Eds.) *Narcotics.* New York: McGraw-Hill Book Company, 1965.

Wilner, D.M. "Research and Evaluation in Social Psychiatry," in: Zubin, J. and Freyhan, F. (Eds.) *Social Psychiatry.* New York: Grune and Stratton, 1968.

Wilner, D.M. "Crime and Delinquency: Is Treatment Effective?" *Medical Opinion and Review,* November 1968.

Appendix 2A
Selected Outcome Measures in Evaluation, 1969-72

1. Alcohol Abuse Interventions

a) Abstinence or near abstinence (one to two drinks per day or less than one episode of drinking)
b) Reduction in regular family disruptions, amount of daily drinking, client assessment, self support
c) Number working at present, abstinence since discharge (complete sobriety), number entering another hospital or institution, number attending AA one or more times per month
d) Percent who worked, cared for family, and interacted socially
e) Total or near total abstinence for six months, referenced global score with items not specified
f) Abstinence or moderation after three months
g) Spitzer Mental Status Schedule
h) Abstinence one to five years after discharge

2. Drug Abuse Interventions

a) Percent who were drug free at follow-up
b) Percent of patients completing hospital treatment program
c) Average length of hospitalization
d) Average reduction of cigarette smoking by 85 percent at follow-up
e) Average percent who did not drop out from treatment
f) Percent returning for recommended treatment, continue to use opiates, lack of employment
g) Abstinence within two to three months of treatment
h) Wechsler-Bellevue, Rorschach, TAT, Figure-Reality Testing (self-concept, frustration)
i) Ratings of class behavior, attendance, homework assignments, academic progress
j) Positive urinalysis results for narcotics
k) Drug free after 18 months
l) Not in prison
m) Urine free of opiates, retention in treatment, employment or school attendance

n) Did clinic meet needs, would respondent continue, would respondent recommend to others

o) Retention rate or still in program after six months

p) Employed full or part time or in training

q) Drug free after six months

3. Mental Health Interventions

a) Time lost from employment, state hospital admissions

b) Return to community after three days, not readmitted for longer term care after two years

c) Patient's self-report of positive gain from use of videotape

d) Social isolation and discomfort, self-assessment of benefits from hospitalization

e) Dropout rate

f) California Test of Personality, Primary; Devereux Child Behavior Rating Scale

g) Self-assessment of discomfort

h) Jastak Oral Reading Test Scores

i) Unspecified ten-point scale of alertness, appearance, attitude, self-confidence, etc.

j) Patient attendance in group, symptomatic and destructive acting out

k) Self-reporting of frequency of symptoms

l) Readmission to hospital within six months, dropout rate, number of days that released patients spent in community prior to readmission

m) Self-supporting, independent living

n) Percent out of the hospital

o) Maintenance in the community

p) Rorschach Test

q) Modified general adjustment, planning scale

r) Quantified mental status

s) Responsiveness to subsequent conventional psychotropic drug treatment

t) Verbal or nonverbal interaction within arm's length

3 Quick Reference Outline of Recent Evaluation Work

Ellen B. Gold

This chapter is a schematic presentation of the 25 recent works on evaluation research cited by the preceding author, D.M. Wilner, as a basis for his state-of-the-art review. The coverage of the subject is not intended to be exhaustive, but rather to act as a guide to selected significant works in the field.

Each work is reviewed in the light of topics relevant to the evaluation field. The list of topics also is not all-inclusive, but it is hoped that the coverage of the literature and major areas of concern outlined in Table 3-1 below will be sufficient to provide the reader with a roadmap to evaluative research. The elements included in the table are:

1. *Background, Definition and Purpose of Evaluation* — key definitions used in evaluative and social research and in methodology (definitions of types of designs); context, function, and nature of evaluation; the objectives and goals of evaluation; the need for evaluation and the concept and background of evaluative research and social action.

2. *Issues and Problems in Evaluative Research* — models for rational decision making; "vague goals, strong promises, weak effects"; sensitivity to unanticipated consequences (positive or negative) of the program that are revealed by evaluation; the changing program scene; inconsistency, parochialism, relativism, and informalism in evaluation; dimensions of evaluation in community action programs; constraint of evaluative research; program strategy and development; politics and evaluation; conceptualization of macrosystem, mezzosystem, and microsystem; and questions evaluators should ask.

3. *Evaluation Resources: Funding and Staffing* — budgeting and personnel; financial support for evaluation; costs of social action programs; economizing problems in research and development programs; national funding of manpower training, health, welfare, housing and education; and estimation of health manpower requirements.

4. *Administration of Evaluation Studies* — the role and problems of the evaluator, manager, and researcher; difficulties in giving advice; organizational relationships and responsibilities in evaluation studies—Congress, the Executive Office, federal agencies, and staff; and evaluation by whom and for whom.

This chapter was prepared in association with the Databank of Program Evaluations (National Institute of Mental Health, MH1R12-22761).

Table 3-1
Quick Reference Outline of Recent Evaluation Work[a]

	Good Reference List	Background, Definition, and Purpose of Evaluation	Issues and Problems in Evaluative Research	Evaluation Resources: Funding and Staffing	Administration of Evaluation Studies (the Role of the Evaluator)	Formulation of Goals and Measurement of Outcome	Evaluation Design and Methodology	Practical Implications of Evaluation Research	Use of Research Findings	Implications for Training in Social Research	Programs and Evaluations in Health and Mental Health	Programs and Evaluations for Social and Economic Problems
American Institutes for Research		Chapter 1	Chapter 6		Chapters 1, 6	Chapters 2, 3, 4, 5	Chapters 2, 5					Chapters 7, 8
Bergin and Garfield	**	Chapters 1, 9	Chapters 1, 2, 6, 8, 9, 11, 20, 21			Chapters 7, 8, 9, 12, 21	Chapters 2, 7	Chapters 7, 8, 9, 12, 20, 21, 22	Chapter 20	Chapters 22, 24	Chapters 3, 4, 5, 7, 10, 13-19	Chapter 23
Caro	**	Overview, Chapters 1, 2, 5, 6	Chapters 3, 4, 6, 10, 14, 15, 16, 19, 20		Overview, Chapters 4, 9, 11	Chapters 7, 15, 16, 19	Overview, Chapters 14, 16, 18	Chapter 8	Overview, Chapters 5, 7, 9, 12, 13		Chapters 26, 27, 28, 29	Chapters 17, 21, 22, 23, 24, 25, 30, 31
Dorfman		Chapters 1, 2	Chapter 2			Chapter 2					Chapter 8	Chapters 3, 4, 5, 6, 7
Freeman and Sherwood	**	Chapters 1, 2	Chapters 1, 4, 5	Chapter 8	Chapters 2, 8	Chapters 3, 6	Chapters 6, 7	Chapter 2	Chapter 3			
Grundy and Reinke			Chapters 1, 2, Annex	Chapters 6, 7		Chapter 3	Chapter 2			Chapter 8	Chapters 4, 5	
Herzog	**	Chapters 1, 5	Chapters 2, 4			Chapters 2, 3, 4	Chapter 3	Chapter 5				

Table 3-1 (Cont)

Mullen and Dumpson **	Chapters 1, 6	Chapters 1, 4, 5, 7, 8, 9, 10, 11			Chapter 3	Chapter 3	Chapters 4, 14	Chapters 5, 6	Chapters 5, 6, 8, 10, 11, 12, 13		Chapter 2
Rossi and Williams **	Chapters 1, 3, 7	Chapter 2		Chapter 12		Chapters 2, 3, 4, 7	Chapters 2, 12, 13	Chapter 13			Chapters 5, 6, 8, 9, 10, 11
Schulberg, Sheldon, and Baker **	Chapters 1, 3, 4, 9, 13	Chapters 1, 6, 7, 8, 9, 13, 14, 15		Chapter 8	Chapters 1, 6, 12, 13, 16, 17, 18	Chapters 10, 11, 12		Chapters 1, 30, 31, 32, 35		Chapters 2, 5, 19, 29, 33, 34	
Suchman **	Chapters 1, 3, 4	Chapters 2, 3, 9		Chapter 9	Chapters 4, 5, 7	Chapter 6		Chapters 8, 9	Chapter 10		
Tripodi, Fellin, and Epstein	Chapters 1, 4	Chapters 1, 2, 3		Chapters 1, 5	Chapter 3	Chapter 4		Chapter 5			
Tripodi, Fellin, and Meyer **	Chapters 1, 2	Chapters 1, 3				Chapters 2, 3		Chapter 4		Chapters 5, 7	Chapters 6, 7
Weiss (Evaluating Action Programs) **	Chapters 1, 2, 3, 4, 5, 7	Chapters 1, 2, 4, 5, 8, 12, 15, 17		Chapters 3, 6, 19	Chapters 1, 2, 4, 9, 13	Chapters 1, 3, 7, 11, 13	Chapters 8, 11, 21	Chapters 1, 4, 5, 19, 20		Chapters 10, 14, 16, 18	
Weiss (Evaluating Research) **	Chapters 1, 2	Chapters 2, 5		Chapters 2, 5	Chapter 3	Chapter 4		Chapters 1, 4, 6			
Wholey, Scanlon, Duffy, Fukumoto, and Vogt **	Chapters 1, 2, 6, 7	Chapters 2, 3, 6	Chapter 5	Chapters 3, 4, 7	Chapters 3, 4, 7	Chapter 6		Chapter 3			
Williams	Chapters 1, 4	Chapters 2, 9, 11		Chapters 2, 10	Chapter 6	Chapter 6	Chapter 4	Chapter 8		Chapters 3, 5, 7	

[a]Chapters may cover more than one topic and will, therefore, appear in more than one box.

5. *Formulation of Goals and Measurement of Outcome* — establishing goal priorities; establishing baselines; variables and indicators of outcomes (developing measures); measurement of therapist and process variables; reliability, validity, and length of follow-up interval; problems in measurement; scales and indices to measure program effectiveness, efficiency and effort; and what change is actually attributable to treatment.

6. *Evaluation Design and Methodology* — types of designs and their problems; advantages and disadvantages of preexperimental designs; quasi-experimental, nonexperimental designs and cost-benefit analysis; and problems with controls, randomization, data collection, analysis, replicability, sampling, bias, internal validity, and statistics.

7. *Practical Implications of Evaluation Research* — do's and don'ts in research; interdisciplinary research; claims and expectations; raising the status and quality of evaluation research; political vulnerability of programs due to knowledge of outcomes; and implications of evaluation for program development.

8. *Use of Research Findings* — relationship of program evaluation to the program planning process; use, dissemination and implementation of evaluation results; feedback to the organization; organizational resistance to innovation suggested by research; and contributions of evaluation research to basic knowledge.

9. *Implications for Training in Social Research* — incorporation of research results into professional curricula; emphasis on research and better training for evaluation; interpretation of data in the education and training of evaluators and researchers; teaching data analysis; and instruction in understanding the structure and function of human service institutions.

10. *Programs and Evaluations in Health and Mental Health* — mother and child health, intensive psychiatric treatment, family planning, general public health practice, preventive services, "social restoration performance of psychiatric hospitals," public health nursing, immunization campaigns, antismoking, multiple screening, narcotics addiction, mental patient aftercare, syphilis control, placebo effect with schizophrenics, placing the mentally retarded in the community, typhoid control, cholera control, tuberculosis control, psychotherapy, ataraxic drugs, counter-conditioning and operant behavior therapy.

11. *Programs and Evaluations for Social and Economic Problems* — cost-benefit analysis of manpower programs, New Jersey Income Maintenance Experiment, antipoverty programs, studies of delinquents, the Neighborhood Benefit Program, Denver Model City Program, Midcity Project in delinquency control, Community Action Programs, correctional effectiveness, outdoor recreation, urban renewal, Area Development Project, Casework Methods Project, New Haven Neighborhood Improvement Project, Neighborhood Youth Corps, "Pursuit of Promise", the Coleman Report, Upward Bound, Head Start, and Sesame Street.

Additional major works were reviewed that are most relevant to evaluative research but very specialized. These works are of great value and are worthy of note.

First, the classic by Donald T. Campbell and Julian T. Stanley, *Experimental and Quasi-Experimental Designs for Research*, is a widely known book devoted entirely to the methodology and design of experiments in evaluation and social research. In addition to the valuable information in its text, this book also has a very useful and extensive bibliography. Another useful text dealing primarily with design and analysis is *The Quantitative Analysis of Social Problems*, edited by Edward R. Tufte. This book presents sample studies relating to each of its five parts: statistical evidence and criticism, experimental and quasi-experimental studies, economic and aggregate analysis, survey data, data analysis, and research design.

Still another very specialized work is Raymond A. Bauer's *Social Indicators*, which presents a detailed discussion of the formulation of organization goals, measurement of impact, problems with social indicators, and feedback loops necessary in organizational structure.

Amitai and Eva Etzioni are editors of a book of readings, *Social Change*, which presents historical, theoretical perspectives of sociocultural evolution by such prominent intellectuals as Karl Marx, Friedrich Engels, Max Weber, Talcott Parsons, James Coleman, Herbert Menzel, and Karl Mannheim. In addition, *The Public Interest* has a special issue, "The Great Society: Lessons for the Future" (number 34, Winter 1974) that deals with the politics and economic and social policies that determined the course of social intervention, health and welfare programs, and education in the 1960s. The contributors discuss the successes and failures, the federal role, and the prospects for the future. Also specialized but quite useful is the September 1969 issue of *The Annals of the American Academy of Political and Social Science* (volume 385), which is devoted to "Evaluating the War on Poverty" and deals in depth with the programs, politics, trends, and perspectives of such antipoverty efforts as Community Action Programs, Model Cities, Head Start, the welfare system, and manpower programs.

The National Institute of Mental Health has a valuable handbook for evaluators and practitioners entitled, *Planning for Creative Change in Mental Health Services: Use of Program Evaluation*. The booklet includes a discussion by Howard Davis of the benefits to be gained from program evaluation, principles to insure high standards of measurement in evaluation, and models and approaches to program evaluation. In addition, the booklet contains a very comprehensive bibliography on evaluation research (about 300 references), as well as abstracts of works on evaluation research.

One rather unique source of information is the four-part set of the U.S., House of Representatives, Committee on Government Operations staff study entitled, *The Use of Social Research in Federal Domestic Programs*. Part I deals with the expenditures, status, and objectives of federally-financed social research. Part II of the study presents statements by experts in a variety of fields on the adequacy and usefulness of federally-financed research for such national social problems as crime, education, poverty, social aspects of medicine and health, social welfare, and urban problems. Part III contains statements by authorities in these fields on the relation of private social scientists to federal social programs. Part IV discusses current issues in the administration of federal social research.

One final, and extremely valuable resource is the journal *Evaluation*. The staff of *Evaluation* have brought together the top persons in program evaluation to discuss the most salient issues facing those involved in evaluation research—social indicators, the governmental perspective, funding for evaluative research, and problems encountered in evaluation.

4

Techniques of Outcome Evaluation in Alcohol, Drug Abuse, and Mental Health Programs
S.B. Sells

Since outcome evaluation is not a common term and the domain is relatively uncharted, this chapter presents a conceptual as well as a methodological analysis. And since there are few well-established guidelines, it is appropriate to mention that the material is colored largely by my own background and experience in work of this kind. This experience is primarily in drug abuse and to a lesser extent in mental health. However, from secondary source information the concepts, models, classes of data, and methodology presented are applicable to a wide range of intervention programs, involving prevention, treatment, and social control, in the three areas of alcohol, drug abuse, and mental health service programs. In order to approach these diverse problems in a common frame the treatment of topics is broad; the translation to specific problems is fairly straightforward.

In recent years there have been a number of important contributions to the theory and practice of evaluation. The books by H.D. Schulberg, A. Sheldon, and F. Baker[1] in the health fields, by P.H. Rossi and W. Williams[2] in relation to social science programs, and the NIMH-sponsored manual by D. Glaser[3] on programs for crime and delinquency, are examples of valuable readings in this general area. However, the topic is covered prescriptively, as it should be addressed, and without cross reference to the opinions and plans proposed by others. Further references related to the approaches proposed here are included in the notes to this chapter.

Evaluation: Function and Characteristic Roles

In order to define and limit the topic, the function and characteristic roles of evaluation must be considered. Evaluation is semantically related, but functionally quite different from two common functions that are often confused with it. These are the *audit* function, which normally emphasizes accountability for funds and resources, and the *program assistance* (or development) function, which commonly involves review of ongoing operations and program practices, but may also include initial planning. Both of these result in judgments of the worth of some aspects of a program, but with limited goals and frankly biased role arrangements.

The auditor (like the inspector in the military) receives his rewards for the exposure of misfeasance and is trained to be suspicious and alert. He is usually in the employ of a funding or external management authority, not the program, and his role is typically that of an adversary. By contrast, the program assistance specialist gains his rewards by satisfying his client, who is generally the director or a staff member of the program involved. He is usually a program consultant and his role is that of an advocate.

Evaluation is an impartial, overall, total program assessment function. It is concerned with the development and interpretation of evidence bearing on the worth of a program or activity in terms of its accomplishment of specifiable goals. Program goals are thought of as including (1) programmed results or effects of particular activities within specified time periods, and (2) costs, in terms of utilization of personnel and resources, risks related to relationships with significant constituencies, and monies expended in connection with particular accomplishments. Outcome evaluation considers only the first type of goal — program results. The other types of goals lend themselves also to independent evaluation. The summary term, cost effectiveness, has most commonly been associated with monetary cost. If it were conceptualized in relation to all of the types of costs mentioned earlier, personnel, resources, and relationships with constituencies, as well as monies, it would approximate the breadth implied by the planners of the 1974 conference on evaluation in alcohol, drug abuse, and mental health programs.

One of the major purposes of evaluation is to support administrative policy decisions concerning the support of various types of intervention programs. Such decisions require impartial, objective evidence, uncomplicated by the influence of adversary or advocate opinion or involvement. In the total spectrum of information required for overall cost-effectiveness evaluation, outcome effectiveness data are particularly critical. They enable the justification of expensive, unpopular, and even controversial programs that have demonstrable desired effects, and also the rejection of those that fail to accomplish expected goals, regardless of their popularity or economy.

While such categorical decisions are often necessary, they nevertheless represent an extreme on the continuum of profitable utilization of well-conducted evaluation studies. In a very practical sense it would be unusual in evaluation research to encounter either a totally worthless program or one near perfection. Any program that is obviously unworthy would be most unlikely to be continued by a responsible authority and programs that require no improvement are equally rare. The types of programs that we deal with in the real world are generally imperfect in particular areas and respects, and evaluation research has the potential of indicating not only their degree of success in attaining overall objectives, but also much detailed information of a diagnostic nature.

This is nicely illustrated by the events related to a recent study of federally supported drug abuse programs by the research group with which I am associated.[4] Our report revealed that the results obtained during treatment, for a cohort of patients admitted to treatment over a two-year period beginning June 1, 1969, while encouraging overall, were differentially effective in respect to subsets of treatments, subsets of patients, and subsets of criteria. For example, the most impressive results were obtained for two of three types of methadone treatment; however, with respect to patients, the results for youth (age 21 and under) were generally poor, and the most favorable results were obtained for older, male street addicts; and with respect to criteria, the most favorable results were obtained in the reduction of drug use, while those in relation to increase of employment were poor. Differentiation of treatments, population subgroups, and criteria, which is intrinsic to the strategy recommended here, frequently reveals interactions of the type illustrated. It is my understanding that in response to the results reported, consideration has been given to modification of the federal strategy for drug abuse treatment programs in respect to the issues disclosed.

In the context presented it appears that outcome evaluation is basically a research function. The problems involved are not routine, but rather extremely complex and demand both substantive understanding of the rationale, philosophical assumptions, and goals of the program and its participants, and methodological expertise in research design, definition of variables and measures to represent them, data collection and management, and analytic procedures. The role associated with this function is therefore that of a research scientist located organizationally outside and independent of the program and its adversaries and advocates. The rewards of scientists come not from whether or not their results support a program, but from the excellence of their research and their publications. For evaluation research there must therefore be acceptable opportunities for publication. Optimally the role also requires communication skills to assure that the results are reported to the users (administrators, program directors, and the public) in terms that are meaningful to them and that facilitate their decision responsibilities. It is often essential to have professional persons in the administrative management (user) group to assist in the explication of the research results.

The problem of integrating outcome evaluation results with those representing other aspects of the total evaluation process is also highly demanding and requires additional and different professional expertise. However, its importance cannot be overemphasized.

Planning for Outcome Evaluation

Although, as already mentioned, the objectivity, impartiality, and independence required for evaluation imply organizational independence for the evaluation staff, it is desirable that evaluation be included in program planning from the outset. This is needed to insure that the objectives, assumptions, and procedures of evaluation are understood by the program staff and that the program practices and information required to support the evaluation effort are explicitly provided for. For example, if random assignment of persons to treatments is an issue, it must be considered at a time when, if adopted, it can be incorporated in the program operations. Or, if certain information is to be obtained from operating records, it is important that the record forms and procedures be adequate to provide that information completely, accurately, and legibly.

It is neither necessary nor desirable for the evaluation staff to be employed by the program to accomplish this. However, by confronting the evaluation issues at a very early stage, it should be possible to propose significant details of operations and data requirements so that a sound design may have a greater chance of being implemented than if the approach were retrospective and based only on existing practices and available data.

Early consultation also has the advantage of facilitating constructive compromise between the reality needs or perceptions of program staff and the design requirements or perceptions of the evaluators, thus fostering mutual trust and cooperation. Experimental designs that enjoy prestigious status in the laboratory may be unfeasible in field studies. On the other hand, clinicians and program directors have been known to raise objections that proved to be invalid when analyzed objectively. There are valid limits on program practice, reflecting ethics, politics, and professional judgment, that may, in certain circumstances, be unalterable. The investigator must have the courage to raise significant issues and be able to explain their implications in support of his recommendations. At the same time he must accept the principle that there is never only one standard or one way to do something. Field research conditions rarely permit the rigorous control and symmetry of design characteristic of the laboratory. However, when the limiting circumstances are finally determined, the practical field scientist must be prepared to make the most of the situation. At least, if he has had an opportunity to be in at the start, he is usually better off than if he were forced to design retrospectively.

Even if the evaluation staff is able to participate in planning early in the development of a program, there is also a problem of when, in the life history of the program, evaluation should be done. New programs to implement even well tried approaches cannot be expected to achieve intended levels of effectiveness at the outset. They need to go through normal processes of organizational birth and development. The evaluation results for these early stages may have limited usefulness. New approaches, in particular, involve considerable trial and error, and frequently formal experimentation as well during their developmental stages. Since full-scale outcome evaluation studies are expensive and demanding, it is questionable whether they should be undertaken too early in the developmental process. Such studies are appropriate at a point where responsible program authorities believe that birth and growth problems have been overcome and a steady state has been reached. From the very outset, however, it is highly desirable to utilize consulting services, program review, management reports, and other self-examination procedures, and to have involved a program historian to record events, decisions, and changes that are all too soon forgotten by the persons involved.

General Strategy

There are a number of reality constraints and postures based on experience that provide a frame of reference and general strategy for outcome evaluation research. Some of the most important of these are reviewed to create a frame of reference for the research design.

Sources of Variance

First, it is obvious that an intervention program relates only to a finite interval in each life that it touches. As a result, many factors and events not directly related to the program, which occur prior to, during, and after the program period, may have effects on the individuals involved and on the measures used to evaluate program effects. In research jargon this involves both confounding and criterion contamination and it is necessary, in the research design, to provide additional information beyond simple pre-postdata points to represent them, as well as appropriate (multivariate) analytic techniques to account for them.

The reference to prior, pretreatment events includes all factors that affect the characteristics of the clients or subjects entering a program and that may account for differential response to the program. This covers a vast area and requires extensive substantive knowledge, experience, and research skill to identify and measure the relevant items. If adequate information is not available in the literature of the field, preparatory research on predictors of outcome may be desirable to aid in design of the evaluation program. The strategic issue raised here is that of determining whether outcomes obtained are true program effects or to some degree results of fortunate (or unfortunate) client sample selection.

Consideration of client characteristics is not, however, merely a matter of isolating unwanted variance. It can be turned to advantage by sorting the client population into subgroups according to their differential prospects for successful outcome. In most situations the range of individual differences on relevant client variables make this a practical possibility and subgrouping on those that predict outcomes might lead to identification of types or classes of clients for whom particular approaches may be beneficial or ineffectual, or even, at the other extreme, contra-indicated. Research in psychiatry and in education has led me to the conclusion that most "people-changing" programs appear to be maximally effective with clients whose backgrounds suggest them to be least in need of the program service. However, that is a philosophical problem that cannot be resolved here. The practical point is that it is desirable to include such information in the research protocol.

Confounding events during and subsequent to the period of program participation are also important to investigate. With large samples it may be appropriate and practically necessary to exclude from the data collected variables that can be expected to vary randomly among individuals. Nevertheless,

when subgrouping is done, sample size should be judged by the size of subgroups, rather than the total sample. On the other hand, nonrandom events
that affect groups of people, such as those resulting from economic depres-
sions, epidemics, energy crises, and wars, should be recorded and taken into
consideration in the assessment of program outcomes, when considered relevant.
Often, when samples composed of persons from different sociocultural environments and varying in such nonrandom influences are compared, attention to
this type of problem can be critical.

Specification of Program Paradigms

A second major concern has to do with the specification of program characteristics. It is desirable that the evaluation staff have complete and detailed
documentation of the program paradigm, including its assumptions, theoretical
rationale, goals, staffing, organization, facilities, location in relation to clients,
time frames (both day to day and overall), activities, rules, records, procedures,
and relations with clients. If there are multiple locations, variations among
units may also need to be studied. If there are multiple (more than one) programs within an organization or system, with different paradigms (as for example,
a multimodality drug treatment program, with methadone maintenance outpatient units, residential therapeutic communities, and outpatient drug-free programs, all under one overall management), then separate consideration of the
diverse program paradigms would undoubtedly be called for. If, as in some mental health programs, treatment is tailored individually to the need of each patient,
then grouping of cases to reflect diagnostic, treatment, patient, and staff factors
involved may be necessary.

Realistically, the documentation is hard to come by. At least, it has never
been adequately available in advance for any program with which I have worked.
However, even it it were, I would still want to verify it in the detail required for
research planning. Therefore, preparation of detailed program documentation
should be taken on as a responsibility of the evaluation research staff, in consultation with and sjubject to the concurrence of the program staff. This would
aid not only in understanding of the program with respect to the questions of
classification already mentioned, but also in the design of almost every aspect of
the evaluation study. This analysis should occur early in the life of the program,
in order to influence program practices and records. Many additional important
decisions, such as selection of criterion variables, definition of the time frame
appropriate to treatment processes, and classification of the treatments included,
depend on this information.

Prospective vs. Retrospective Designs

Prospectively oriented, longitudinal tracking of clients or patients is the optimal data collection and design strategy for effective evaluation research. There are many arguments in support of this position, two major ones concerning the sampling base appropriate for evaluative research, and the requirements for data collection and management. With respect to the first point, it must be recognized that the universe of clients or subjects for any intervention program consists of all individuals that enter the program. It is not uncommon to read evaluation reports based only on individuals who complete the program, which is highly misleading, or others that compare individuals who complete with a sample of those who fail to complete, which may be equally misleading. The prospective orientation is more likely to identify the population universe correctly and, if sampling is undertaken, to facilitate inclusion of the entire universe in the sample design.

From the standpoint of data collection and management, the prospective approach is the only approach that insures the opportunity for completeness of reporting over time and avoidance of excessive missing data that may be impossible to recapture at a later date. In the latter connection it is also impossible to overstate the importance of a well standardized and professionally supervised reporting system for longitudinal tracking. Traditional clinical progress notes and unsupervised record keeping involve so many obstacles to research that they cannot be regarded as a viable alternative.

Criterion Problems

Perhaps the most important data required for evaluation are those that define and measure the outcomes by which program success is evaluated. Four of the main problems in this area are (1) definition, (2) measurement and data acquisition, (3) multiprogram or system criteria, and (4) composite measures.

On the first point, the client behaviors that are adopted as criteria to measure program effects should reflect program goals as completely as possible. It follows, of course, that if goals are only vaguely formulated, criterion development will be affected. This has been the downfall of many evaluation efforts and should also be an obituary note to a large amount of psychotherapy research. For the purpose of this discussion, criterion variables are defined as concepts and criterion measures as the specific observations recorded to represent those concepts. The criterion variables should be conceptualized to capture all aspects of behavior programmed as targets of the program and in terms appropriate to the behavioral units involved (for preventive and social-control programs the units may be population groups and for treatment, the units may be individual patients). The criterion measures should be valid to represent the respective variables, reliably measured, and quantifiable. Validity is a serious problem with so-called intrapsychic variables and also with information obtained by subjective methods, whether by rating or by interview with patients (or clients). In my own research on drug abusers, for example, almost all of the patient data have been obtained by interview and questions of validity are frequently raised. Although this is true of the educational system, the civil service, the medical and correctional systems as well, it should be understood that the burden of establishing the credibility of data remains with the investigator.

Second, one of the advantages of a longitudinal reporting system is that information acquisition becomes systematic (although never routine) and questions relevant to criterion assessment become familiar aspects of the setting, rather than one-time, critical events. Longitudinal reporting provides a basis for observing trends, for evaluating extreme values, and for relating variations to known events that can be presumed to be related. Thus, it provides a basis for assessment of reliability and validity of data collected.

Third, a special criterion problem will be encountered when an evaluation program embraces a network or system of diverse programs, with varying goals, or a highly individualized (and therefore, heterogeneous) program that permits varying treatments and varying goals for individual clients. If one of the evaluation objectives is to compare treatment effectiveness across groups (or types) of clients, or within groups, then it is essential to have uniform criteria for all cases. A decision must be made concerning the feasibility of uniform criteria. In many cases this is feasible and then the different goals can be included as part of the various treatment descriptions. If it is not feasible, then the groups must be evaluated separately and cross comparisons may be difficult.

A fourth aspect of the criterion area requiring caution is the construction and use of generalized measures of success or failure. Such composites, combining information from diverse criterion measures, appeal to common sense and facilitate communication of results. Unfortunately, however, if the separate measures are uncorrelated, as they usually are, combinations would not only be arbitrary, but counterproductive to the extent that they might mask significant outcome patterns. Although multiple criteria involve greater complexity in analysis and in reporting, arbitrary composites may be too misleading to warrant their use.

Time Perspective

Time perspective is very important in the design of evaluative research in order to answer questions concerning the duration as well as the extent of effects obtained. It is convenient to conceptualize two major phases within which effects should be assessed. The first is during the period of program participation or during treatment, and the second is the indefinite period thereafter, or posttreatment. Depending on the characteristics of the program and the resources available, a number of data points could be considered within each. During-treatment effects are of interest to provide early feedback on whether expected goals are being achieved, but they do not indicate whether or how long they may endure.

In many ways posttreatment evaluation provides the real payoff. However, if both during-treatment and posttreatment evaluations are performed, it is possible to design the research to answer additional important questions, such as how performance during the program is related to posttreatment success.

We have already argued strongly for a reporting program to track subjects throughout the period of program participation. One important item, relating to the collection of during-treatment data, concerns the frequency of reporting. There is no magic about this. In general, the period covered by each report should be determined by the type of data required, records available, the resources available for interview and report preparation, and program length. The number of data points required to study trends should also be considered. The analyst who has the opportunity to select his final measures after studying the intercorrelations and trends observable in a data set is far better off than one who must make do with what is available.

The optimal design for posttreatment followup would of course be a projection of the during-treatment series. Unfortunately, this is not practical in the world of reality. Often one must settle for only one posttreatment data collection point, particularly if it involves locating and interviewing individuals and if invasion of privacy is an issue. This point should occur long enough after program completion to allow the individuals to function independently, but as early as possible to minimize confounding influences. For many types of programs in the areas of concern to this conference, this may be within one to two years.

For a treatment program of twelve months duration the cycle from beginning of planning through during-treatment evaluation and then posttreatment follow-up study, for a single client cohort could easily take seven to eight years and I see no practical way to reduce it. This means that information based on rigorous evaluation research cannot be made available in the quick turnaround mode expected from an audit or a site visit. Further, the implications of constant and rapid change in technology, cultural and economic norms and values, and other significant aspects of population and environment may lead us to wonder whether the problem may not itself change by the time that results are available. Indeed, it may, and it has. Evaluation should optimally be a continuing feature of program administration and not a one-time effort. Only then can we build up a body of knowledge that would enable productive diagnosis of situations and reliable predictions derived from a valid data base. Unfortunately, this idea is still regarded as novel in many circles and decision making continues to be based on "expert" opinion, often unsupported by relevant empirical information.

Problems of Field Research

Evaluation research provides many satisfactions to the social scientist who prefers to work on problems of the real world and to contribute knowledge that may have relatively direct application. However, it lacks the control that is frequently available in the laboratory and is fraught with many frustrations, not the least of which are the problems of funding such expensive activities and of coping with administrative and clinical policies and decisions that appear to interfere with research requirements. These are realities with which we must learn to live if we intend to survive.

The problem of funding is not merely one of research support, but rather that it involves the overall approach of our society and our governmental institutions to problem solving in areas of major concern. This is a long-term educational problem. In the perspective of present conditions, there is much room for improvement in the way we document the rationale of evaluation and in communicating evaluation needs and plans to administrators and legislators. Unfortunately, the present inflation has added greatly to our problems in this as in many other areas.

One of our main concerns is how to engage in field research and still remain a "respectable scientist." An illustrative case is the issue of random assignment of persons to treatments. There is no doubt that sample bias is a critically important source of error in experimental studies and that the advantages of random assignment have been demonstrated in as widely separated fields as agriculture and psychopharmacology, even with human subjects. However, this brings into sharp relief some differences between laboratory and field research with respect to philosophy and procedure.

Methodological caveats have traditionally received priority in the laboratory, while in the field they have frequently been subordinated to clinical, ethical, and administrative concerns. In a typical laboratory study, for example, the distribution of types of subjects across treatments would be balanced and assignment to treatments would be random. However, in a typical field study, certain assignments might be prohibited for clinical reasons (such as the assignment of youth or recently addicted persons to methadone maintenance treatments), for ethical reasons (such as the assignment of a person to a treatment against his will), or others, including decisions based on funds available. It is the duty of the investigator to make certain that the prohibitions are substantively compelling and not unjustified or capricious. It is easy to compound error as a matter of expediency, but there is another type of error that must also be avoided; that is the error of distorting proper, ethical, and humane practice in the name of research. Both must be avoided. We need to find a tolerable middle ground between the artificiality and sterility of unrealistic practices appropriated improperly from laboratory research and the biases and errors that remain everpresent pitfalls in the field. In the real world we must expect to be forced to compromise and it is here that the mettle of effective field research is tested. When we are required to accept conditions that are less than optimal we must find ways of coping with them. This is, of course, one of the strongest endorsements of multivariate methodology; in addition, we must be prepared to point out the limitations of our data in the interpretation of results.

Ethics in Evaluation Research

Problems of invasion of privacy, anonymity, human dignity, and respect for the client are currently prominent in evaluation research, as they should be. The failure by social scientists in the past to observe proper responsibility in relation to human subjects has contributed at least partly to the present mood although they are not the only culprits. In spite of the importance of the results sought, there is no justification for treating any human being other than with the same respect, consideration, and concern that we would each demand for ourselves. We must also be tolerant of the right of an individual to refuse to be interviewed and take appropriate steps to assure the anonymity of the information he provides. With pressure from the federal government, we are gradually doing a better job, but there is room for improvement. The dangers of unwitting disclosure, not by the investigator and his staff, but by others into whose hands data files might pass must also be emphasized; these are real and it is our responsibility to take all steps to insure that information received as confidential stays confidential.

Use of Computers

We are living in the age of the computer and computers are uniquely adapted to the file maintenance and analytic requirements of evaluation research, which usually involves samples of large size, measured in the thousands of cases. Contemporary computer technology lends itself to efficient and economic operations and, in comparison with what could be achieved even ten years ago, enables analyses that could not otherwise even be considered feasible. However, variations in cost, of great magnitude, can be incurred, depending on the skill with which this equipment is used. It is therefore urgent that major attention be given to systems design and programming for large data files and that these problems be thought through with the utmost care. Misuse of computer files (popularly referred to as "data banks") is not a property of the computer, but rather of the way that people design and use them. If we subscribe to the ethical principles that I assume we all accept, the imputed dangers can be contained by building appropriate safeguards.

Reactive vs. Nonreactive Measures

The final topic under strategy is one that received wide attention following the publication in 1972 of a small book entitled *"Unobtrusive Measures: Non-reactive Research in the Social Sciences,"* by E.J. Webb et al.[5] In the present context, a reactive measure could be illustrated by information obtained by interview, such as do you own and operate a car? while a nonreactive measure would be the same information obtained by checking car registrations and drivers' license registries. The possibilities of using nonreactive measures, particularly in developing criteria for evaluation research are intriguing. The advantages are numerous. However, in a climate of concern about privacy and anonymity this approach involves a number of sensitive issues that must be resolved with the utmost circumspection and wisdom. It is mentioned here mainly to generate some productive dialogue, but not as a recommendation at this time.

Research Design and Procedures

This final section is limited to three topics not covered previously, and an integrative concluding discussion. The three topics involve data organization, data management, and analytic models.

Data Organization by Entry Cohorts

Whether the unit of study involves population groups, such as schools or clinic units, or individuals, such as patients in treatment, the organization of data for evaluation research differs from that usually followed in administrative analyses for management purposes. In the latter case the concern usually focuses on activities, expenditures, and other transactions that occur during given calendar periods, as for example, the number of doses of a particular drug, their cost, and personnel involved, in relation to all patients treated during a particular period. This is required for administrative accountability, but is inappropriate for evaluation research. The population in treatment during any period may include individuals who started prior to the beginning of the period as well as others who entered during and even near the end of the period, and terminations during the period do not directly reflect tenure. As a result, data organization by period of treatment fails to treat the participation of every subject comparably. An alternative, which is called *cohort design*, is to organize data by time of entry, following every individual in the cohort an equal time from his entry up to termination or the end of the study, which ever occurs first. This involves the use of sequence numbers (or their equivalent) for months following admission, rather than calendar dates, and results in an organization of data comparable to an overlay, starting every case at time zero, with periods of equal length for comparison, up to the end of the time adopted for tracking.

If the evaluation study were to include only the status at admission and one data point after entry, the equivalent of a pre-postdesign, then sequence numbers would be of no concern. However, if multiple, periodic points are employed to track patients or clients through treatment, then it is desirable to incorporate sequence codes for data processing.

Data Management

In this discussion it is assumed that a computer is available and will be used and that the data will be transferred from records, data forms, and interview records to a computer file. The important data management problems include (1) client (patient) identification, (2) coding of all nonprecoded items of information, (3) computer input, (4) editing of computer input, (5) handling of missing data, (6) development of algorithms for classification, data conversion, and scaling, (7) sequential preparation of the final data matrix, and (8) the importance of backup tapes and files. Since effective data management is a major concern in evaluative research, brief treatments of each topic follow:

1. **Client Identification.** Codes should be used that are compatible with the commitments concerning privacy and anonymity, even to the extent of preventing inadvertent identification from data profiles. The ID coding should ordinarily identify each record as unique and separate codes should be used for clinic or location, and other items, such as age, race, sex, and the like, that may be treated as classification or data variables.

2. **Coding.** Precoded information is easier and more reliable to handle than free response, and this format can be used advantageously for most information if adequate planning and pretesting are allowed. This is a professional function and should be taken seriously. Free response information is often difficult to bring into a uniform coding system and the apparent advantages of free response may be lost in the process of coding. Closely related to this, client self-report forms are too often the source of more errors and cost than the apparent savings that persuade some people to adopt them. Since the raw data are the fundamental basis of the research, data collection procedures and staff should receive high status in the project and qualified, trained interviewers and staff members should be assigned, with adequate supervision. If some information to be included is not precoded, all coding should be completed and checked before the input step is initiated.

3. **Computer Input.** Optical scanning technology is available to transfer coded records directly to a computer. However, the forms required are bulky and this technology is still imperfect. It requires editing and verification and

alertness to the idiosyncracies of various types of equipment. The investigator has options of going from forms to cards, which are then read into computer tapes or directly from forms to tape. The decision should be based on a study of comparative costs in the use of equipment, time, and personnel.

4. Editing of Computer Input. It is possible to write computer programs to examine the completeness, reasonableness, and logical consistency of data entered into a computer file. Such programs can list and count incomplete and missing items, responses using invalid codes, and responses to different items that are logically incompatible, such as a single woman living with her legal husband. These can then be checked against original records and verified. We recently found that there were twelve patients recorded as male housewives in a carefully edited file of 44,000 patient records; of these, six reflected coding errors that were previously undetected. When it comes to the control of human error, it seems impossible to be overzealous. The best way to control error, however, is to minimize it at the source.

5. Missing Data. Excessive missing data, reflecting carelessness (which may be randomly distributed) or bias in reporting (which is usually nonrandom) can cripple a study. It is therefore important to adopt procedures to prevent or minimize omissions in the process of data generation and data processing. However, even then there will be missing data. Investigators and statisticians who have studied this problem believe that except in the most extreme cases, it is preferable to treat the omissions as variables than to discard records that are incomplete. Random omissions that are not excessive can be estimated by various procedures, but estimation of dependent, criterion variables should be considered only with caution.

6. Algorithms for Data Transformation. For the final analysis it may be desirable to compute a variety of index variables to represent combinations of items in the original field data. For example, in one study in the drug abuse treatment evaluation research at TCU we developed a patient typology, based on a profile of variables (including race, age, sex, frequency of use of eight drug groups and of alcohol), a treatment typology, of comparable complexity, and eight criterion measures, several compiled from multiple items. Each of these was described by a set of computational rules, or an algorithm. It was then possible to write computer programs and to compute these index values for each patient, for use in the final analyses. These steps in the final stages of the research are clearly of major importance. In addition to organizing the data for efficient analysis, it is possible to compute measures that meet statistical criteria and that are optimally suited for the types of analyses planned.

7. Preparation of Final Data Tapes. The final analyses are most efficiently carried out using specially prepared data tapes that incorporate only the edited and computed items and indices required. The preparation of this tape is an important process. First, some cases may be excluded for various legitimate reasons, such as excessive missing data, failure to qualify as belonging in the cohort sample (perhaps because of date of entry into the program), or failure to participate in the treatment evaluated. Although such exclusions should be made when justified, the data should be retained for the study report. Then the basic information required for analysis, which may be dispersed in the process of computation of algorithms, must be merged into the final tape. When this is accomplished, the exciting final stage arrives, which compensates for all of the drudgery in the lengthy process of data preparation.

8. Backup Tapes. As noted recently in the press, electronically stored information can be accidentally erased. Indeed, the possibility of human error, as well as fire, heat, and other dangers, makes it imperative to make duplicate copies of all valuable files and to keep them in safe and secure storage.

Analytic Models

An evaluation study resembles a scientific experiment in that it exposes subjects to treatments that are hypothesized to produce certain effects and evaluates the effects obtained under specified conditions. The essence of the experimental method is control of factors that affect the dependent (or criterion variable) in order to isolate the effects that can properly be attributed to the treatment. In the classical laboratory experiment—the experimental control model—factors other than the treatment tested, are generally dealt with as extraneous, to be controlled by exclusion. That is, the conditions of treatment are rigidly standardized and variations, interruptions, and changes are not permitted; the effects of previous experience are cancelled out by random variation between experimental and comparison control groups, and various other techniques are employed to remove the influence of factors that can neither be controlled experimentally nor randomized, usually by additional comparison groups. The net result is a degree of control of extraneous sources of variance that enables evaluation of treatment effects under the assumption that all other factors are eliminated. Of course, total control is seldom achieved, but the thrust of this model involves both advantages and disadvantages. The advantages lie in obtaining answers that are subject to good control, so that treatment effect is rigorously tested. The disadvantages include: first, that such results cannot be easily generalized to the real world in which extraneous, but in a practical sense, possibly important influences do exist; and second, that their elimination precludes any assessment of their influences.

For reasons that have already been discussed, the experimental control model is often impossible to implement in field research, particularly in evaluation of alcohol, drug abuse, and mental health programs. In the field study, however, while it is not possible to exclude experimentally the non-treatment factors that account for criterion variance, it is possible to compute their effects and to assess them independently of the treatment effects. The models that have proved useful for accomplishing such analyses belong to a class of statistical operations known as multivariate methods. These include multivariate analysis of variance and analysis of covariance, multiple regression, multistage regression analysis, canonical analysis, and other variations of what statistical analysts refer to as the general linear model. Although multivariate methods have led to the design of more powerful laboratory experiments, their advantages in field research are of particular importance here. An example of this general approach can be found in a study by Spiegel and Sells[6] evaluating eleven treatments for drug abuse for twelve patient types during the first year in treatment, using measures for eight criterion variables.[7] Some useful general references include R. Bottenberg and J.H. Ward,[8] F.A. Graybill,[9] J. Cohen,[10] J.E. Overall and D.K. Spiegel,[11] G.W. Joel,[12] and J.E. Overall and C.J. Klett.[13]

These models are not only highly sophisticated and powerful tools for analyzing the complex data involved in evaluation research, but unlike the experimental control model, they are also uniquely suited to the field situation. Their most obvious advantage is that they deal with the complex field situations as they occur and are therefore generalizable to such situations. However, in addition, they have the power to provide rather complete analyses of the effects of the extraneous, but often interesting factors, that are not part of treatment per se, but that frequently interact with them in real life situations. As a result their use has turned what may at first have appeared as an adverse situation into a decided advantage for evaluation research.

Notes

1. Schulberg, H.D., Sheldon, A., and Baker, F. *Program Evaluation in the Health Fields.* New York: Behavioral Publications, Inc., 1969.
2. Rossi, P.H. and Williams, W. *Evaluating Social Programs; Theory, Practice and Politics.* New York: Seminar Press, 1972.
3. Glaser, D. *Routinizing Evaluation: Getting Feedback on Effectiveness of Crime and Delinquency Programs.* Washington, D.C.: U.S. Government Printing Office, 1973.
4. Chatham, L.R. and Sells, S.B. *Evaluation of Treatment for Drug Abuse Based on the Joint NIMH-TCU Drug Abuse Reporting Program (DARP).* For presentation at the National Drug Abuse Conference, Chicago, Illinois, March 31, 1974; Spiegel, D.K. and Sells, S.B. *Evaluation of Treatments for Drug Users in the DARP: 1969-1971 Admissions.* IBR Report No. 73-10, June, 1973.

5. Webb, E.J., Campbell, D.T., Schwartz, R.D., and Sechrest, L. *Unobtrusive Measures: Nonreactive Research in the Social Sciences*. Chicago: Rand McNally & Company, 1966.

6. Spiegel and Sells, *Evaluation of Treatments*

7. Sells, S.B. (Ed.). *Studies of the Effectiveness of Treatments for Drug Abuse, Vol. 1, Evaluation of Treatments*. Cambridge, Mass.: Ballinger Publishing Company, 1974 (in press); Sells, S.B. (Ed.). *Studies of the Effectiveness of Treatments for Drug Abuse, Vol. 2, Research on Patients, Treatments and Outcomes*. Cambridge, Mass.: Ballinger Publishing Company, 1974 (in press).

8. Bottenberg, R. and Ward, J.H. *Applied Multiple Linear Regression Analysis*. Department of Commerce, Office of Technical Services, 1960.

9. Graybill, F.A. *An Introduction to Linear Statistical Models*. New York: McGraw-Hill, 1961.

10. Cohen, J. Multiple regression as a general data-analytic system, *Psychol. Bull., 70*, 426-443, 1968.

11. Overall, J.E. and Spiegel, D.K. Concerning least squares analysis of experimental data, *Psychol. Bull., 72*, 311-322, 1969.

12. Joe, G.W. Comment on Overall and Spiegel's, Least squares analysis of experimental data, *Psychol. Bull., 75*, 364-366, 1971.

13. Overall, J.E. and Klett, C.J. *Applied Multivariate Analysis*. New York: McGraw-Hill Book Co., 1972.

5 Evaluation Research in Mental Health:
Lessons from History

Adeline Levine and *Murray Levine*

Research and inquiry always occur in some social and historical context and are always in a state of reciprocal influence with that context. We associate the term "research" with an emphasis on observable, measurable events or results, reflecting the scientific mode of examining phenomena, generally adhered to for the last two or three centuries.

When we append the adjective "evaluative" to qualify the term research, we recognize that we are dealing with a phenomenon somewhat distinct from other kinds of research. The differences between evaluative and other kinds of research reflect differences in their social context.

Reaction to the statement that contemporary problems and approaches to evaluation research are not new and in fact have a close kinship with the past will illustrate one important distinction between evaluative and other research. If the reaction is dysphoric, depressive, discouraged in tone: "Oh, good heavens, we have made no progress over the last hundred and fifty years," then you are reacting in the culture of the evaluative researcher. If the reaction is one of curiosity, and mild interest; if you say to yourself, "How did they formulate the problem then? What approach did they take? What problems did they encounter?" then you are probably in the culture of the researcher not involved in evaluation.

The evaluation researcher, aligned with the clinician, is concerned primarily about a result, an outcome, a product, *in relation to a time-bound program*. Theory building and the determination of causality belong to the pure researcher and those concerns are essentially timeless. The pure researcher, although influenced by ambitions for a career and professional reward, does not really care when he gets an answer to a problem.[1] The pure researcher resonates with the problems of the ages. Thus, Donald Hebb, in an address to the American Psychological Association, in August 1973, was able to discuss the mind-body problem, which, in its modern form, dates back more than 300 years, to Descartes, Berkeley, Hume, and other thinkers of the enlightenment. It is still a relevant problem for the psychologist as a scientist: His scientific culture condones seeing the problem as timeless with no pressure to achieve a solution.

The pure scientist's basic social reference group consists of members of his professional discipline, an historical stream of workers in the past, and in the future. The failure of any specific study or the inability to confirm some particular hypothesis does not reflect on the total scientific enterprise. We have learned a little more, or have discovered another blind alley, but science itself goes on.[a]

The evaluation researcher, working with the clinician, cannot adopt a timeless perspective, for his context is different. The evaluation researcher is constrained by the fiscal year of the sponsor, for example, and by the requirement that he show evidence of productivity in order to justify requests for the allocation of the limited resources of public funds.

The clinician and evaluation research team are part of a system of accountability, the clinician accountable to his sponsor, typically a governmental executive, in turn accountable to the legislator, who responds to his people through the electoral process. If this appears to be an overidealized view of the responsiveness of a service system to the political accountability process, consider the background of the National Mental Health Act of 1946.[b] The scandalous conditions of the state hospitals in a number of states in the late 1940s were perceived as political threats by the governors and state legislatures, and it was they who in successive meetings of the Governors' Annual Conference, provided a good part of the political support and pressures on the Congress to act positively and meaningfully in the area of mental health.[2]

In brief, then, it is a critical difference that the researcher not involved in evaluation is responsible primarily to his professional colleagues, while the evaluation researcher feeds information into an elaborate political system of accountability. The first researcher contributes to the development of theory and conceptual knowledge, while the evaluation researcher contributes justification for the continuance or discontinuance of a service competing for scarce resources.

Scientific thinking—with which both types of researchers claim common ancestry—evolved from the period of the Enlightenment, when the basis for widely held cultural values moved from spiritual and mystical concepts transmitted by people in positions of religious or political authority to material, positive, observable, quantifiable, experimental concepts, proposed by philosophers, scholars and scientists involved in empirical discovery and verification. David Hume's statement summarized the new views of what was to be accepted as knowledge.

---

[a]In an era of "big science" and public support of science, the concerned reference groups become larger, and we see an increased pressure for results pertinent to the solution of urgent social problems.

[b]In an earlier age the political skills and influence that Dorothea Dix exercised with state legislatures, in controlling appointments to superintendencies, and in influencing the very nature of the day-by-day programs of state hospitals should be recalled. Miss Dix was a fanatical reformer with a program designed to prevent the abuses of mental patients. A reduction of incidents of abuse was her primary criterion for judging program success. So successful was she in arousing backing from voters and tax payers, that Bockoven attributes much of the security-conscious atmosphere that helped to destroy moral therapy in the mid and late nineteenth century hospitals directly to her efforts (Bockoven, J.S., *Moral Treatment in Community Mental Health*. New York: Springer, 1972).

If we take in our hand any volume . . . let us ask "Does it contain any abstract reasoning concerning quantity or number?" No. "Does it contain any experimental reasoning concerning matters of fact and existence?" No. Commit it then to the flames: for it can contain nothing but sophistry and illusion![3]

During the same period, the economic world was characterized by an increase in entrepreneurial capitalism; the industrial revolution and scientific advances began to move forward, rapidly and together. Technical advances were responsible for tremendous growth in material wealth; profit-oriented use of wealth made possible the exploitation of technical advances. In this same period there was a renewed humane concern for people. For example, major prison reforms occurred in the late 1700s to early 1800s. The early 1800s saw a new emphasis on childhood and children as special. Robert Owen initiated his experiments in cooperative living as a response to the human problems of the industrial revolution. While humanitarian values were often pushed and shoved aside by the emphasis on the materialistic, nonetheless, we need to give credit where it is due, simply to appreciate the complexity of the forces influencing programs and their evaluation.

Consider how a scientific-capitalistic-materialistic orientation has influenced the evaluation of programs for the treatment of mental disorders. Our present system of care for the mentally ill arose during the late eighteenth and early nineteenth centuries as a reaction to the view that the insane were possessed by demons, or were being punished for having sinned. In an earlier time those who deviated too greatly, who were demented, or who were severely threatening, were confined to one or another of various institutions: workhouses, almshouses, or jails, or in some places given to the lowest bidder for care. Wealthier people who were insane were frequently hidden away in attics or basements. The care of all was equally bad for it was believed that the insane were best handled roughly. Even his Majesty, King George III of England, was put in restraints and the royal personage was manhandled by his attendants, by design.

By the late eighteenth century the rise of scientific thinking and the accompanying optimism that grew out of the new confidence that science could indeed conquer all led many to approach the insane from a naturalistic viewpoint. Expanding concepts of physiology, and a beginning knowledge of the workings of the brain, contributed to that optimism and to people's willingness to try new approaches. Humane values motivated the allocation of public resources to the medical care of the mentally ill, also. T.S. Szaz[4] has argued, in fact, that it was the reconceptualization of the problem into the medical model that permitted humane care to be extended to the mentally ill who were previously abused. It was within that historical period that Phillipe Pinel in France, Samuel Tuke in England, and Benjamin Rush in the United States, among others, moved to develop a humane but scientifically based therapy for the insane, and a little later for the severely mentally deficient as well.[5]

Given that care for the mentally ill and the mentally retarded grew out of a scientific spirit, it is surprising that gross and even fraudulent misuse of data characterized some of the earliest efforts to evaluate treatment programs unless accountability is seen as an important factor. A *scientific* spirit requires that the available data be fed back to test the next hypothesis. A *justificatory* spirit uses data within a system of accountability, diminishing the motive to truly know. For example, in 1839 the Swiss physician Johann Jacob Guggenbuhl convinced the Swiss Association of Natural Science that it would be a good idea to establish an institution for the cure and prophylaxis of cretinism, by treating very young children. He proposed to use a combination of diet, healthful living, baths, massage, exercise, some drugs, and educational and psychological methods of developing sensory perception in his charges.

Guggenbuhl's first problem was to develop resources for his project, and he won the support of a layman who had been interested in the reform of prisons and almshouses. His supporter helped him to obtain the facilities that grew into the Abendberg institution, the forerunner of all subsequent institutions for the care and treatment of the feebleminded throughout the world. Guggenbuhl successfully publicized his work, and achieved support for it from notables of the day. He travelled and lectured extensively, and the Abendberg Institute drew large numbers of visitors, philanthropists, physicians, and writers who published glowing reports about what they had seen. A political and social movement of some proportion developed on an international scale to urge governments to build similar institutions in many other countries. Guggenbuhl received innumerable honors that some felt when to his head, especially when he presented his institution as one of God's miracles, with himself as the instrument of God's work. Partly in response to his manner of presenting himself and partly because others recognized that idiot children were not cured by Guggenbuhl's or by anyone else's methods, enemies began to be more openly critical. A British official went to visit almost 20 years after the institution had opened, and discovered abominable conditions in the institution.[c] He complained, and an official Swiss government investigating commission was formed.

Among other things the commission reported that Guggenbuhl had never cured a single cretin at Abendberg, and, in fact, the report accused him of smuggling in normal children whom he presented to the public as cured cretins! Ironically, the report ended his career and his institution, just at the time when individuals in many other nations were taking up the work.[6]

Subsequent biographers and reviewers maintained that Guggenbuhl was in many respects quite sincere and have credited him with initiating the concept of an institution for the care and treatment of the feeble-minded.

---

[c]The conditions were probably not too unlike those described by Blatt (Blatt, B. and Kaplan, F., *Christmas in Purgatory*. Boston, Mass.: Allyn & Bacon, 1966; Blatt, B., *Exodus from Pandemonium*. Boston, Mass.: Allyn & Bacon, 1970) for some of our modern day institutions.

We can, of course, write Guggenbuhl off as a narcissistic sociopath, a bad example of the clinical scientist at work. But what then do we say about the physicians of the period of moral therapy in the United States who juggled recovery rates, claiming 70, 80, 90, and even 100 percent cures? Are we to say they are simply innocent when we discover they computed the percentage cured on the basis of the number discharged and not on the basis of the number admitted; or that they included those who died among the successes; or that they determined who was ill a year or less before hospitalization only after it was known whether the patient was cured, and that they then developed statistics only for those, ignoring all the rest? If a patient was not cured after some period, his case would be reviewed, and it would then be determined that he had been ill longer than one year. The patient would not be counted among the new cases treated.[7] Such practices were *not* uniform. J.S. Bockoven[8] recently reanalyzed and reinterpreted some of the early surveys, and he concluded that Samuel Woodward, the first superintendent of the Worcester State Hospital, and a primary innovator of moral treatment methods in the United States, provided figures that were essentially accurate. The rate of recovery was really quite adequate, hovering around 50 percent of all cases admitted. But it was apparently a widespread practice in those times, in the mid-1800s, to present misleading figures in annual reports of hospitals and in journal articles as well.

Even if the pioneer physicians were innocent and eager, and not really sophisticated about evaluation, what then do we say about John Rosen's work in the late 1940s, with the psychotherapeutic treatment of schizophrenics? His claims of a high rate of stable cures were simply not borne out at all by an independent team that followed about half of the patients he claimed to have treated.[9] The few patients who showed stable recoveries were not properly diagnosed schizophrenic, and the remainder had histories of further treatment and hospitalization in direct contradiction to Rosen's claims.

We might argue that we can understand the enthusiasm of the clinician. We might point to a survey such as G.A. Foulds'[10] on the relationship between claims of efficacy for treatments for mental illness, and the use of control groups. Foulds shows that claims of success are found more than three times as often when a control group is not used than when it is.[d] We can say simply that we cannot trust the clinician, that we wish to see hard data and controls before we are convinced. But there are many examples of innovators who by all accounts were sincerely devoted to the welfare of their charges, who at various points in their careers made absurd claims, absurd statements, that were refuted when events simply could not sustain the claims. Neither Guggenbuhl nor others

---

[d]In the field of education similar claims of success as justification for programs can be found (Levine, A. and Levine, M. (Eds.). *The Gary Schools*. Cambridge, Mass.: MIT Press, 1970; Levine, M. and Graziano, A.U. "Intervention Programs in Elementary Schools." In S.E. Colsun and C. Eisdorfer (Eds.) *Handbook of Community Mental Health*. N.Y.: Appleton-Century-Crofts, 1972).

could cure cretins with his methods. The moral therapists could do nothing about the rate at which chronic patients filled the hospital beds. We do not know what stimulated the follow-up study of Rosen's patients, but we would not be at all surprised that it had something to do with the readmission of patients he claimed had been cured.

Since events themselves disconfirm unsupportable claims it is puzzling that for 140 years reputable, well trained (for their day), conscientious, and innovative clinicians had distorted, sometimes deliberately, the results of clinical innovations. Their behavior is ironic in view of the origins of the clinical innovations and the decision to evaluate in the empirical spirit of scientific thought. The data, in a scientific tradition, would have been fed back as a test of an hypothesis, and a new hypothesis should have been tested. It is too easy to dismiss these examples as the consequences of the aberrant personalities of a few, for their work was designed to influence an audience, and it is that factor which confirms for us that they were working within a social context whose influence needs to be examined and understood.

Pliny Earle is a well known name in mid-nineteenth century American psychiatry. An early advocate of moral treatment, he installed his version of it when he became superintendent of the Northampton State Hospital in Massachusetts in 1864. Earle ran a model institution in many respects with a full program including recreation, work, and other forms of therapy. During his 21-year tenure at Northampton Earle never exceeded his budget, and in fact, accumulated a cash surplus of some $34,000. Moreover, the state hospital property increased in value over 60 percent. "This gain came from the high cultivation of the enlarged farm, the better labor of the employed patients, the systematic handling of all expenditure, and for a time, the increased income from private patients."[11] Because he was able to reduce costs, and indeed, show a profit, Earle was intensely admired by the hard headed, practical men who run our public affairs.

In contrast to an earlier generation of moral therapists who claimed *high* rates of cure, Earle argued strongly for a concept of the incurability of mental illness.[e]

Apparently, over the middle decades of the nineteenth century, discharge

---

[e]In a series of publications Earle reevaluated statistical data showing high rates of cure in the earlier period. He showed that the overall rates of people who had been discharged and never readmitted as ill was lower than the 70 to 100 percent claimed in the earlier time. The earlier claims were overstated because they included discharges of patients repeatedly readmitted.

Some authorities credit him with selling American psychiatry on the proposition of incurability to the point that rates of those discharged as recovered declined from the 50 percent or better characteristic of the early period of moral treatment to rates of about 5 percent by the 1920s.

However, Earle overlooked the significance of the number of discharged patients who apparently did well. Even his reanalysis of the earlier data clearly showed that 50 percent or better of patients admitted did do quite well on long-term followup (Bockoven, *Moral Treatment* supra note b).

rates were becoming lower than in an earlier time. The reason for those poorer discharge rates were complex, probably having to do with a combination of declining resources for treatment, and more complex cases emerging from the increasing urbanization, immigration, and attendant poverty of that day. The hospital superintendents of the time, rather than fight politically against declining resources, had docilely adapted, and had subverted some of the aims of moral treatment by developing the most efficient means of processing the large numbers of patients left under their care.[12] For a while superintendents apparently made heroic efforts to conceal the facts. When Earle led the fight for a concept of the incurability of insanity, he justified their positions and made it possible for them to accept the fact of a declining rate of cure.

Earle's position that mental illness was incurable was justificatory in another way. According to Earle's biographer (Sanborn) there was a connection between a high proportion of working patients, low discharge rates, and the excellent financial condition of the hospital. "It was to this steady but not compulsory discipline of labor that the financial success of the hospital was due in great part; and though the record of recoveries at Northampton showed small numbers . . . there were many unrecorded *virtual* recoveries—patients who, while still insane, were capable of self-support and self-direction under kindly supervision"[13] In other words, the financial status of the hospital, and the cost of care superceded the cure rate as an index of effectiveness. Cure rates, or rates of discharge, as an evaluative criterion were subordinated to financial criteria, and less effort was made to discharge patients.

The interplay of financial and recovery criteria was present right along. Horace Mann was a prime mover in selling the concept of a hospital to treat the insane to the Massachusetts legislature in 1830. He argued in part that a hospital would be cheaper to the state because it would remove persons once cured, from the welfare roles. That was not his sole argument by any means, but it was an obvious argument whose values combined both capitalistic and scientific material-isms.[14] Many years later an annual report of the Worcester State Hospital, sum-marizing 30 years of its operations, claimed that 3,131 men and women had recovered and been discharged. Projecting from actuarial tables, the author esti-mated that an aggregate of "82,090 years of labor and self-sustenance" had been given back to these patients and to the Commonwealth as a result of the hospital's care. The hospital had thus given the state 50 percent more "labor and aid" than it would have had, reducing the overall expense to the community.[15] It would not take much for an economist to put a dollar value on the hours of labor, and maybe some additional amount as value for the enjoyment of life and come up with a cost-benefit analysis to make the claims of that 1863 report fully modern.

Efforts at program evaluation focusing only on costs or discharge rates reveal very little about the conditions under which patients recover, nor do they help us to identify the characteristics of patients more and less likely to recover. Ques-tions of conceptual or scientific interest are not answered by such data. Program evaluation stated exclusively in terms of numbers of patients recovered and in terms of the cost per recovery is directed toward legislators who share deeply in the value system of production, units of output, and cost per unit. Since legislators are part of the social context of evaluation research, their interests become critical in shaping the form, the substance, and the interpretation that is placed upon the research. The inclination of the clinician and evaluator to collect and present data in a way suited to the interests of powerful others, reflects the more elaborate context of evaluation as compared with scientific knowing.

The historical evidence suggests a reciprocal relationship between financial criteria and recovery or discharge criteria. Public funds may be conserved through a rate of discharge that will insure society that people will continue to participate in the labor force. If such a discharge rate is not maintained, then funds will be conserved by minimizing the expenditure for care of intractable problems. This cost-benefit equation, in terms of dollar expenditure, omits from consideration the humanitarian benefits of providing the service in the first place. We shall return to this issue of humanitarian benefits later in this chapter.

The selling of any new program is part of the prehistory of the creation of any service setting,[16] and becomes part of the context of its evaluation. Any new treatment program, any social reform, is based partly on implicit or explicit criticism of the existing mode of solving the problem. While adversial interaction is a critical part of the scientific process in the short run, in social programs, uncritical advocacy puts a premium on claims of success, creating obstacles to a later careful determination of the issues.

In the case of moral therapy, ideas came across the Atlantic frequently on the basis of relatively brief visits to showcase installations.[17] Pinel's *A Treatise on Insanity*[18] depicts fully the problems in management of the insane, but did those who diffused the innovations take the problems with sufficient seriousness when they went home? Guggenbuhl was able to convince many visitors who came to see the Abendberg only briefly, and they were encouraged to return to their homes with missions to establish similar facilities.[f]

Visits are opportunities for crude evaluations and, generally speaking, visitors, be they professionals, journalists or laymen with an interest in a particular problem, tend to accentuate the positive.[g] There rarely is any sound basis for believing that the innovative method will, in fact, solve the problem, but

---

[f]See Kanner, L., *A History of the Care and Study of the Mentally Retarded*, Springfield, Ill.: C. Thomas, 1964. In another field we have demonstrated that the Deweys endorsed the Gary, Indiana plan of education for New York City and for the nation at large in their book based upon a single visit to Gary of *no more than three days* (Levine and Levine, *The Gary Schools*, supra note d).

[g]Gary, Indiana had a steady stream of visitors to its schools in the early 1900s. These visitors included wealthy and influential members of the lay group, the Public Education Association of NYC, and prominent journalists such as Randolph Bourne. These visitors influenced the New York School Board in its decision to adopt the Gary plan for the New York schools. For a program to be adopted, not only do professional judgments count,

concerned persons seem to have a tendency to believe that it will, and to sell the new program to others as if it will do the job.

Aside from the enthusiasm of the proponents, the need to develop political support behind any program contributes to the tendency to present the program in the most positive terms, deemphasizing the doubts and uncertainties.

When legislators (or other persons entrusted with allocating huge funds) act, they prefer to act on the basis of some consensus. When experts disagree or are ambiguous, legislators are liable to back off from taking definitive action. After all, why should politicians stick their necks out, if the experts disagree, or have serious doubts about the efficacy of the expensive programs they propose?[h]

A contemporary example is found in the report of the Joint Commission of Mental Health and Illness in its recommendations for revitalization of the state hospital system. Knowledgeable individuals claim that the plan presented was a compromise to insure a united professional front to the politicians.[19] It was neither presented nor sold as an hypothesis to be tested.

During the prehistory or selling stage difficulties tend to be minimized, and the efficacy is emphasized, if not oversold. The program, once sold, becomes institutionalized, in the sense that it becomes deeply embedded in law, and in the budgetary process. The capital investment in mental hospitals provides one good example. The attempt to ameliorate social problems through prohibition (expressed in the form of a constitutional amendment) and federal enabling legislation, is another good example of how the helping force can become deeply embedded in the social structure. The political constituency developed for programs of the Office of Economic Opportunity allowed those programs to fend off attempts to close them out, and, of course, evaluative research became deeply involved on both sides of the question, typically in justificatory arguments for keeping or doing away with programs. Albert Shanker has recently been citing evaluation research on Title I programs of the Elementary and Secondary Education Act in an effort to insure that federal funds for education be continued. In few instances was there any real attempt to determine and to understand just what any intervention accomplished in a conceptual sense.

Historically, reformist, humanitarian, and religiously based motives underlay the development of many human service institutions, some of which institutions

---

but the support of influential laymen, and politicians responsive to those lay opinions are also necessary (Levine, A and Levine, M. (Eds.), *The Gary Schools*. Cambridge, Mass.: MIT Press, 1970; Levine, A. and Levine, M., "The Social Context of Evaluative Research." In R.L. Handy (Ed.) *Education and the Behavioral Sciences*. St. Louis, Mo.: Warren H. Green. In Press).

[h]The public wearies of complex, unresolvable arguments. Sinclair, in writing about the public reaction to claims and counterclaims made about the benefits of prohibition, feels the public controversy was detrimental to the full and careful consideration of the benefits of prohibition (Sinclair, A., *Era of Excess. A Social History of the Prohibition Movement*. Boston, Mass.: Little Brown, 1962).

we now decry. The penitentiary was developed as reform for the system of
mutilating and killing offenders. The mental hospital was developed as a reform
for the horrors of the almshouse, or for the system of auctioning off the care of
the insane to the lowest bidders. But, humanitarian goals were obscured when
they were fused with production-oriented values in the overstated argument
that restoration of the disabled individual's productive capacity would reduce
the drain on the taxpayer caused by dependence. The emphasis on production,
on cure, in the early development of the mental hospital, put the emphasis on
the acute patient who could be helped. The chronic patient became a positive
liability to be ignored, hidden or moved out of the institution if possible. In
the case of the mental hospital the game led to statistical manipulation of cases
to justify the existence of the service by demonstrating a high rate of cure. The
game led to an obscuring of the problem of the chronic patient, and, moreover,
since a high rate of cure was promised, the lower overall 50 percent rate, which
certainly did not support a concept of incurability, was interpreted as a failure
of the treatment method. Eventually, the resources devoted to the care of the
mental patient declined. By the late 1940s the situation in the hospitals had
deteriorated to a scandalous level.

One cannot claim the decline was solely due to the materialistic criteria
employed in evaluating mental hospitals. However, the humanitarian values,
and the sense of community that at least in part, motivated the establishment of
programs to assist the less fortunate were less explicitly considered in evaluating
the goodness of the institutions designed to implement those values. In part
the mental hospitals of the past deteriorated because they became separated from
the communities they were meant to serve, and no effective attention or measurement was devoted to monitoring that separation. The hospitals of the past
developed reputations as places that dealt only with the indigent or the violent,
and as places from which a patient would never be released as cured once admitted. Of course, the laws establishing those institutions sometimes unintention-
ally guaranteed the institutions would develop such reputations, but, for whatever reason, the institutions became inaccessible to many, if not in actuality,
then in a psychological sense, and when they became inaccessible, they lost value
as a social symbol of mutual assistance. Instead of embodying the sense of community, or making explicit and concrete the concept that people care for one
another, and provide for each other, hospitals became the embodiment of separation and exclusion.

However weak and halting it is, the contemporary movement to increase
consumer and community participation in programmatic efforts, as a way of
dealing with contemporary problems of distance and alienation, has potential to
modify the social context within which programs are evaluated to increase the
pertinence of measures of dehumanization and of perceived helpfulness for evaluation. The patient's rights movement in the courts may also serve to support
this direction for evaluation of our institutions. The mistrust of the citizenry for

government, may also make it a propitious time, from the viewpoint of government officials, to assess the feelings of trust and the degree of reliance people feel in service institutions as highly pertinent criteria for evaluation. Moreover, the recent reaction against hard line positivism and behaviorism and the renewed interest and legitimacy of phenomenological approaches in the social sciences suggest that values in the scientific component of the social context of evaluation are changing. There may be a professional climate more supportive of the study of soft variables such as satisfaction, alienation, or dehumanization as coequal in importance with hard data production variables. In keeping with the concept of reciprocity between science and its context, we would urge that social scientists educate their sponsors to the relevance and importance of such issues.

There should be a clear-cut separation between studies designed to determine relationships between treatment modes and effects, and evaluation studies. The former studies should be undertaken within a pure science context, and probably should not enter into the argument for increased resources, or of important change in the form of practice, until there is strong evidence that a given result may be obtained regularly and predictibly.[i] For evaluation purposes it is necessary to monitor treatment programs to see that any given approach does not fall below some experientially determined lower limit of production. It apparently was the case that mental hospital discharges fell far below optimal levels over a period of years. We certainly should determine that we are not doing harm.

However, when we are dealing with problems that have proved to be relatively chronic or intractible, or relatively refractory to most of the modes of treatment whose properties we know fairly well, the connotative significance of the term evaluation should be modified to emphasize examination of the degree to which the service itself reduces alienation, or in S.B. Sarason's terms, increases the sense of community.[20] Evaluation should be directed toward determining the degree to which the service preserves the integrity and dignity of each person served, and if the patient population is chronically dependent, then the degree to which as full a life as is feasible is provided. Evaluation should also concern itself with the implications of the nature of the service for the personal development of the staffs of service agencies, of the degree to which the human potential

---

[i]Lick has suggested that intensive clinical trials with carefully defined clinical populations should precede efforts to evaluate in the more expensive experimental mode (Lick, J., "Statistical Versus Clinical Significance in Research on the Outcome of Psychotherapy." *International Journal of Mental Health*, 2, 26-31, 1973). Zusman and Bissonette have also argued that most agencies should not engage in regular evaluation of outcome on the grounds that good evaluation is sometimes more difficult and expensive than it is worth, and poor evaluation gives the whole enterprise a bad name (Zusman, J. and Bissonette, R., "The Case Against Evaluation (with Some Suggestions for Improvement)." *International Journal of Mental Health*, 2, 11-125, 1973).

of the staff is realized and not stultified.[j] From a social point of view, helping institutions are not only established out of need, but also as visible and concrete manifestations of the view that members of a community care for each other, and are willing to provide mutual assistance. From that viewpoint continuous assessment and determination of the accessibility of the service to its surrounding community, and the degree to which the service is viewed by various components of the community as caring and concerned, are critical issues for evaluation.

The scientific spirit that allowed us to develop treatment programs for the helpless, the dependent, and even the repulsive in society has, in one of its distortions, led us to overlook the subjective satisfactions that services should have yielded for the providers and the recipients of services. The emphasis on the fiscal value of services to society allowed us to accept the premise that only the minimum of resources necessary to salve our collective consciences should be committed to those services that could not prove their value by productive criteria. Perhaps if our predecessors had measured the quality of institutional services in the dimensions suggested, we would not have allowed the institutions to deteriorate as they did. The contemporary movement to empty mental hospitals, evaluated as it is by criteria of patients discharged, and costs of maintaining patients in the community, without regard to the quality of life for those patients, is already leading to a reaction against the concept of community treatment for the mentally ill. It will not be long before journalists will be exposing the exploitation of patients living in the community, and politicians responsive to the complaints of citizens will be demanding that the mentally ill be returned to the hospitals. When that happens, the fault will lie, at least in part, in the failure to develop and evaluate programs from a truly humanitarian perspective. We hope the professional evaluator will rethink his mission in those terms.

Notes

1. Merton, R.K., "Behavior Patterns of Scientists." *The American Scholar.* 38 (Spring): 197-225, 1969.
2. O'Gorman, M., *Every Other Bed.* Cleveland, Ohio: World Publishing Co., 1956; Brand, J.L., "The National Mental Health Act of 1946. A Retrospect," *Bulletin of the History of Medicine, 39,* 231-245, 1965; Felix, R.H., *Mental Illness. Progress and Prospects.* New York: Columbia University Press, 1967.
3. Hume, D., *An Inquiry Concerning Human Understanding.* New York: Bobbs Merrill, 1955 (originally published, 1748).

[j]For a sophisticated discussion of this set of issues, See Goldenberg, I.I., *Build Me a Mountain.* Cambridge, Mass.: MIT Press, 1970.

4. Szaz, T.S., "The Uses of Naming and the Origin of the Myth of Mental Illness." *American Psychologist, 16*, 59-65, 1961.

5. Alexander, F.G. and Selesnick, S.T., *The History of Psychiatry*. New York: Harper and Row, 1966; Caplan, R.B., *Psychiatry and the Community in 19th Century America*. New York: Basic Books, 1969; Grob, G.N., *The State and the Mentally Ill. A History of the Worcester State Hospital in Massachusetts, 1830-1920*. Chapel Hill, N.C. University of North Carolina Press, 1966.

6. Kanner, L., *A History of the Care and Study of the Mentally Retarded*. Springfield, Ill.: Charles C. Thomas, 1964.

7. Caplan, *Psychiatry and the Community*, p. 9.

8. Bockoven, J.S., *Moral Treatment in Community Mental Health*. New York: Springer, 1972.

9. Horwitz, W.A., Polatin, P., Kolb, L.C., and Hoch, P.H., "A Study of Cases of Schizophrenia Treated by 'Direct Analysis.'" *American Journal of Psychiatry*, 114 (March), 780-790, 1957-1958.

10. Foulds, G.A., "Clinical Research in Psychiatry." *Journal of Mental Science, 104*, 259-265, 1958.

11. Bockoven, *Moral Treatment*, p. 49.

12. Gish, L., *Reform at Osawatomie State Hospital*. Lawrence, Kansas: The University of Kansas Press, 1972.

13. Bockoven, *Moral Treatment*, pp. 52-53.

14. Grob, *The State and the Mentally Ill*.

15. Caplan, *Psychiatry and the Community*.

16. Sarason, S.B., *The Creation of Settings and the Future Societies*. San Francisco, California: Jossey-Bass, 1972.

17. Grob, *The State and the Mentally Ill*.

18. Pinel, P. *A Treatise on Insanity*. Sheffield, England: W. Todd, 1806.

19. Connery, R.H., Backstrom, C.H., Deener, D.R., Friedman, J.R., Kroll, M., Marden, R.H., McClesky, C., Meekison, P., and Morgan, J.A., Jr., *The Politics of Mental Health*. New York: Columbia University Press, 1968; Felix, *Mental Illness*.

20. Sarason, S.B., *The Psychological Sense of Community: Prospects for a Community Psychology*. San Francisco: Jossey-Bass, 1974.

Part II

Evaluation in Practice

6

Comprehensive Approach to Evaluation and Community Research

Peter Sainsbury

At the time the community psychiatric service evaluation described here was undertaken, evaluative research was relatively uncharted territory. Consequently, some difficult decisions had to be made, in particular: selecting objectives that would be feasible and also have practical value; questions of experimental design, such as the practicability of obtaining base-lines and of using a "control" for a program as diverse as a community psychiatric service; various problems of method, including the choice of appropriate variables to depict the services and characterize their users; and defining the criteria of evaluation—that is, those measures and indexes that would reliably describe the operation of the service and its effects.

Other related problems were: anticipating a suitable statistical analysis, and insuring that the data would be in the required form; and finding ways of storing and handling a lot of information on many patients. A last, and by no means the least formidable, hazard was the efficient administration of a survey of this kind: to arrange matters so that all participants recorded their observations in the agreed-on manner, that the requisite data were systematically filed and checked and so on.

Psychiatric Services in Britain

Among the salutory consequences of introducing the National Health Service in Great Britain were improved standards for the care of the mentally ill and an extension of services available to them. Mental hospitals not only began exploring better ways of caring for patients within the hospital, but also of bridging the gulf between hospital and community.[1] The result of these endeavors was the Mental Health Act of 1959. This removed the administrative distinctions between mental and general hospital patients, and the remaining barriers between the mental hospital and its community. It also made the provision of community services mandatory; an evolution that has culminated in a recent statement of policy by the Department of Health and Social Security (DHSS). This official enthusiasm for the extramural care of the mentally ill was pre-empted by Dr. J. Carse at Graylingwell Hospital as early as 1956. He also anticipated the need to assess the consequences of introducing a new policy, for, rather surprisingly, the Health Department has only recently joined the cause of operational and evaluative research.

95

Graylingwell Hospital and the Worthing
Experiment

Graylingwell is situated in Chichester, the county town for West Sussex.
The county is the catchment area of the hospital; it has a population of 400,000
and Worthing, the largest town, has some 80,000 inhabitants.

The planning of hospital and related services in England is undertaken
regionally. So in 1956 it was the Hospital Regional Board that approved
Dr. Carse's request to set up "an experimental outpatients service in Worthing."
The proposal was to open a day hospital and community service center there;
to increase the outpatient clinics and to introduce a scheme of domiciliary treatment, to discover "whether the provision of greatly extended outpatient treatment facilities would reduce the number of patients admitted to Graylingwell
and thereby ultimately overcome the crowding problem that was beginning to
cause anxiety."[2]

After consultation with local family practitioners it was agreed that patients
living in the Worthing district would be admitted to Graylingwell only if a
psychiatrist found them unsuitable for community care.

Chichester and District Community Service

The success of the scheme in Worthing led to its introduction in 1958 in the
Chichester district to test whether it would be equally successful in a rural area
with a more dispersed population (120,000), and whether the hospital's psychiatric staff could run the service without additional personnel.[3]

The distinguishing features of the community psychiatric service in Chichester were:

1. No patient could be admitted without first seeing a psychiatrist, either at
    home or at the day center or at one of the outpatient clinics. The initial
    contact was about equally divided between these three alternatives, options
    that offered considerable flexibility in caring for patients as there were now
    three possible avenues for treatment other than in the hospital.
2. Close collaboration with the local general practitioners was considered
    essential.
3. Because the service was run by the staff of the psychiatric hospital, its em-
    phasis was more on clincial than on social care; so at this stage the local
    social services only provided transport to and from the day hospital and the
    clinics.

The extent to which the immediate goal of the service was realized is shown
in Figure 6-1. From this it can be seen that admissions to Graylingwell from
Worthing and from Chichester each decreased by over 50 percent.

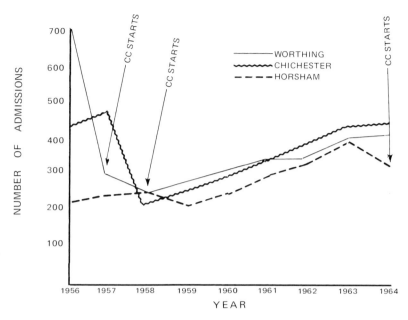

Figure 6-1. Admissions to Graylingwell and the Introduction of Community Care

MRC Clinical Research Unit

To complete the setting of the scene requires some mention of research at Graylingwell.[4] Since 1948 the Regional Board had supported a research department in the hospital. This was taken over by the Medical Research Council in 1957. When the evaluation began in 1959 a psychiatrist, three social workers, and a clerk were available to undertake the research. Though the research unit was now administratively independent, its psychiatric members still had honorary contracts with the hospital, and exercised the same privileges as other members of the staff. This arrangement solved the first obstacle it is essential to overcome at the outset of an evaluative research project, namely: to insure that the investigators are *independent* of the service studied while at the same time persona grata with the clinicians and administrators running it.

The second obstacle is that, by and large, people do not like having their work inspected. At the start of the Worthing Experiment, the idea of evaluating it was loudly applauded. When the research plans were actually formulated, however, they provoked a quite unanticipated degree of alarm and resistance. Those whose carefully considered policies are being assessed, whose favored ideas may appear to be in question, whose expectations would seem to be demoted from certainties to possibilities, understandably see the evaluator as a threat of as superfluous. Consequently, they will use all manner of cajolery in order to share in the planning of the project to make sure it will become a self-fulfilling prophecy. The investigator will then have to point out that it is improbable that a plan drawn up by experienced administrators will be exposed as unworkable, but what will probably emerge is some indications about the patients most likely to benefit from their policies and how their schemes might be modified to increase their effectiveness.

Collaboration with Service Personnel and Efficient Organization

A third essential is fostering the harmonious participation of those providing the services. From the outset, promoting the interest and willing cooperation of the service personnel in the purpose of the research and its planning, and then maintaining their active support by regular meetings in which their difficulties can be discussed, their criticisms invited, and their contribution appreciated, are vital and worth every bit of the time they take.

Another little-considered aspect of research of this kind is its efficient administration; it is more likely to flounder on this than on anything else. Evaluative research entails keeping uniform records, the systematic registration of patients to insure that no cases are missed, seeing that time-schedules are strictly observed, and so forth. In our experience time must be set aside to supervise clerks and collaborators, and to check regularly on procedures.

Goals of a Psychiatric Service and Evaluative Research

As a matter of practical fact, the usual purpose of evaluating services is to determine whether certain service objectives are being met, and the factors prompting the investigation stem from questions asked and comments made by those responsible for planning or implementing it. The stated goal of the Worthing Experiment, for example, was to reduce admissions to an overcrowded hospital. The research aim, therefore, was to see whether this was achieved. It was not a difficult test and the answer has already been demonstrated in Figure 6-1.

But the objectives and expected gains in setting up new services are often couched only in general terms. It can usually be assumed that the objectives are: either to reduce morbidity in patients and in the community at large, or that both patients and service personnel will gain in other unstated respects, such as better standards of care and improved efficiency of service.

Furthermore, objectives will differ in emphasis, if not in content, depending on to whom they are addressed—those who will administer them, those who will operate them, or those who will make use of them.

The first requirement, therefore, is to formulate the goals of the services clearly and exactly; and it will usually evolve on the research worker to clarify the issues. Once this has been done, defining the research aims and selecting priorities that are likely to help those providing the services becomes easier.

In addition, the evaluator must be prepared to anticipate some of the consequences of innovations that the planners had not taken into account; for example, assessing the effects on the morale of staff whose responsibilities would be affected, or the demands made on those who will need to assume new roles.

Our aims in evaluating the community services in Chichester were therefore determined by a combination of factors:

1. The stated objectives of the service
2. The unstated but implicit goals in providing new facilities for treatment in the community (for example, we assessed the operation by describing the characteristics of patients using the facilities and whether community patients too readily lost contact with them)
3. The more general purposes of service evaluation such as reducing morbidity and increasing efficiency by making better use of the available resources in personnel and money
4. The unexpected and unconsidered problems that we anticipated a service of this kind might create, such as placing an undue burden on patients' relatives or household
5. The feasibility of each objective in terms of research design and method

Aims of the Research[5]

The aims we eventually chose, or which emerged as the result of these pressures, were the following:

1. To see how the introduction of a community service affects *who gets referred* to the psychiatrist. We wanted to examine the referral rates of the different social and clinical categories of patients to see whether it was meeting new needs.

2. To see how the community service affects *who gets admitted* and who gets treated in the community. What considerations, for instance, determine admission when opportunities for treatment at home and in a day hospital are provided and what the bed needs and rates of contact with the community facilities were. Was discharge also facilitated, and hence whether or not the numbers of long-stay and institutionalized patients were increased.

3. To determine the effect on the community of treating patients outside the hospital who previously would have been admitted. As members of the patient's household and his neighbors will be those most closely concerned, how were they affected? And what were their attitudes to the new service? This policy was introducing a novel element in that the burden previously borne by the hospital was now transferred to the patient's relatives. Equally, we were interested in the attitudes of the general practitioner, as he also would be taking on a greater responsibilities for the sick member of the family than previously.

4. To assess the effects of the new service on patients' clinical and social outcome. We wanted to know whether morbidity was reduced, either because more patients had a better outcome or because of a shorter duration of illness, and how this was achieved in terms of the number and type of contacts with the service needed to attain "recovery." Was the service using its manpower more efficiently in containing morbidity?

Many aspects of the service that might be considered more salient were omitted: a comparison of the quality of patients' care and of their daily lives within and outside hospital, especially the chronically handicapped; staff morale and satisfaction; a full-scale, cost-benefit analysis; and a detailed look at the effects on selected groups of patients such as senile dementias, psychopathic personalities, and schizophrenics who respond poorly to treatment and present a particular challenge to community care programs.

Feasibility and Pilot Studies

Once the aims had been precisely stated, the research plan and the criteria of the evaluation could be settled. But to do this, it was necessary first to find out what was feasible. Because evaluative research is expensive and time consuming, the temptation is to include too many aims, and this can be self-defeating. Moreover, a research design that is appropriate to settle one question will not necessarily be suited to another. So the matter of relating priorities to one's overall plan and resources (in time, research personnel, etc.) entails painful sacrifice.

With such questions in mind, Dr. J.D. Morissey and I undertook a pilot study to see whether an evaluation of certain aspects of the service, using a before-and-after comparison, was practicable.[6]

We concluded that such a design would be feasible only if it were planned before the start of a new service, because uniform base-line data could not be obtained retrospectively from hospital records. The operation of a new service, moreover, is not typical during its first year and a year or two should be allowed to elapse before assessing its efficiency. However, we were able to show that the new service had pronounced effects that related to patient characteristics such as class, marital status, and diagnosis. Accordingly, we inferred that an evaluation was possible, but that the preferred design would be to compare the Chichester Community Service and another psychiatric service not planned on community lines.

Planning the Evaluation

Having come to this conclusion, our plan was to combine two familiar research strategies: that of an epidemiological survey, and that of a controlled clinical trial in which services instead of drugs are the main dependent variables. Nevertheless, each posed very difficult problems of a methodological and organizational kind.[7]

Some questions, notably those posed in the first two aims—the effects on referral and admission of patients—could be answered by comparing the rates of referral and admission in the new service and in a control one; but on what criteria should the comparison service be selected? To fulfill the epidemiological needs of the research, every patient referred to the psychiatrist from two defined populations (the community care and the control districts) would have to be identified, and uniform information recorded on each of them. Furthermore, selecting and defining the items needed to describe the patients and the services they received would be a most exacting task.

Valid criteria would have to be devised to measure the effects and effectiveness of the service. Many of our criteria were epidemiological indexes: rates of referral, of duration of stay, or of contacts with the various facilities. But as few generally accepted standards or norms were available for assessing such aspects of the effectiveness of a service as family burdens and needs, new instruments would have to be devised.

Comparison or Control Service

Although we had decided that, for the most part, it was not going to be practicable to compare the community service with the one provided beforehand, to a limited extent this approach can be suitable; for example, when information on patients is required for statutory returns, because it is then accurately registered. We therefore compared admission, discharge, length of stay, mortality, and suicide rates before and following the introduction of the service. This approach to evaluation can best be illustrated in reference to suicide.

One criterion on which the overall effectiveness of a psychiatric service might be appropriately assessed is the incidence of suicide in its target patient population; indeed, critics of community care often cite the increased risk of suicide it might expect to incur. Dr. D. Walk[8] therefore examined the incidence of suicide in the five-year period (1952-56) before the service started, and again following its introduction (1959-63). First we calculated the suicide rate of patients *resident* in the hospital, since an open-door policy that allows patients freedom to come and go as they wish might have been expected to increase the likelihood of suicide. We found an identical rate in the two periods, indicating that patients had not been given a license to commit suicide, rather we found evidence that when there is less need to "kick against the bricks" suicide is resorted to less often.

Second, we had predicted that if the community service was more success-ful than its predecessor fewer patients who had been in contact with it the past year would commit suicide. This hypothesis was supported in the case of the elderly, in whom suicide decreased significantly. The "before and after" mode, then, had demonstrated a definite if restricted usefulness.

Comparison Between Services

An alternative design was to prevail upon a neighboring county hospital to accept the invidious role of being labelled the "traditional, conservative, or conventional" service. As it happened, the medical superintendent of the Old Manor, Salisbury, was very justifiably proud of the service his hospital gave. But he was also satisfied we were more curious than committed; we had no pre-conceived notions that the community service heralded a new era of psychiatry. Indeed, by this time we had abandoned the simplistic view that an evaluation would label one service as "better" than another, instead we hoped we might be able to say something about the needs of different types of patients—those whose requirements would best be met by admission and the skilled manage-ment the mental hospital provides, and those whose needs would be realized by staying at home or by a place in a community facility.

The gratifying consequence was that Dr. Simpson and his staff collaborated unstintingly in the comparative evaluation. The Salisbury service, it should be added, was hospital-based, the majority of patients being directly referred to the hospital by their general practitioners, although the hospital psychiatrist offered domiciliary consultations and held outpatient clinics in Salisbury and the out-lying towns.

Similarities and Differences Between
the Two Services

Salisbury might have been tailored to our requirements: It is a replica of Chichester, geographically and demographically. Both are relatively prosperous county towns set among chalk downs. The only obvious demographic difference is the higher proportion of elderly people who have retired to the Sussex coast. The population of each district is about 121,000.

The material and economic resources of the two services—their quota of beds, personnel, and general practitioners—are the same. The only rather paradoxical difference is that the Old Manor Hospital has a larger psychiatric social work department. In neither area were there any psychiatrists in private practice, and very few patients are sent to London for an opinion. Consequently, all the mentally ill in both populations needing psychiatric advice were referred exclusively to their respective service.

If a total district service is being compared with another, the ideal procedure of randomly allocating patients to each is out of the question; but this procedure would be preferable, practicable, and ethical when comparing facilities *within* a service.

The final plan of the study, therefore, was: first to compare the social and clinical characteristics of all patients referred during a least one year to the community service, with similar data on all referrals to the hospital-based control. As the catchment area of each service was an administrative district, for which there was a population census, we could then compare rates of referral, admission, and discharge, and also the specific rates of the different demographic and social categories.

The second part of the plan was to take a random sample of all referrals to each service, and by interviewing the responsible relatives, to compare their household circumstances, and the burden of the patient on the family. We then planned to follow the samples through two years to assess their subsequent contacts with the service, and to compare their clinical outcomes.

Collection of Data

Certain decisions had to be made about the collection of data, involving (1) our criteria for including cases in the evaluation; (2) what social and clinical items of information it was essential to record on each case in order to realize our aims; and (3) how to insure that these data were reliable and uniformly recorded in each case. In practice the last presented the greatest problems, depending (as it must) on the willing cooperation of one's colleagues, and efficient machinery for checking that all the records were available in the required format.

1. *Definition of a case*: We aimed to include all new patients referred to the psychiatrists for whatever reason and from whatever source (the family doctor, the social agencies, the physicians in the general hospital, etc.) For various, and now regretted, reasons we defined a new case as someone who had not seen a psychiatrist for the preceding six months.

2. *Selecting and defining the other variables*: The psychiatrists at both hospitals agreed to complete a coded clinical item sheet, instead of hospital case folders they ordinarily used. In this way they recorded some 80 items of information on each referral, which could easily be transferred to punch cards. All this was done without adding to the time psychiatrists needed to take a routine history.

The selection of clinical items did not present undue difficulties. However, we did need more social and family background data than is customarily recorded. Choosing these meant keeping our goals in very clear focus—a prerequisite of this kind of inquiry. Had the referrals been randomly allocated to the services, this would have controlled many confounding variables. Instead, we needed to have data on such variables as severity of symptoms; whether retired; or any other factors on which the two services might not have been balanced. Predicting which ones were most likely to be troublesome is necessarily chancy.

3. *The case register*: The systematic recording of data on all referrals meant, in effect, setting up two "case registers," one for each service. An indispensable tool for collecting routine, descriptive statistics of a service, a case register enables basic identifying, personal, social and clinical data to be obtained in a standardized form and avoids suplication. This is especially valuable where patients are in contact with a variety of facilities—hospitals, hostels, social work services, and domiciliary visits, for example. A case register also allows data to be accumulated on subsequent events, such as patient contacts with the different amenities within the service, or failed appointments, or whatever other information might be appropriate to the aims of the evaluation, for example: costs and welfare needs. Another advantage is that a case register provides a sampling frame, and this was crucial to our plan.

Accordingly, the evaluator can, on the one hand, construct stratified samples of matched patients with specific characteristics, such as he would need if he wanted to compare hospital and domiciliary care of chronic schizophrenics. On the other hand, he can, if he wants, draw a random sample of the referrals. This was the case with us. In order to assess the effects on the family of having a mentally ill member at home—their social needs and attitudes to mental hospital and home care—the homes of an approximately one-in-three sample were visited and the responsible relative or head of household interviewed. The two service cohorts were then followed up for two years. When the families' burdens were assessed a second time, the extent to which their needs had been met was scored, and a number of outcome measure made. Their general practitioners' attitudes to the services were also estimated at this time.

4. *Reliability of case register data*: The agreement between psychiatrists on data they recorded in the coded item sheet was assessed by having two psychiatrists independently examine the first 90 patients. It was found to be surprisingly high on most major items.[9]

Criteria of the Evaluation: Indexes and Measures

Crucial to any evaluative study of services are the standards by which the new service is to be measured. What they should be will depend on having defined clearly the objectives of the service and the aims of the research. These standards may be set out in terms of the community's need, those of the patients and their households, cost-efficiency, the quality of service, acceptance of and satisfaction with services by users and staff, clinical and social outcomes such as reduction in morbidity (especially by prevention). Among the indexes and measures we used were the following:

Epidemiological Indexes

The first step was to delimit the target population. To realize our first two aims (to see who gets referred, admitted, and discharged following the introduction of a community service), the relevant populations were those of the two districts. The national census gives a breakdown by age, class, household composition, and by other demographic and social variables, thereby furnishing the denominators for calculating rates for specific categories of patients of referrals, contact with day hospitals, and domiciliary visits.

The second step is to insure that all indexes are precisely defined, relevant to the objectives, and reliable. This may entail designing and pretesting new instruments to provide the appropriate measure.

Measures of Burden on Family [10]

The problem can be illustrated by reference to one of our major aims: to assess the effects on the family of a mentally ill member. Our criteria were the effects on simple, uncontroversial, and objectively definable aspects of family life—those activities that could be reliably rated, such as members having to stay home from work, reduction in family income, and the health of the informant (the responsible relative). A questionnaire was constructed upon which these and other pertinent items could be rated as having "no," "some," or a "severe" effect.

The family interview schedule contained 72 items from which a number of indexes were obtained: 13 items for the effects on the family; 11 describing the patient's behavior found by the family to be most worrying; 2 rating the health of the informant; 8 assessing the family's economic circumstances and quality of housing; and the other 27 pertaining to facts such as composition of household, patient's employment, and demographic details. [11]

Similarly, the needs of the family and the extent to which these were being met was estimated by marking a checklist of needs at the first visit, then recording social work visits actually made in each service during two years, with final assessment after that period of which needs had been met.

Outcome Measures

A variety of clinical and social outcome measures were used. The clinical ones included: (a) mortality rates; (b) the service psychiatrists' ratings of improvement (i.e., change in clinical status) at follow-up and at the time of discharge; and (c) the research psychiatrist's ratings of outcome, that is, how well the patient was at the two-year follow-up. Combined measures of improvement and consumer satisfaction were also used, including a self-rating of improvement made by the patient; another made by the responsible relative; and last the general practitioner's rating of improvement.

Measures of improvement that were independent of clinical symptoms were derived from the change in the effects-on-the-family scores, and by the reduction in family problems scores at the end of the two years compared with those at referral; we called these indexes "relief of burden." The idea was that the more disturbed the patient, the greater would be his effects on his family; a reduction in burden would therefore be a measure of his improvement.

Quality and Acceptability of Services

Quality and acceptability of services were not included among the major objectives of the project; nevertheless, some measures of satisfaction with the services were possible. On the one hand, the general practitioners were asked to rate whether each of their patients treated in the community had involved them in more work; and also whether they were satisfied with the service provided. And on the other, the responsible member of the patient's household rated their attitudes to the patient receiving his treatment at home, to admission, and whether they were satisfied with the disposal that had actually been recommended.

Reliability and Validity

In the interests of both validity and reliability, we included only those items that could be defined objectively. For example, one of the items for assessing effects on the family was income change through having the patient at home. This was rated as having "no effect" if the total loss of income had decreased by by less than 10 percent; a decrease of 10 to 50 percent was rated "some effect;" and more than 50 percent was rated "severe effect." Where no objective criteria were available, ratings were based on a description of the patient's behavior and on concrete examples of its effect on the family. Anchoring examples and definitions for rating were given in an instruction book.

The reliability of the schedule was examined by the three psychiatric social workers visiting 30 consecutive families in pairs; the interviews being randomly distributed between the two districts. Their level of agreement was above 80 percent on most items.[12]

Insuring the validity of this kind of material is a problem that cannot be wholly solved, but it may be helped by concentrating on "hard" data, by defining items operationally, and by using independent measures of the same item. For example, we categorized "educational status" by both school-leaving age and by type of schooling received; and "social status" by income level as well as by occupational category. The correlated scores then provide a measure of the validity of the variable.

We used this technique to assess "severity of illness," one of the most salient clinical measures, because if the referrals to the two services are clinically comparable, interpretation of the findings is greatly simplified.

Severity of illness at referral was first compared by ranking the frequency with which the 28 symptoms were recorded in each service, and a high correlation of 0.88 was found. Second, the effects of the patient on the family provided an independent and, in this context, a very appropriate measure of severity. As can be seen in Table 6-1, there was again very little difference between them.

We concluded that although more patients per 1,000 of the population were seen in Chichester, they were clinically very similar to those in Salisbury, and

Table 6-1
Effects on Families When the Patients were First Referred

		CHI (N:271)	SAL (N:139)
Problem Scores		%	%
	0 - 1	38	32
	2 - 3	25	24
	4 - 5	14	15
	6+	23	29
Burden Ratings		%	%
	None	40	29
	Some	42	46
	Severe	18	25

that the higher total rate in the community service was not primarily due to more patients in any one category being seen.

Some Findings and Their Practical Applications

In order to stress their practical relevance, some of the findings are related to the new proposals of the Department of Health and Social Security for the care of the mentally ill in England.[13] The plan is to close the mental hospitals and substitute psychiatric units in the District General Hospitals, day centers and sheltered accomodations in the community to be run in collaboration with local and social services. Guidelines to beds and "places" needed to achieve this have already been established.[a] The results are presented in the context of the four principal aims, the first of which was to see how the introduction of a community service affected the referral of patients.[14]

Referral Rates

The referral rates to the community care service were higher for nearly every demographic, social, and clinical category; but the rates of certain categories were very significantly higher in Chichester than in Salisbury (see Figure 6-2).

There were, for example, two referral peaks in both services: one in the age group 24-35 and the other at 65 and over, which probably indicate categories most at risk for mental disorder, as they occur irrespective of type of service. Yet, it was just these age groups that had a significantly higher referral rate in the community care service. Further analyses showed the peak at 65 and over was due to the high rates of the single and widowed of both sexes, especially those living alone, and the peak at 24-35 was accounted for by married women. Moreover, the high rates of the former were due to more depressive illness and organic dementias being referred to the community service and in the latter to neurotic and depressive disorders.[15]

It would therefore appear that the new service was especially responsive to the needs of the neglected elderly and of the seriously mentally disordered in the community, rather than recruiting more people with minor disorders.

Table 6-2 shows that the community care policy was also preferentially

---

[a]Dr. Grad de Alarcon and I are currently evaluating the introduction of this policy in Southampton, where we have been fortunate in being able to divide the city in two—the services in one half to be in accord with the new policy, and in the other to be centered on the local mental hospital.

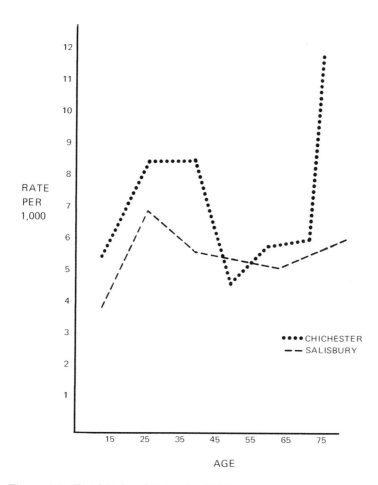

Figure 6-2. Total Referral Rates for 1960

Table 6-2
Social Class: Rates per 1,000 Population of Occupied and Retired Males in Three Social Classes

Social Class		Chichester	Salisbury
Upper	I and II	10.4	8.8
Middle	III	4.3	3.9
Lower	IV and V	5.0	2.6

providing a service for the socially disadvantaged as the rates of referral are
relatively higher in the lowest socioeconomic class.

Last, it is evident from the higher referral rates in Chichester than when
services are extended they are more widely used, consequently some caution
must be exercised in predicting future needs from statistics describing current
practice, as the Department of Health and Social Security appears to have done.

On the other hand, when the mean duration of illness at referral of community and control patients were compared, it was significantly shorter in the
former, indicating that the community policy provides better opportunities
for early, and therefore more effective, treatment.

Admissions

Comparison of the two services showed that only 14 percent of referrals
were admitted in the month following referral to the community service in contrast to 52 percent to the hospital-centered one (the admission rates were 1.0
and 2.8 per 1,000 respectively). This lower admission rate in the community
service was maintained throughout the two years (Table 6-3).

The length of stay in hospital of patients below the age of 65 was the same
in Chichester as in Salisbury; but for the elderly it was significantly shorter in
the community service—29 weeks as compared with 42. It was apparent that

Table 6-3

**Proportion of Patients Admitted to Mental Hospital at any Time During the Two
Years in Both Areas**

A.	% of live cohort ever admitted:		
		CHI (N:223)	*SAL (N:120)*
	Patients aged 15-64 years	34	55
	Patients aged 65+ years	52	79
	***All Patients	38	59
B.	Time spent in hospital—all patients in the cohort:		
		Mean Weeks	
		CHI (N:223)	*SAL (N:120)*
	Patients aged 15-64 years	15	34
	Patients aged 65+ years	7	11
C.	Time spent in hospital by admitted patients only:		
		Mean Weeks	
		CHI (N:84)	*SAL (N:71)*
	Patients aged 15-64 years	20	20
	Patients aged 65+ years	29	42

***$p < 0.001$

the procedures of screening patients rigorously in the community to determine whether to offer care in one of the extramural amenities results in a selected group of patients being admitted: those who were not suitable for treatment at home. Hence, patients who are admitted to the new units in the District General Hospitals may also be difficult to discharge, and their length of stay may well be longer than expected.

When the clinical, social, and family factors affecting admission were examined in detail, this supposition was borne out; because social factors were clearly affecting the admission of cases to a greater extent in the community than in the comparison service.[16] Thus, the lower socioeconomic groups, elderly patients living with their children, patients whose families had negative attitudes to them, and families with high burden scores were factors determining admission in Chichester; whereas clinical considerations were more evident in Salisbury. Furthermore, the clinical groups most likely to be admitted in the community service were those whose symptoms were socially disruptive, for example patients showing aggressiveness, embarrassing behavior, and suicidal tendencies. But these symptoms usually responded to treatment, and will not necessarily delay discharge; whereas the socially determined admissions present a more intractable problem whose solution will depend largely on the resourcefulness of the social services team.

Calculations based on the referral and admissions rates of the two services during 1960-61, and the figures for patient-weeks in hospital obtained from the cohorts that were followed up, show that the bed needs in the Chichester Community Service were about the same as the 0.5 per 1,000 population now proposed by the Department of Health and Social Security. Bed occupancy for adult patients (excluding dementias in the aged) was 0.6 per 1,000 total population, as compared with 0.8 in the hospital-based service in Salisbury.

Bed needs in the community service for *severe* dementias, on the other hand, were 1.8 per 1,000 population aged 65 and over, which is less than the Department's estimate of 2.5-3, but in excess of the control (Salisbury) service's needs of 2.4.

Another finding that has important implications for the new policy, and an aspect that is causing much concern with claims of insufficient attention being given to the problem, is the build-up of *new* long-stay patients—those who remain in hospital for more than one year. We found their bed needs were still considerable. In Chichester, for the elderly this was 0.5 beds per 1,000 over 65, whereas in Salisbury it was 0.8. These demands would soon block the available beds.

In forecasting needs for beds and residential places, therefore, allowances should be made not only for a likely increase in referrals and the build-up of new long-stay patients, but also for the finding that cases with social problems will be selected for admission.

Other analyses were undertaken to see what categories of patients were treated in which of the community facilities. Home treatment was extensively used in Chichester, most often in providing care for widowed women with dementias. The day-hospital preferentially accepted elderly, married depressives. And nursing homes admitted many more psychogeriatric patients in Chichester than in Salisbury because the staff were willing to look after them when they could count on psychiatric assistance, which augers well for the feasibility of the new supervised accommodation in the community.

The social as well as the clinical characteristics of the patients were therefore determining whether they were looked after at home, in the day hospital, or elsewhere.

Effects on the Family

It has already been suggested that the extramural treatment of patients throws much of the burden previously borne by the mental hospital's trained staff on to the patient's household and family. Using quite conservative measures, we found this to be substantial in terms of effects on the health of the closest relative and on the children; on loss of work and income; in physical demands; and in disruption of domestic routine, and of social and leisure activities.[17] Thus, at the time of referral to both services, the burden on two-thirds of the 410 families was rated as moderate, and in 20 percent as severe (see Table 6-4).

These figures reveal the high cost in personal and social hardship that families with a mentally ill member pay. Considering the further fact that, at the point when the patient was referred, 60 percent of the families had incurred these burdens for more than two years, the importance of looking carefully at this aspect of community psychiatry is apparent. For example, in order to define

Table 6-4
Family Problems

	% Families		
Effect on	Some Disturbance	Severe Disturbance	Total Burden
Health of closest relatives:			
Mental	40	20	60
Physical	28	–	28
Social and leisure activities of family	14	21	35
Children	24	10	34
Domestic routine	13	16	29
Income of family	14	9	23
Employment of others than the patient	17	6	23

the families' problems in clinical terms, we recorded which aspects of patients' behavior had been worrying them. Most troublesome was constant harping on bodily complaints, with fears that the patient might harm himself coming second. But, unexpectedly, behavior conspicuous enough to provoke comment from neighbors was the least frequently reported item. Burden also increased with the patient's age, with the demented elderly and psychopathic personality being the two most taxing diagnostic groups (Table 6-5).

When the cohorts in each service were followed up for two years, and the burden at the beginning, during the period, and at the end compared, all indexes showed that the community service left families more heavily burdened. But of particular importance was the finding that the mental health of the closest relative was impaired. Over half complained of excessive anxiety due to worrying about the patient, one-fifth attributed other neurotic symptoms, and a third disturbances in their children's behavior to this cause. This obliges us to consider whether the cost of keeping certain patients at home will be more illness in the community.

However, when the most severely affected families were separately considered, their burden was equally relieved in both services, in spite of the fact that the community service admitted fewer patients from these families (Table 6-6). Similarly, the families with patients over 65 years old, and those with patients who were never admitted, were not significantly more burdened in the community service. So failure to admit is not a sufficient explanation for their having more problems.

Further examination of our data then showed that relief of the families' burden in the community service was less satisfactory than in the comparison one whenever it omitted to provide adequate social support to families (see

Table 6-5
Patient's Behavior Described by Family as Worrying

Behavior	% Families (410 Patients)
Frequent complaints about bodily symptoms	38
A danger to himself (suicide or accident)	34
Importunate and demanding	34
Behaving oddly or expressing peculiar ideas	27
Unco-operative and contrary	26
Constantly restless or overtalkative by day	23
Troublesome at night	21
Threatening the safety of others	12
Objectionable, rude, or embarrassing	8
Causing trouble with neighbors	7

Table 6-6

Percentage of Families Relieved of Burden After Month and Two Years Later

	Relieved			
	At One Month		At Two Years	
	Chichester	Salisbury	Chichester	Salisbury
Some burden at referral	24	36	59	86
Severe burden at referral	62	61	66	68
Any burden at referral	35	44	60	82

Table 6-7). In fact, the research social workers' assessments of family needs, and whether these were being met, showed certain families in Chichester were receiving *less* support than those in Salisbury. We concluded that the psychiatrist visiting a patient's home does not make an adequate social assessment, that collaboration with a social worker is essential.[18]

Community care is as effective in relieving the burden of looking after a patient as is a hospital-centered service, but only when the combined skills of the therapeutic team, social worker, and GP are available to the family. If the service fails to provide this, it is likely to add to the community's mental health problems, since both family and patient then fare worse than in a conventional service.

Table 6-7

Social Work Done in the Two Services

Type of Work	% Patients Chichester (186)	65 Years Salisbury (105)	% Patients Chichester (85)	65+ Years Salisbury (34)
Social assessment made	8	38	5	21
Support, advice, or casework given	5	36	7	26
Help with employment problems	6	17	0	3
Rehabilitation arranged	1	15	0	0
Help with housing or money problems	9	15	6	12
Help with children or domestic problems	2	7	1	0
Institutional placement	2	1	12	6

Last, outcome in terms of mortality figures was identical in the two services.[19] But the psychiatrist and patient agreed that, in general, the course and outcome of the illness was more favorable in the hospital service, although the community service was more effective with one major disorder—depressive illness. In contrast, neither relatives nor the family doctors (whose appraisal was probably largely based on social behavior) observed a difference in outcome between the services (see Table 6-8).

When relief of burden on the family is used as an independent measure of outcome, we found that the outcome of patients who caused a severe burden was the same in Chichester as in Salisbury. The probable explanation for this is that the psychiatrist was able to recognize, and so take steps to remedy, circumstances in the household likely to have obviously adverse effects on the course of illness. On the other hand, outcome was consistently less satisfactory in Chichester where family burden had been rated *moderate*, again because the psychiatrist probably fails to see the less conspicuous hardships and stresses within the family, and fails to take the kind of action that a social worker would.

In spite of the extra demands made on families in Chichester, they expressed greater satisfaction with the type of care provided. They usually preferred having the patient at home, providing that welfare, social and medical support was readily available.

These data strongly suggest the success of the Department's policy. To develop a form of community care in which general hospital units, day care, general practitioner, and local authority social services jointly provide a comprehensive service for the patients in a district, will depend upon the efficiency with which the collaboration between the psychiatric team and social services are organized.[20] Our findings emphasize the importance of supplementing the clinical care of patients treated outside the hospital with a systematic appraisal of

Table 6-8

Outcome of Psychogeriatric Patients in Chichester and Salisbury After Two Years

Outcome	Findings
1. Research psychiatrist's rating of mental state at follow-up	Better in Salisbury
2. Treating psychiatrist's rating of improvement	Better in Salisbury
3. Patient's rating of improvement	Better in Salisbury
4. Relative's rating of improvement	No difference
5. GP's rating of improvement	No difference
6. Rating of symptom remission	Better in Chichester (more depression remits)
7. Rating by social cost (burden on family)	No difference
8. Death rate	No difference
9. Suicide rate	Decreased in Chichester

the needs of the family and then meeting them adequately. Failure to achieve this is likely not only to prolong the patient's illness but also to effect the mental health of his relatives.

Notes

1. Sainsbury, P. "Social and community psychiatry," *Am. J. Psychiat., 125,* 1226-1251, 1969.
2. Carse, J., Panton, N., and Watt, A. "A district mental health service: the Worthing experiment." *Lancet,* i, 39-41, 1958.
3. Morrissey, J. "The Chichester and district Psychiatric Service," *The Millbank Memorial Fund Quarterly, 44,* no. 1, part 2, 28-36, 1966.
4. Sainsbury, P. "Research report: Medical Research Council Clinical Psychiatry Unit," *Psychological Med., 1,* 429-436, 1971.
5. Sainsbury, P. and Grad, J. "Evaluating the Community Psychiatric Service in Chichester: aims and methods of research," *The Millbank Memorial Fund Quarterly, 44,* no. 1, part 1, 231-1966.
6. Morrissey, J.D. and Sainsbury, P. "Observations on the Chichester and district Mental Health Service." *Proc. Roy. Soc. Med., 52,* 1061-1063, 1959.
7. Sainsbury and Grad, "Evaluating the Community Psychiatric Service."
8. Walk, D. "Suicide and Community Care," *Brit. J. Psychiat., 113,* 1381-1391, 1967.
9. Kreitman, N., Sainsbury, P., Morrissey, J., Towers, J., and Scrivener, J. "The reliability of psychiatric assessment: an analysis," *J. Ment. Sci., 107,* 887-908, 1961.
10. Grad, J. "Psychiatric social workers and research," *Brit. J. Psychiatric Social Work, 7,* 147-152, 1964.
11. Sainsbury, P. and Grad, J. "Evaluation of treatment and services." In *The burden on the community,* pp. 69-116, Oxford University Press, for the Nuffield Provincial Hospital Trust: London, 1962.
12. Grad, J. "Psychiatric social workers and research."
13. Department of Health and Social Security. Hospital Services for the Mentally Ill. H.M.S.O., London, 1971.
14. Grad, J. and Sainsbury, P. "Evaluating the community psychiatric service in Chichester: Results." *Millbank Memorial Fund Quarterly, 44,* no. 1, part 2, 246-287, 1966; and in *Research Methods in Health Care,* Ed. John B. McKinlay, Prodist for Millbank Memorial Fund: New York, 1973.
15. Grad, J. and Sainsbury, P. *Psychological Medicine* (in press).
16. Grad, J. and Sainsbury, P. "Evaluating the community psychiatric service in Chichester: Results."
17. Grad, J. and Sainsbury, P. "Mental illness and the family," *Lancet,* i, 544-547,

1963; Grad, J. and Sainsbury, P. "The effects that patients have on their families in a community care and control psychiatric service: a two year follow-up." *Brit. J. Psychiat., 114,* 265-278.

18. Grad, J. and Sainsbury, P. "The effects that patients have on their families."

19. Sainsbury, P., and Grad, J. "Evaluating a service in Sussex." In *Roots of Evaluation,* Ed. Wing, J.K. and Hafner, H., Oxford University Press for Nuffield Provincial Hospitals Trust: London, 1973.

20. Sainsbury, P. "A comparative evaluation of a comprehensive community psychiatric service." In *Policy for Action,* Ed. Crowley, R. and McClachlan, G., Oxford University Press for Nuffield Provincial Hospitals Trust: London, 1973.

7

The Ideal and the Real: Practical Approaches and Techniques in Evaluation
William G. Smith

In the early 1960s the Illinois Department of Mental Health was reorganized into seven geographic regions. Even prior to the Community Mental Health Act of 1963, the state began to move toward implementation of the community mental health model. Each decentralized region was placed under jurisdiction of a regional center. The regional center has responsibility for organizing the delivery of public mental health services to the entire population of the area.

One of these centers, the H. Douglas Singer Zone Center, was opened in late 1966. This center serves the ten northwest counties of the state, home of nearly 700,000 people. The center houses 220 beds and provides an inpatient backup for locally based outpatient programs. Consultative assistance in planning, funding, recruitment, and training is also supplied to local communities. The goal of the center's clinical services is to prevent the need for long-term hospitalization and to maintain patients in their communities at a maximal level of social functioning. In addition to traditional patient management techniques (medication, psychotherapy, etc.), a heavy emphasis is placed upon crisis intervention, a readiness to assist *all* persons from the territory who come for help, and a vigorous effort to link patients to any community resources necessary to maintain their social functioning.

To carry out these functions the center is organized into five clinical units. Two of the units are general adult psychiatric services, each responsible for different portions of the territory. The other three units serve the entire region addressing problems in alcoholism, mental retardation, and children's disorders. Each unit provides incare services, limited outcare services, and program consultation within its domain of responsibility.

When the center began operation, there were few formal psychiatric services in the region—one community clinic and a handful of private psychiatrists. Since there were so few services and because the area was typical of much of Midwest America, the center had a natural laboratory in which to conduct various studies assessing the effectiveness and costs associated with the community mental health approach.

Evaluation Section

From its beginning the center had a permanent evaluation section charged with the task of monitoring regional programs. The evaluation section has a threefold purpose:

1. To provide scientific information about the successes and failures of a large community mental health program.
2. To provide the regional administration with data necessary for planning and the allocation of available resources, and
3. To provide a continuous monitor to assist regional staff in gauging their progress toward specified goals.

The annual regional budget is approximately $8,000,000. Of this amount, $150,000 (1.8 percent) has been allocated for data processing and evaluation. Besides the director (part time), the evaluation section consists of four bachelor-level research assistants, a data processing systems analyst, a computer programmer, a machine operator, two key-punchers, and two secretaries.

Over the past eight years the evaluation section has experienced a number of problems.

1. There has been difficulty maintaining support for evaluative research. In 1967 the entire blueprint of evaluation work was presented to NIMH in a grant application. This request was denied. While a great deal of lip service has been paid to the importance of evaluative research, it has been a constant struggle to obtain operating funds from the state. With every change in the Department of Mental Health's central office personnel (and they occur fairly frequently), the evaluation program had to be rejustified. The section has been reasonably successful in surviving but at great cost in energy and manpower.

2. Difficulty has been encountered in obtaining and maintaining cooperation from clinical staff. The work of evaluation personnel continues to be viewed with suspicion, in spite of repeated explanations and reassurances.

3. There have been many technical research design problems. It is hard to keep adequate scientific controls in a real-life service organization. A compromise has to be struck between scientific purity and the constraints imposed by sound patient care.

4. Finally, it has taken considerable effort to insure that study findings actually make an impact on clinical programs. Even high-level staff resist change in their way of doing things, regardless of the evidence. To get changes evaluators must involve themselves in the internal political process of the organization.

Against the background of these problems, highlights of evaluative work conducted at the center will be presented along with some of the lessons that have been learned.

Indexes of Effectiveness and Productivity

Adequate data is essential for rational program planning. To this end the evaluation section gradually implemented a patient information system.[1] This semiautomated system included patient movements, detailed demographic and clinical data, as well as detailed information on the quantity and kinds of treatment each patient received. A great deal of care went into designing input documents that are simple to use and to integrate their generation by clinical staff with routine patient management tasks. In spite of these efforts numerous input errors continue to occur. It has become clear that data needed for overall program design and resource allocation is of little direct value to clinicians. Hence, they do not have strong intrinsic motivation for maintaining consistent administrative input. Hence, as long as staff are not paid on the basis of services reported and patients are not billed for the exact services they receive, it will not be possible to obtain accurate service reporting.

On the other hand *standardized* clinical information has not proven necessary for reaching decisions regarding program modification and has not been highly valued by clinical personnel. Hence, in retrospect, the center would not have automated detailed clinical data and would have greatly simplified its information system.

Over time, however, the region's leadership came to rely heavily upon basic patient flow and cost data to monitor program effectiveness. One of these statistics is called the incare effectiveness index. It is composed of three indicators: mean length of hospitalization, a readmission-discharge ratio, and the ratio of patients received from long term institutions relative to the number of patients sent to such facilities.

The mean length of stay obviously reflects the goal of reducing chronic hospitalization. It is possible, however, that a low average stay rate could be achieved either by premature discharge or by sending patients to state hospitals. Hence, the other two parameters were added to offset these possiblities. Each parameter was standardized to a score of 100 based upon a year's experience. The final index for any given time period consists of the mean of the three standardized indicators. For instance, suppose a unit had an average stay of 20 days, a readmission ratio of 30 percent, sent 10 patients to a state hospital, and received 12 in return, that is, a 1.2 received-sent ratio. The empirical standards for these three parameters are 30 days, 25 percent, and 1 respectively. Thus, the length of stay indicator would be $(30 \div 20) \times 100 = 150$; the readmission ratio $(25 \div 30) \times 100 = 83$; the received-sent ratio $(12 \div 10) \times 100 = 120$, and the incare effectiveness index 114, that is, $(150 + 83 + 120) \div 3$.

In order to get an idea of each clinical unit's productivity, calculation is carried a step further to generate a cost-benefit ratio. This incare productivity index consists of total program cost divided by patient workload times the incare effectiveness index. Patient workload for a unit consists of the average in-hospital census plus 20 percent of the admissions and 10 percent of the average outpatient census.

Admissions were weighted by 20 percent in order to give some workload credit for the extra staff effort required to evaluate and plan a treatment approach for new patients. In addition, several time studies have indicated that 10 percent of clinical effort has been spent in outpatient work; hence, this factor was added to the inpatient census to reflect a unit's true workload more accurately.

Thus, in the above example, with an average census of 50 patients, 60 admissions per month, an average active outpatient census of 150 and a monthly cost of \$40,000, the unit productivity index is derived as follows: $\$40,000 \div [(50 + 0.2\,(60) + 0.1\,(150)) \times 114]$ or \$4.23. In making long-term comparisons it is important to adjust cost-benefit ratios to offset the effect of general inflation.

These indexes are heavily used in quarterly program reviews and in reaching decisions concerning staffing levels and changes in the design of clinical services at the Center.

The person at high risk of long-term hospitalization is the specific concern of the state. As one of its responsibilities the regional office funds local facilities to provide emergency and aftercare services for such patients. Some means were necessary to assess the cost-effectiveness of these community agencies. Currently a simplified patient information system specifically designed for community clinics is under development. Until such a system becomes operative, the region created a community monitor index from its own data base.

The index is composed of four variables. The first two indicators comment on the effectiveness of front-line programs in screening patients and in utilizing alternatives to hospitalization; the last two indicators focus upon the effectiveness of the aftercare network:

1. *Ratio of crisis to intermediate stay admissions.* Since the regional center is a backup facility to local resources, it should manage patients who cannot be adequately handled in the community. Persons who are sent to the center, but require fewer than five days of hospital care, can usually be managed locally and are designated as "crisis" (inappropriate) admissions. On the other hand persons who stay at the center more than two weeks are most likely appropriate and are designated as "intermediate" admissions. The exact number of days that distinguish an inappropriate from an appropriate admission is arbitrary, but does separate, in a rough way, persons likely to have needed care at the center from persons who probably could have been managed at the local level—hence the crisis-intermediate ratio.

2. *Ratio of the proportion of admissions from an area relative to that area's*

general population. One reasonable way to allocate the regional center's beds is on the basis of population. If a subregion has ten percent of the region's population, the annual admissions from this subregion ought not to exceed ten percent of the center's admissions.

3. *Percentage of patients hospitalized more than two months within a year at the center.* This percentage of long term admissions is based upon the assumption that adequate community aftercare programs should decrease the need for long-term hospital care.

4. *Annual per capita days hospitalized for mental illness.* A high per capita rate of days hospitalized indicates excessive use of the incare option.

Each of the above indicators is standardized around a score of 100, based on several years experience. The arithmetic mean of all four indicators comprises the community monitor index. Progress is indicated by a rising index.

Dividing per capita state dollars (allocated to community programs) by the community monitor index yields a community productivity index. While such a statistic cannot be used mechanically, it has been quite helpful in assessing the gross outcome of community programs and in distributing funds among them.

It has become clear, however, that no routine information system yields data adequate for definitive comment on the effectiveness of a care network. Information systems can address themselves only to questions of the volume of patients served and the cost of services. These data do not comment upon the more important questions of clinical outcome and quality of care. Routine records had to be supplemented by special studies.

Outcome Studies

Among its principal goals, the community mental health approach aims at reducing disability due to mental illness through early crisis intervention. Is the community-oriented approach with its short-term intervention and social support better able to alter the course of serious mental disorder than the traditional state hospital system? Two major outcome studies have been carried out by the evaluation staff to test this question.

In the first study[2] a systematic ten percent sample of all adult public admissions from the ten-county region during 1967 was selected. The sample included 47 center patients and 51 state hospital patients. These cohorts were followed for a full three years by means of intensive interviews at six month intervals with patients and significant others. Outcomes were measured in terms of social competence and economic cost.

A success was defined in terms of minimal social competence. To be counted a success, a patient had to achieve the following conditions:

1. Did not spend more than 30 days per six-month period in a mental hospital or nursing home for psychiatric reasons
2. Was not in any trouble with law enforcement agents for suspected criminal activity or unacceptable public behavior, and did not have any commitment procedure initiated against him
3. Derived at least half of his economic support from his own resources (including employment, savings, retirement pensions; excluding disability payments for mental illness, family gifts, funds from illegal activity)
4. Belonged to a primary group, that is, both the patient and family or family surrogate group agreed that the patient was a member in "good standing"

Economic costs, standardized to offset the effect of inflation, included all psychiatric care cost plus losses due to vocational disability.

The results were disappointing. Although the level of humanitarian care had improved, no evidence was found that the community-oriented approach was superior in decreasing social disability. Costs at the center also proved to be appreciably higher.

It was noted, however, that this study was loaded with unfavorable cases. Only 26 percent were coming into the hospital for the first time. The balance of patients in the study had a history of repeated hospitalizations. The average patient's hospitalization prior to the study year was 320 days. Thus, almost three quarters of the sample had already lapsed into chronicity. Although the study pointed out that the community-oriented approach was not showing better results with chronic patients than the state hospitals, it did not say enough about outcomes achievable with first admissions who, presumably, were not already in a chronic phase of illness.

Therefore, a second four-year investigation was undertaken.[3] Only first admission patients without a diagnosis of organic brain syndrome were followed. A matching procedure selected a representative sample of 26 center patients and 26 state hospital patients. Methods of outcome assessment were identical with the first study. The results were more positive. The regional center cohort accumulated fewer days institutionalized and less occupational disability. They received three times as many outcare services; yet, the overall cost of care for four years was more than $1,300 less. The center's patient group achieved a higher level of social success. In regard to consumer satisfaction, center patients and their families were more frequently satisfied with services they received.

In spite of these marked differences in outcome, there was still no essential difference in the number of patients who completely failed to make a community adjustment. There were five such persons in the state hospital sample and three in the center sample. Neither system of care was significantly more effective in preventing chronicity.

The findings did not substantiate the widely held conviction that crisis intervention prevents chronic disability. Neither the state hospital nor the regional center approach was succeeding with hard-core patients. The eight chronic patients, 15 percent of the combined sample, accounted for 68 percent of the hospital days. Persistence in the use of an intensive crisis mode of treatment with chronic patients actually escalated costs without resulting in improved outcome.

Public facilities for the care of the mentally ill came into being and continue to exist precisely because of the expensive care associated with long-term mental illness. Apparently there is no clear technology available to prevent chronicity in some patients. If this conclusion is correct, the community mental health approach must be modified as follows: A continued search for better rehabilitative methods must be pursued; the task of managing chronic patients must be given a more recognized status and the means must be provided for its accomplishment.

As a consequence of these findings, the regional center will continue to promote the development of crisis intervention programs for *acute* patients in need of intensive short-term hospital care. At the same time resources are being focused on a search for ways to provide fuller and more useful lives for patients with long term illness. At present a clubhouse program for socialization and a work-oriented lodge program have been started by the center. Studies are being launched to identify potentially chronic patients as early as possible.

Recently a special alcoholism treatment study has been initiated. In the basic follow-up research described above, alcoholics tended to accumulate fewer hospital days, but failed as frequently as other diagnostic groups on the other indicators of community adjustment. The alcoholism unit has been operating a four-to six-week program with high-staff density and an emphasis on insight psychotherapies. This program is quite expensive and achieved only moderate success (40 percent) according to the center's four indicators of social competence.

One area in the region has a well organized network of alcoholism services including a detoxification center, a halfway house, a number of active AA groups, and a specialized alcoholism clinic. The other half of the region has no specialized services. After reviewing the literature, an alternative incare treatment program was designed around the theme of patient-initiated self-help. This program utilizes less than half the staff density of the original program.

Thus, a one year's cohort (approximately 400 patients) of admissions will be followed for eighteen months after random assignment to one of four programs:

1.   High staff density—insight, with a service network
2.   High staff density—insight, without a community service network
3.   Low staff density—self-help, with a service network
4.   Low staff density—self-help, without a community service network

This investigation is currently in progress and has the purpose of clarifying two major questions in the field of alcoholism treatment:

1. What level of incare and outcare resources is necessary to maximize successful outcomes in the treatment of alcoholism?
2. Are there patients with identifiable characteristics who respond more favorably to distinctly different treatment approaches?

The results should greatly assist the region in redesigning its alcohol treatment services, and, since all alcoholics who require hospital care will be included, should have considerable general application to the profession at large.

Quality of Care

While outcome studies continue, it has become apparent that attention also has to be directed to quality of care. Even if some desirable "absolute" outcome cannot be achieved with some patients, it is important that competent care be provided for every patient. As a result the center has implemented the problem oriented record[4] to foster improved and individualized patient care and has incorporated T.J. Kiresuk and R.E. Sherman's[5] goal attainment scale in its regular follow-up studies.

Thus far a systematic ten percent sample of 106 cases has progressed through the first of three six-month intervals. A group of three researchers interview each patient and his responsible staff person. They then independently describe and scale a series of goals for each patient. These expected outcomes are intended to describe the patient's functional status one and a half years after admission, given the present state of the art and the patient's initial condition. The three raters also meet to perform a "consensus goal-setting" in order to strengthen the validity of the method. Each scale is then weighted according to its relative importance. Finally, a weighted average score is calculated. The reasonably expected outcome, represented by this score, is the criterion of quality care.

Inter-rater reliabilities have been quite satisfactory ($r = 0.85$). At the six month milestone, 40 percent of patients had succeeded in reaching their clinical goals; 60 percent had not. It is not possible to draw conclusions this early since goals had been set for an eighteen month interval, but an individualized quantitative method has now been incorporated in the center's evaluation process. It is expected that each year's cohort will contain about 250 patients in this continuous follow-up program.

Prevention Study

The high personal and social cost of serious mental disorder naturally directs attention to preventive programs. A study was undertaken to investigate the relationship between onset of serious mental disorder and the occurrence of crisis or stress events.[6] The study focused upon 37 crisis markers suspected of being clinically important in contributing to mental disorder. All admissions from the region (880 patients) over a two-year period were compared with a stratified random sample (2,414 persons) of the entire state population on the occurrence within the previous year of each of these potential risk markers.

Most of these critical life events did not occur more frequently among hospitalized patients than in the general population. Seven events were so associated: being hospitalized for mental disorder, a suicide attempt, trouble with the police, onset of heavy drinking, loss of job, divorce/separation, and a family member beginning heavy drinking. None of these markers were related to specific diagnoses. Only two markers, divorce and onset of drinking in a family member, tended to *precede* the onset of mental disorder. These two markers may be useful as foci for a widespread primary prevention program. The other five positive markers might be used in a program of early treatment or secondary prevention.

While specific life stress may be important in the etiology of emotional disorder in particular persons, few could be demonstrated to be major epidemiologic factors in mental disorders requiring hospital care. If they do contribute to populationwide breakdown, the relationship is complex, perhaps the confluence of many stresses over a longer time span. As a result of this study the center backed away from any present attempt to initiate an extensive program in primary prevention.

In addition to these major studies, the evaluation section regularly fills special requests for administrators, clinical leaders, community programs, and, occasionally, line staff. This work usually involves three steps: (1) providing the consumer with help in translating his problem into operational terms; (2) expediting the retrieval of information through data processing; and (3) interpreting the results to the consumer. Because of the section's availability and prominence at the center, there is a rather marked emphasis on data in the decision-making process.

Lessons Learned

From eight years experience, a number of lessons have emerged:

1. It is essential that any serious evaluation effort have a stable source of funding. The grant process, whether state or federal, is much too whimsical to serve as a firm base for continuing work. If it is to survive, evaluation work must be funded as part of the regular operational budget of a mental health program. The experience at the Singer Zone Center indicates that between one and two

percent of the operational budget is needed to sustain a respectable evaluation program. Although the section has become part of the center's operating budget, it has been repeatedly singled out for questioning. Until funding agencies are willing to truly underwrite applied research, all the talk about the importance of evaluation will remain empty rhetoric.

2. It is not possible to carry out useful evaluation work unless an agency is willing to specify its goals. Though available research tools are primitive, some definition of objectives is required. Findings must be tempered by careful interpretation and executive judgment, but progress toward sound scientific decisions can be made through successive approximations. As counterpoint to the need for goal definition, evaluation staff must organize studies around the real needs of management and clinical staff, if evaluation research is to be creditable and relevant. Esoteric investigations are not germane and will command little attention or support.

3. Do not bite off more than you can chew. There are so many needs for information that it is difficult to avoid becoming overextended. In several instances the center's evaluation program started projects it was unable to complete with its limited resources. One such project was called the Polygraph Monitor system. The purpose of this study was to assess the general mental health of the community by monitoring a broad spectrum of indicators related to mental health, for example: rates of imprisonment, suicides, alcohol-related arrests, public assistance enrollees, immigrations, school dropouts, and divorces. The idea was to plot the covariance of these variables, using various time lags, and to correlate them with major community events, such as floods or school desegregation. The project seemed worthy, but there was never adequate time to follow through.

Other ideas were rejected after preliminary study. For instance, the center explored the feasibility of a regional case register to track the course of disordered persons and to act as an integrating force among helping agencies. The great expense (relative to forseeable benefit), legal problems of confidentiality, and technical difficulties finally led to a decision to abandon the project.

4. A firm link must be forged between the evaluation staff and the principal policy makers of the organization. Large organizations resist change. Unless executive personnel are personally involved in efforts to understand evaluation and to sanction such efforts, the work is likely to have little impact on program change. Although the head of evaluation at the center was also an associate regional director, it was still difficult to get the program to shift its attention to the needs of chronic patients. Evaluation personnel must take the necessary steps to establish working relationships with program leadership and line staff. If they hope to be effective, evaluators also need to develop skills in negotiation and persuasion to complement their technical expertise.

5. The bulk of evaluation work must be carried on by a separate staff. Clinical personnel are necessarily biased as well as being unable, in the press of daily work, to attend to the nuances and constraints of the scientific method.

6. A variety of methods are necessary to support an evaluation program. Four kinds of assessment data are required: (a) workload, (b) costs, (c) quality of care information, (d) outcome monitoring. Routine information systems can only address workload and cost factors. Since information systems cannot answer the more important quality of care and outcome questions, they are not, in themselves, adequate vehicles for evaluation work. Many administrative and preliminary research questions can be answered from a data bank, but, inevitably, key problems in longitudinal research require specially designed projects. Many such projects can be implemented by bachelor-level staff, provided they have ready access to more experienced consultants.

It appears that resources for the delivery of mental health services are reaching a plateau. In such an atmosphere it is more important than ever to use these scarce resources wisely. A sound evaluation program must become an essential element in any rational scheme that proposes to insure quality care for the human casualties of our society at a reasonable price. Intuition and fervor are not enough!

Notes

1. Kaplan J., and Smith, W.G.: Evaluation Program for a Regional Mental Health Center, in *Progress in Mental Health Information Systems: Computer Applications*, J. Crawford, D. Morgan, and D. Gianturco eds., Cambridge, Mass., Ballinger-Lippencott, 1974.
2. Smith W.G.: Evaluation of the Clinical Services of a Regional Mental Health Center. *Community Ment Health J* (in press).
3. Smith, W.G., Kaplan, J., and Siker, D.: Community Mental Health and the Seriously Disturbed Patient—First Admission Outcomes. *Arch Gen Psychiatry* (in press).
4. Weed, L.L.: *Medical Records, Medical Education and Patient Care.* Chicago, Year Book Medical Publishers, Inc., 1969.
5. Kiresuk, T.J., and Sherman, R.E.: Goal Attainment Scaling: A General Method for Evaluating Comprehensive Community Mental Health Programs. *Community Ment Health J*, Vol. 4 (6), 1968.
6. Smith, W.G.: Critical Life-Events and Prevention Strategies in Mental Health. *Arch Gen Psychiat*, 25:103-109, 1971.

8 A California Five-county Cost-effectiveness Study

Marshall R. Hanson

In recent years there has been an increasing demand for information from public programs and services regarding actual accomplishments along with reporting of costs and services delivered. This demand for greater accountability in the field of mental health is perhaps best reflected by the evaluation requirements specified in Assembly Bill 2649, which were subsequently incorporated in the California Welfare and Institutions Code as the following sections:

> Section 5656. To enable the department to determine the relative cost-effectiveness of the programs and services included in the county plans, the department shall conduct a series of evaluations of the cost-effectiveness of the different types of programs and services being provided for each of the target groups. The department shall conduct these evaluations in at least five counties providing different types of programs and services for the same target group and shall conduct these evaluations in such a manner as to enable the department to compare the relative cost-effectiveness of the same or similar programs or services provided in different counties.
>
> Section 5657. Evaluation studies shall be designed to provide the department, the Legislature, and the counties with at least the following information:
> (a) Detailed description of the target group served
> (b) Detailed description of the kind of programs or services provided and their cost
> (c) Detailed description of the results of the programs or services — at six-month intervals — for at least 18 months after the programs or services have been initiated
>
> Section 5658. After July 1, 1972, a primary responsibility of the department shall be to conduct such evaluation studies. In conducting evaluation studies, the department may contract for research and evaluation with counties, state agencies, or other public or private agencies.
>
> Section 5660. On or before July 1, 1972, the department shall present to the Legislature detailed plans for conducting such evaluation studies — including the counties selected for evaluation studies, each of the target groups to be studied, and the methods to be used in conducting the studies.

In order to satisfy the above legislative mandate, the (then) Department of

131

Mental Hygiene adopted the strategy of assigning responsibility for independently developing an appropriate study design and methodology to designated sections within the department and several outside contractors. Proposal completion and review dates were specified that would permit submission of the department plan to the legislature on or before July 1, 1972.

Department managers, representatives of the legislature, community mental health directors, outside contractors, and department staff attended the two planning and proposal review meetings. These sessions provided an opportunity for management at both state and county levels of government to participate in the planning and decision-making process.

Management involvement in the initial planning/formulation phase of a study is a highly desirable state of affairs that will yield dividends in the form of support throughout the study period. Periodic feedback to management and participants during the conduct of a study is, in the author's opinion, a mandatory requirement.

It was decided that project personnel would be designated as a group — an organizational element that was unique in terms of the department's table of organization. The group reported directly to the chief deputy director of the (then) Department of Mental Hygiene and later to his counterpart in the newly organized Department of Health. This arrangement helped insure the integrity of project staff during the life of the project and provided a ready channel of communication to the department's top level management.

After a study design and the study counties were selected, project staff met with program treatment staff in the respective counties in order to brief them on the project and to elicit their assistance in the development of the study instruments. The "Services Assessment Summary" form used in this study was based on and developed from inputs received initially from approximately 200 clinicians in the study counties; so both management and nonmanagement personnel were provided opportunities to participate in the study right from the start. Without the continued support and many constructive suggestions from both organizational levels, this project could not have been completed.

Since a state evaluation system would eventually entail participation of community mental health programs in all 58 California counties, it was deemed advisable that some mechanism to keep the nonstudy counties informed of project progress, and enable them to make inputs to project staff, should be established. The Research and Evaluation Subcommittee of the Conference of Local Mental Health Directors generously consented to serve as an advisory committee to the project, at which point the foregoing communication problem was, to a large extent, resolved.

The study design of the cost-effectiveness portion of this project utilized pretreatment and posttreatment measures of change in impairment and social functioning as indices of program effectiveness. It treats programs as if they were black boxes in that no information is gathered regarding types or mixes of intervention techniques used by treatment staff to achieve the observed change. This study design yields information on "apparent" program effectiveness, since it does not provide for experimental and control groups, take into account differences in staffing patterns and mixes of intervention techniques, or control for socioenvironmental changes that might account for or contribute to differential outcomes. Modes of service – inpatient, partial day, and outpatient – are conceptualized as same or similar programs. Providers are compared within modes of service.

The major data collection instrument was a set of three "Client Episode Outcome Summary" forms. *Form 1* provided demographic data for purposes of identification, case linkage, and analysis. *Form 2* – "Services Assessment Summary" – is a rating scale consisting of 30 problems, which is filled in by the clinician at time of entry and at completion of treatment. Column A identifies presenting problems; column B identifies the problems to be treated and the primary problem that represents the major focus of the intervention efforts. Columns C and D record entrance and final impairment for each problem on a four-point scale. A "global impairment" rating, which represents an overall sickness index, is also obtained at time of entry and at completion of treatment. Global impairment ratings are required because the effects of various problem constellations are unknown and indeterminate at this time. At the present time the Services Assessment Summary is a combination of nominal and ordinal scales. Interrater reliability tests have been conducted and the data is presently being analyzed. *Form 3* was used to collect fiscal information by mode of service per episode.

Although we used three separate forms to collect information during the study, the final instrument, which will be used for the state evaluation system, is a single-page form containing essentially the same data. Separate forms resulted in some rather severe linkage problems, for example, different entry dates, missing forms, and so forth. Both sides of the page are used in order to resolve the experienced linkage problems.[a]

It was originally intended that pretreatment and posttreatment data on social functioning would be collected from two sources: (1) other agency records, and (2) completed Personal Adjustment and Role Skill Scales (PARS) – a rating scale filled in by relatives or significant others designated by clients who consent to participate in this portion of the study. Unresolved issues and legal questions pertaining to the general area of "confidentiality" of client records precluded access to client data from other agency records at this time, so the PARS was the sole input document for assessment of changes in social adjustment.

The study has been conducted in five California counties during the past 18 months. The five study counties represent both small and large counties in terms of geographic area, population density, percentage of low income families, and ethnic composition. Three counties in the study are agricultural (Butte, Fresno, and Santa Barbara), one is industrial-recreational (San Diego), and one is

---

[a]Copies of the instrument and final report may be obtained by written request to the author.

forestry-recreational (Siskiyou). The counties range in size from 1,657 square miles to 6,325 square miles. The population of the smallest county is 33,000, while the population of the largest county is 1,358,000 people.

During the course of the study clinicians have provided Services Assessment Summary forms for approximately 22,000 treatment episodes. Based on a preliminary analysis of the data and inputs from users of the instrument in the study counties, the Department of Health is installing this evaluation data collection system on a statewide basis. By January 1, 1975 all county-operated and-contracted providers will be required to complete a Client Episode Outcome Summary form on all service episodes where evaluation, treatment, or maintenance services are funded totally or in part by Short-Doyle or Short-Doyle Medi-Cal funds. This requirement will be applicable to the programs of approximately 800 service providers.

At the planning and proposal review sessions, top level management of the Department of Mental Hygiene expressed a desire that some provision for assessing the overall integrity and efficiency of a total county organization for mental health in regard to its form and its administration be incorporated in the study. Results of this portion of the study are reported in a document titled "Management Review Handbook."[b] A summary of the major premises and procedures of the Management Review System follows.

Management Review: An Overview

It was recognized by staff that local mental health service delivery systems vary as to organization, size, complexity, and content. It was also recognized from business management studies that different management styles and organizational arrangements can be equally effective and efficient as reflected by year end balance sheets. The management review process and associated instruments described in the following sections represent an attempt to minimize the subjective component inherent in the review process. The assumption underlying this process is that a relationship exists between system performance in terms of defined standards and the overall integrity and efficiency of a total county organization for mental health.

The management review is a structured process through which selected aspects of a local mental health program can be assessed in a limited amount of time and with limited staff. It accomplishes on-site review activities with minimal disruption of local mental health program operations, utilizing a structured approach to develop factual evidence that allows for an independent review leading to essentially

---

[b]Assisting the author in the construction of this handbook were: Katherine Ruland, Edward D. Shafer, and Melvin H. Voyles. Copies may be obtained on written request to the author.

the same conclusions. It develops a data base that permits periodic assessment of progress or change in local mental health program operations, limiting the scope of the investigation required to ascertain compliance of the local mental health program.

The process is structured by use of a "protocol" containing 17 provisional standards that define the scope and depth of the investigation. The standards meet the following criteria: They are based on legislative intent, law and regulation, or other mental health program practices generally accepted by mental health professionals as requisites of a good mental health program; they are limited in scope and intent to looking at administrative mechanisms and procedures. They encompass the whole range of program management from policy and planning to service accessibility and fiscal practices, and include: emergency services; accessibility of services; case records; referral system; case review specifications; indirect services; public information; citizen participation; research and evaluation; primary prevention; 24-hour care services; detention services; indirect services to out-of-home operators; fiscal administration; reimbursement procedures; contract administration; training programs.

Each standard is organized as follows:

1. A statement of the provisional standard in terms that specify the scope and intent of the review of that standard
2. The documented evidence to be compiled for use in assessing the degree of compliance of the local mental health program with the provisional standard
3. The rating criteria on which judgment of compliance will be based
4. Comments that define terms as used for purposes of the provisional standards and that clarify scope and intent where needed.

Rating consists of placing a check mark on those criteria that are fully met. The local mental health program does not satisfy the provisional standard unless all criteria are checked.

The standards have been tested in nine California counties and have been finalized based on the results of these tests. As experience is gained with the management review process, additional standards may be developed to cover other aspects of local mental health programs and to make the instrument more comprehensive.

Management Review Process

A management review may be initiated either by a request from the local mental health program director or by a directive from Department of Health management. Each individual management review will require a director, teams of regular members, a field coordinator, and ancillary team members as needed. The size of the staff needed to conduct any one review can vary depending upon the size of the program and the time allowed. The staff, as a group, must have expertise in administrative, fiscal, research, and clinical fields.

Teams are formed as required for each review. The number of teams required is determined by the size and complexity of the local mental health program to be reviewed. Teams are organized in terms of the knowledge and background of the team members, and provisional standards are assigned accordingly.

Experience has shown that a minimum of three teams, composed of at least two persons, is usually advisable to conduct any review because of the wide range of knowledge required and the variety of activities that are a part of the management review process. One member of each team is designated as the leader of team activities during the review and is responsible for write-ups on each provisional standard assigned to his team.

When the management review director has been designated, he contacts the local mental health program director to confirm the dates for the review and to make all other necessary arrangements such as making a general timetable of major events in the management review process, selecting team personnel, and assigning the provisional standards for which each team will be responsible.

He also appoints a field coordinator whose duties include: establishing liaison with local program coordinator, preparing materials for introductory packets and provisional standards, and orienting local mental health program staff to the management review process.

Following orientation the field coordinator and the local program coordinator meet to plan data collection. The field coordinator briefs local mental health program data collectors on their provisional standards, and supervises the data collection including review and editing of preliminary packet inputs. The field coordinator collects final inputs from the local program coordinator and reviews the material to insure that it is both complete and appropriate. Corrective action is taken as necessary.

The on-site review is then scheduled and the management review teams briefed and provided with their introductory packets. Following this briefing the members of each team meet to review the provisional standards for which they are responsible, and delegate responsibilities for the conduct of the review. After meeting with local mental health program staff, the review teams begin to conduct the on-site interviews according to the schedule. In each interview the team: provides feedback of their perceptions regarding the local mental health program's performance on the provisional standard, based on the documented evidence; attempts to find answers to questions left unanswered by the documented evidence; and provides the local mental health program staff an opportunity to introduce new evidence and respond to the teams' findings.

Once the initial interviews have been completed, the teams visit agencies and programs to interview staff as required by the provisional standards to corroborate and validate the information gathered from previous sources.

After completion of team interviews, each management review team meets to discuss its findings on each provisional standard, and to develop the exit interview presentation that describes the degree to which the local mental health program satisfies each criterion within the provisional standards.

On the final day of the on-site review each management review team presents its findings to the local mental health program staff designated by the local mental health program director. This feedback provides an opportunity for the local mental health program staff to offer additional information or to challenge the conclusions drawn regarding performance on the provisional standards.

The management review director is responsible for the collection of all team inputs and the writing of the final report. The final report contains an introduction, a section for summary conclusions and recommendations, and a section that details the findings on each provisional standard.

9
Development of a Generic Cost-effectiveness Methodology for Evaluating the Patient Services of a Community Mental Health Center

Daniel B. Fishman

This chapter reports on the progress of an NIMH-sponsored project involving the development and pilot-test of a generic cost-effectiveness methodology for developing the patient services of a community mental health center (CMHC). The specific methodology developed was named the "cost-outcome/cost-effectiveness" (C*O*C*E) methodology. At the time of this report, March 1974, the development phase of the project was nearing completion and the pilot-test phase was about to begin.

The C*O*C*E methodology consists of two general components: a *conceptual model* of cost-effectiveness analysis as it applies to CMHC patient services; and a *data support system* consisting of source documents and computer software that generates the data needed for analysis. This chapter will focus on the C*O*C*E conceptual model by explaining (1) the assumptions employed in developing it; (2) the determination of treatment effectiveness; and (3) the determination of treatment cost.

Assumptions Employed in Developing the C*O*C*E Methodology

Limited Version of Cost-benefit Analysis (Cost-effectiveness) Appropriate for Evaluating Mental Health Services

Cost-benefit analysis is generally defined as a technique that attempts to specify and evaluate the social benefits of different investment projects, to help decide which of the projects has a greater claim to limited resources.[1] In order to make a meaningful comparison between different projects, it is necessary to reduce the various social costs into one set of common units. Usually, when dealing with health, education, and welfare programs, it is fairly straightforward to reduce the social costs of various projects to the common denominator of money. In contrast, the reduction of the social benefits of such programs to a common denominator is very problematical.

A.M. Rivlin[2] offers a good illustration of the problems involved with her example of the two different publicly supported programs—one to teach poor children to read, the other whose goal is to find a cancer cure—that each need additional funds. Funds are limited so that only one program can receive them,

139

and the cost-benefit analysis task is to determine which should get the additional funding. To answer this question Rivlin asserted that a method must be devised for reducing the benefits of each program into common terms, for example hypothesizing the market value of (a) education, and (b) health, in terms of investments "to improve the nation's productivity and the individual's earnings." However, she adds, "analysis based on future income ignores what most people would regard as the most important benefits of health and education. Cancer is a painful and frightening disease. People would want to be free of it even if there were no effect on future income. Reading is essential to culture and communication and opens the door of the mind."

A similar case in point cited by Rivlin was the Salk vaccine:

> Judged in terms of private benefits alone, the Salk vaccine would have been a poor national investment, since polio never attacked more than a miniscule portion of the population. Freeing the whole country from the fear and anguish it caused was clearly worth a lot, but how much in monetary terms?

An additional dilemma in applying cost-benefit analysis (also noted by Rivlin) is that:

> The private benefits of different types of social action programs may go to entirely different groups of people. People who have cancer are not the people who cannot read. Even if we knew that the benefit-cost ratio was higher for reading programs than for cancer programs, we would not necessarily choose to devote more resources to reading. The decision would depend in part on the values attached to benefitting cancer victims and illiterates. (p. 58)

Another aspect of this same issue further complicates the problem. It is probably true that better cost-benefit ratios are obtained for educational programs involved with brighter students, job-training programs involved with more skilled trainees, and health programs involved with less sick individuals. However, it would not seem reasonable then to conclude that health, education, and welfare programs should be funded only for brighter, more skilled, and less sick individuals.[3]

As Rivlin and others point out, there is an application of cost-benefit analysis that does not run into the "common unit of benefit" problem discussed above. This occurs when a comparison is made of the relative effectiveness of different treatment programs for groups composed of the same type of individuals who have the same target problems. Since the target problems are the same, whatever measurement of benefit is employed for one group is applicable to other groups. For example, if one group of neurotic depressives receives psychotherapy alone and another group of neurotic depressives receives drug therapy alone, the measures of treatment effectiveness relevant for one group— for example, decreased depression and improved family relationships—are as relevant for the other group. In the present conceptualization this type of cost-benefit analysis is called *cost-effectiveness analysis*, which we define as: a technique that attempts to specify and evaluate the social costs and social benefits of different investment projects, to help decide which of the projects should be undertaken, when the projects involve the same type of target population and have identical predefined goals, that is, identical, predefined desired benefits.

Cost-effectiveness analysis is conceptually related to the "planning-programming-budgeting system" ("PPBS") that was introduced into the Department of Defense in 1961 and extended by President Johnson in 1965 to other government agencies, including Department of Health, Education, and Welfare. More specifically, as Charles Schultz pointed out in his 1967 testimony to Congress, cost-effectiveness analysis is a final step in PPBS after objectives have been specified, alternative means for reaching those objectives have been defined, and the costs of each alternative computed. According to Schultz the fourth and very crucial step is cost-effectiveness, which involves "analyzing alternatives, seeking those which have the greatest effectiveness in achieving the basic objective specified . . . or which achieve those objectives at the least cost."[4]

Cost-effectiveness analysis in health, education, and welfare programs thus involves five preliminary steps:

1. Specifying the goals to be obtained, that is, specifying a particular target population and the types of changes that are desired in that target population
2. Operationalizing the goals so that extent of goal attainment can be explicitly measured
3. Developing alternative programs for reaching the goals
4. Determining the cost of each program
5. Assessing the effectiveness of each program, that is, assessing the extent of goal attainment of each program

Once these five preliminary steps have been accomplished, cost-effectiveness analysis proceeds by comparing the relative cost and effectiveness of each program.

To illustrate cost-effectiveness analysis for mental health, suppose two groups of representative outpatients were seen at a particular community mental health center (CMHC). More specifically, suppose each group was seen in individual therapy for two months and then, on the basis of a three-month follow-up interview, each group was objectively rated along a seven-point scale ranging from "1—Much Worse Now Compared to Status at Intake," to "7—Much Better Now Compared to Status at Intake." Consider the following two hypothetical statements:

1. The patients in one group were each seen both for initial evaluation and for

subsequent therapy by a paraprofessional at an average center cost of $50, and these patients obtained an average outcome rating of "6–Moderately Better Now Compared with Status at Intake."

2. The patients in the other group were each seen both for initial evaluation and for subsequent therapy by a psychiatrist at an average center cost of $150, and these patients also obtained an average outcome rating of "6–Moderately Better Now Compared with Status at Intake."

The five steps mentioned above can now be applied to these two statements as follows:

1. *The goal to be attained:* success in treating representative outpatients
2. *The measurement of goal attainment:* an objective rating based upon a three-month follow-up interview
3. *The alternative programs:* treatment by a paraprofessional or treatment by a psychiatrist
4. *The costs:* paraprofessional treatment is $50 per patient and psychiatrist treatment is $150 per patient
5. *The benefits:* the paraprofessional and psychiatrist treatment were equally effective in their treatment

Cost-effectiveness analysis of these data is then quite straightforward, with a conclusion that the paraprofessional treatment was less costly but as effective for treating a representative sample of outpatients.

Cost-effectiveness Viewed as Comparison of
Two or More "Cost-outcome" Statements

In the area of mental health patient services, cost-effectiveness analysis can thus be defined as the comparison of two or more statements about the same type of patient, with each statement summarizing the cost per patient and the outcome of the patient's treatment, for example, the two hypothetical statements presented above about representative outpatients.

A cost-outcome statement for a community mental health center can be viewed as a summary of the answers to three questions about the patient services "output" of a CMHC program: (1) What types of individuals are being served, that is, what are the characteristics of the patients served by the program? (2) On the average how much does it cost in "input" dollars to serve each individual in the program? (3) On the average how much help does each individual receive as a result of the program?

Technically, the outcome aspect of cost-outcome involves an assessment of the extent of change between a client's level of functioning at intake and his level of functioning at follow-up. For the individual client there is no way of documenting scientifically whether this change was actually caused by the treatment or was simply concurrent with the treatment. Moreover, the same logic holds for a cost-outcome analysis of a group of patients. For example, if a group of 50 neurotic depressives shows strong improvement after three months of a particular type of treatment, there is no scientific way of documenting that the improvement was due to the treatment as opposed to other concurrent factors in the patients' lives. However, at the level of cost-effectiveness analysis, the causal relationship between treatment and change over time can be investigated. For example, if two groups of comparable patients each receive different treatments and then are assessed with standard procedures at follow-up, any differences between the two groups at follow-up can be ascribed to the differences between the treatments. This is because the only systematic difference between the two groups is the difference in treatment. Any other factors that might be related to change in functioning over time can be considered equally potent in both groups. In other words, these other factors are *controlled* when the two groups are compared.

The nature of cost-effectiveness analysis is clarified by considering E.D. Suchman's[5] five categories of criteria according to which the success or failure of a program can be evaluated. These are:

1. *"Effort" criteria*, involving the quantity and quality of activity that takes place, that is, the quantity and quality of "input or energy, regardless of output"
2. *"Performance" or "effectiveness" criteria*, measuring "the results of effort rather than the effort itself"
3. *"Adequacy of performance" criteria* involving "the degree to which effective performance is adequate to the total amount of need"
4. *"Efficiency" criteria*, involving "a ratio between effort and performance—output divided by input"
5. *"Process" criteria*, involving "how and why a program works or does not work"

It is clear that cost-effectiveness analysis explicity involves efficiency criteria (with respect to cost) and performance criteria (with respect to effectiveness.) Cost-effectiveness analysis also involves indirectly "adequacy of performance" criteria (in terms of the "performance" aspects of these criteria). On the other hand, one should note that cost-effectiveness analysis does not focus on effort or process criteria. In other words, the cost-effectiveness-oriented decision maker looks at a mental health program in terms of how much money it costs to treat a patient and what the effectiveness, outcome, and impact of the treatment is; he does not concern himself with the details of how the input dollars are employed in order to produce a particular output. Such effort and process questions are deemed the province of specific program administrators, who are held accountable by the decision maker in terms of cost-effectiveness data.

Rivlin argues cogently for the advantages of decision making based upon output, cost-effectiveness criteria as opposed to input, effort and process criteria:

> Stating accountability in terms of inputs—through detailed guidelines and controls on objects of expenditure—spawns red tape and rigidity without introducing incentives to more outputs. Hence a new approach is in order: State the accountability in terms of outputs, and reward those who produce more efficiently. Free to vary the way they spend the money as long as they accomplish specified results, recipients of federal grants could be rewarded for producing beyond expectations . . . just as in large corporations plant managers are free to vary production methods, but are rewarded and promoted according to sales and profits. (p. 127)[6]

Outcome of Mental Health Treatment Best
Assessed by Multidimensional Approach
Involving Group of Standard, Substantive
Dimensions

As Rivlin points out, single measures of health, education, and welfare program performance generally lead to "distortion, stultification, cheating to 'beat the system,' and other undesirable results . . . . Multiple measures are necessary to reflect multiple objectives and to avoid distorting performance." In the mental health literature this point has been documented again and again. This literature has been reviewed carefully and extensively by A.E. Bergin and Hans Strupp under an NIMH contract, and on the basis of their review, Bergin[7] makes the following conclusions and recommendations:

> The most obvious thing to be concluded from the various intercorrelations of therapy outcome criteria . . . and from the divergent results obtained by using different criteria with the *same* client group . . . is that the process of therapeutic change in patients is multifactorial . . . . We feel quite strongly that researchers and therapists should begin to think more precisely in terms of *kinds of change* rather than in terms of a general multiform change.
>
> The clearest issue in criterion development and selection at the present time is whether evaluation should be based chiefly upon external behavior or internal states of experience . . . . Since "internal" and "external" criteria measure different human characteristics, since these characteristics are significant, since changes occur in both domains

during therapy, and since important decisions regarding the value of different techniques continue to be based on the extent of change induced by them, we recommend that future studies include representative measures derived from this dichotomy. (pp. 257-258)

Two general types of approaches to outcome measures have been developed: generic-dimensional measures;[8] and individualized-goal measures.[9] With the *generic-dimensional* approach a patient is assessed at the beginning of treatment in terms of a limited number of standard dimensions of functioning, such as productivity and affective distress. At follow-up the patient is again assessed in terms of the same standard dimensions. Outcome is measured in terms of level of functioning on each variable at follow-up as compared with the level of functioning on the same variable at the beginning of treatment.

With the *individualized-goal* approach, at the beginning of treatment an individualized, unique set of goals is developed for each individual patient. Outcome is measured in terms of level of functioning relevant to the various goals at follow-up as compared with the desired level of functioning that was set as a goal at the beginning of treatment.

While in fact the generic-dimensional and individualized-goal approaches to outcome assessment are complementary in their various distinctive assets, time economy of the assessment procedure necessitated the choice of only one approach for the C*O*C*E methodology. The generic-dimensional approach was deemed the more appropriate, and the specific procedure chosen was a structured, fixed-alternative, person-to-person interview with the patient. The advantages of such a generic-dimensional interview over the individualized-goal approach to outcome assessment are noted in the paragraphs below.

Psychometrics. Psychometrically, the generic-dimensional interview has the advantage of continuing a series of standardized questions that are asked of each patient, thus yielding data as to the psychometric properties of items and scales—for example, the shape of the frequency distribution of the item and the concurrent validity of the item. In contrast, the individualized-goal approach involves items that are tailored to different individuals, and thus there is no standardized set of items to be psychometrically studied.

Training and Reliability. A structured, fixed-alternative interview is relatively easy to teach so as to obtain consistent and reliable administration. This type of interview was developed by B.P. Dohrenwend[10] for an epidemiological study, and he found it feasible to have the interview conducted by a polling organization employing many interviewers with no specific training in mental health. In contrast, to generate goals on an individualized-goal measure at the beginning of therapy involves an interviewer with some specialized mental health training.

Moreover, the individualization aspect of the procedure makes it intrinsically open-ended and somewhat unstructured, thus creating training and reliability problems.

Interview Effort. In employing the generic-dimensional approach, it is possible to equate groups initially (by random assignment and/or by matching on demographic and clinical information) and then assess relative treatment effectiveness by administering a generic-dimensional interview *at follow-up only*. This is possible because since the groups are equated initially, any differential changes that take place in the groups are reflected in differences in their level of functioning at follow-up. In contrast, an individualized-goal measure intrinsically requires both initial and follow-up interview sessions.

Public Accountability. The generic-dimensional approach is superior to the individualized-goal approach in meeting many public accountability questions. The public in general and its elected representatives are interested in knowing the effectiveness of a particular mental health program in dealing with particular types of problems such as work impairment, emotional distress, drug and alcohol abuse, and marital disruptions. This type of effectiveness data is yielded by a generic-dimensional approach. In contrast, the individualized-goal approach only yields information as to what degree a patient's individualized goals are achieved; since the goals are individualized, no standardized information is yielded concerning generic problem areas.

Need Assessment. A frequently employed approach for assessing unmet mental health needs in a community is to assess the percentage of nonpatients in the community who manifest levels of functioning that are as impaired or more impaired than those of identified patients (e.g., see Dohrenwend and Dohrenwend,[11] Leighton, Leighton, and Armstrong,[12] and Srole et al.[13]). A structured, fixed-alternative generic-dimensional interview is often chosen as the most appropriate assessment technique for such epidemiological studies; for example, J.A. Ciarlo,[14] B.P. Dohrenwend,[15] and G.J. Warheit and C.E. Holzer[16] are presently employing this type of assessment technique in ongoing epidemiological studies of this sort. Specifically, in this type of study the same generic-dimensional interview is used for assessing the level of functioning of a representative sample of nonpatients in the community, of patients at intake, and of former patients at follow-up. Comparisons between the functioning of these various groups can then answer such questions as:

1. What percentage of the nonpatient population is functioning at the same level as identified patients at intake? This percentage can be interpreted as one indicator of the unmet need for mental health services.

2. Is the distribution of types of functional impairment in the community similar to the distribution of types of functional impairment of patients at intake? The answer to this question is one indicator of the extent to which a particular program is meeting the priorities of problems in the community.

3. To what extent does the functioning of former patients at follow-up improve relative to their functioning at intake and approach the average level of functioning in the community? The answer to this question provides an indication of the absolute meaning of the effectiveness of data in the context of meeting mental health needs.

Thus, the same generic-dimensional assessment technique can be used both for measuring patient outcome and for unmet community mental health needs. In contrast, an individualized-goal assessment technique is not appropriate for the assessment of unmet community mental health needs. This is because the intrinsic nature of an individualized-goal technique is such as to yield goals that are based upon the unique situation of each individual being assessed; and therefore it is not possible to compare the goals generated by identified-patients as a group versus nonpatients as a group. Moreover, there does not appear to be another need assessment model for which the individualized-goal approach would be an appropriate assessment.

Meaning of Single Outcome Assessment
Limited by Time Context in which Obtained

Cost-outcome or cost-effectiveness statements must be qualified by the time context of the associated outcome assessment procedures. For example, suppose a group of neurotic depressives is randomly assigned at admission to Treatment A or Treatment B, and at follow-up three months later Treatment A is found to be $100 more expensive but also 50 percent more effective in reducing depression. The following statement can then be made: The additional expense of Treatment A will increase the extent to which depression can be reduced *during the first three months after admission.* What the cost and impact of Treatment A is relative to Treatment B *after* the three months simply is not known until further follow-ups are completed. For example, at six months follow-up it might be that Treatment A was actually less expensive in the long run than Treatment B, or that Treatment A was actually less effective in reducing depression. Ideally, the decision maker should have data from multiple follow-ups so that a graph can be generated in which the relative cost and effectiveness of various treatments are shown as a function of varying time periods between admission and follow-up. Such a graph can be important since there are numerous examples in which programs require a high initial cost in order to achieve a long-term effect that does not manifest itself until one year or more later.

In light of these considerations our earlier definition of *cost-effectiveness* for a CMHC program can now be refined as the comparison of two or more cost-outcome statements, with each such statement a summary of the answers to three revised questions about the patient services "output" of a particular CMHC program:

1. What types of individuals are being served, that is, what are the characteristics at admission of the patients served by the program?
2. On the average how much does it cost in "input" dollars to serve each individual in the program *over a specified period?*
3. On the average how much help does each individual receive as a result of the program *over the period between intake and follow-up?*

To Facilitate Decision Making, Multidimensional Indexes of Mental Health Treatment Outcome Combined, via Decision-Maker's Values, into Single Summary Outcome Measure

The gap between the accumulation of cost-effectiveness-related data and the decision-making process has been widely discussed (for example, see G. Buchanan, Horst, and Scanlon,[17] H.R. Davis,[18] E.D. Suchman,[19] and R.A. Walker.[20]) The problem can be illustrated by the following research design. One hundred neurotic-depressive patients are randomly assigned in equal numbers to two treatments: a drug-therapy-only treatment and a psychotherapy-only treatment. While the cost of each treatment is reduced to a single monetary figure, the outcome of each treatment is measured by an instrument especially developed for the C*O*C*E methodology called the "C*O*C*E adult interview"; and this interview yields separate scores on 36 scales. In order to make a cost-effectiveness comparison between the drug-therapy-only and the psychotherapy-only treatments, the decision maker first needs to anser the question: For which group of 50 patients was the treatment more effective, the drug-therapy-only group or the psycho-therapy-only group? One way of answering this question is to perform 36 separate *t*-tests comparing the two groups on each of the 36 outcome variables. However, this procedure has the disadvantage of yielding, in many cases, conflicting results, with one group improving more on some of the measures, and the other group, on other measures. This is a problem for the decision maker who is trying to decide which type of treatment is more effective with neurotic-depressives. Walker[21] gives the following example to illustrate the decision maker's problem with multiple outcome measures.

In a program on manpower training each month a data report was generated that supposedly enabled the administrators "to determine the overall effectiveness of the program by providing summary statistics on program activities." This report consisted of a summary of outcomes and transactions for all enrollees terminating the program during each report month. On a single sheet of paper 246 scores were displayed. In addition, the local program staff developed a supplementary performance report and added to the data base an additional 51 measures. In effect, each program month, project management and staff were deluged with 297 program indicators in hopes of "determining overall effectiveness of the program . . . . Since the data report did not tell the decision-makers the relative importance of each of the 297 measures, the report was in effect a smorgasbord of offered choices dependent upon the capricious value judgments of the program managers." Walker points out: "As all indicators were apparently of equal value, it would be possible for fickle management to select a new indicator each month that need not be repeated until twenty-four years had passed!" (p. 47)

If a decision maker is presented with a series of 36 comparison outcome scores, all of which do not consistently favor a particular treatment group, he probably will either employ a subjective, unsystematic, arbitary procedure, as described in the Walker example above, or he will probably try to generate his own type of summary score, for example, by simply counting the percentage of the 36 outcome scores that favor each treatment group and then selecting as more effective that treatment group with the higher percentage. As an attempt to improve upon this rough method of outcome determination, a more explicit and systematic procedure has been developed for the C*O*C*E methodology. This approach is called "decision-maker effectiveness matrix" (DEM) analysis. In brief, DEM analysis is a method for combining the results of multiple outcome scores into one summary score. However, instead of simply an additive procedure, DEM analysis provides for differential weighting of the various outcome scores as a function of the *values* of the decision maker along two dimensions: (a) type of behavioral outcome (for example, weighting more for improvement in job productivity than for improvement in emotional distress); and (b) degree of severity of behavior involved in outcome (weighting more for improvement of a severe impairment in job productivity than for improvement of a mild impairment in productivity). A detailed description of the application of DEM analysis to the C*O*C*E adult interview follows.

Determination of Treatment Effectiveness in the C*O*C*E Methodology

The C*O*C*E adult interview consists of 200 questions with precoded alternative answers that are summarized into 13 scales of functioning, and a 14th scale that assesses a CMHC patient's satisfaction with the services he has received—his "consumer satisfaction." The 14 scales are:

1. Productive hours (weekly hours of "productive" activity in a job, school work, housework, childcare, or volunteer work)
2. Productivity impairment (impairment in functioning during productive hours)
3. Social impairment (impairment in social relationships)
4. Emotional distress (anxiety and depression)
5. Psychotic thinking
6. Alcohol abuse (frequency of alcohol intoxication)
7. Alcohol-induced impairment (impairment in a variety of areas of functioning due to alcohol abuse)
8. "Soft" drug abuse (frequency of using illegal "soft" drugs)
9. "Hard" drug abuse (frequency of using illegal "hard" drugs)
10. Drug-induced impairment (impairment in a variety of areas of functioning due to drug abuse)
11. Illegal behavior (presence of antisocial, illegal behavior)
12. Welfare use (present receipt of welfare assistance funds)
13. Mental health service use (present receipt of mental health services)
14. Consumer satisfaction (patient satisfaction with the services he has received from a CMHC)

In order to create a decision-maker effectiveness matrix for the 13 functioning scales (the consumer satisfaction scale is discussed later), the scales are first arrayed into a matrix having two dimensions: (a) ranges of scores on a particular scale (as the columns of the matrix), and (b) the 13 scales (as the rows of the matrix). Each cell of the matrix thus consists of scores for a particular scale that fall in a particular scoring range. In order to make the meaning of the score ranges consistent across all the scales, the first process in creating a DEM matrix is to administer the interview to a standardization population, for example, a representative sample of all patients who are admitted or readmitted to community mental health centers. The raw scores achieved by this standardization sample on each of the 13 functioning scales are then transformed into t-scores, that is the raw scores are transformed so that the new scores have a mean of 50 and a standard deviation of 10. If the standardization sample includes patients at admission or readmission to a CMHC, such a score, which is below 30, can be viewed as reflecting severe impairment, since it represents functioning that is more than two standard deviations below that of the average CMHC patient at admission or readmission. Similarly, scores of 30 to 39 can be viewed as reflecting marked impairment; those of 40 to 49, low average impairment; those of 50 to 59, high average impairment; those of 60 to 69, mild impairment; and those of 70 and above, minimal impairment.

The consumer satisfaction scale is added to the matrix by using a t-score standardization sample of representative CMHC patients at three-month follow-up. The meaning of these scores can be viewed as comparable to those of the functioning scales, with a t-score below 30 viewed as reflecting very strong dissatisfaction, since it represents satisfaction that is more than two standard deviations below that of the average CMHC patient at three-month follow-up. Likewise, scores of 30 to 39 can be viewed as reflecting strong dissatisfaction; those of 40 to 49, low average satisfaction; those of 50 to 59, high average satisfaction; those of 60 to 69, strong satisfaction; and those of 70 and above, very strong satisfaction.

On the 13 functioning scales patients can be assessed both at intake and at follow-up, and thus change scores can be derived. While the consumer satisfaction scale is only administered to patients at follow-up, change scores comparable to the functioning-scale change scores can be generated by automatically assigning patients consumer satisfaction scores of 50 at intake and by t-scoring consumer satisfaction scores at follow-up in terms of a representative sample of CMHC clients at three-month follow-up.

In sum, the DEM matrix consists of six columns composed of score ranges (0-29, 30-39, 40-49, 50-59, 60-69, 70-99) and 14 rows consisting of the 14 scales. Such a matrix thus includes 84 cells, with each cell representing a particular score range of a particular scale. In addition, change scores on each scale between intake and follow-up can be summarized in terms of so many points change within one or more of the 84 matrix cells. Moreover, since clients can potentially change in positive or negative directions between intake and follow-up, there are thus 168 possible types of change (84 boxes indicating types of changes multiplied by two directions of change). In the C*O*C*E methodology the decision maker is asked to employ his own values in weighting (assigning points to) each of the 168 different types of change. For example, the productivity impairment scale might be weighted more highly than the emotional distress scale; changes within more impaired levels of functioning might be weighted more highly than changes within less impaired levels; and improvement might be weighted more highly and in an opposite direction from deterioration.

Because common scales and a common DEM are used for weighting those scales, the derived summary outcome scores can be comparable across disparate clients. It is thus possible to say, for example, that a group of schizophrenics has an average change score of 30, and neurotic depressives an average change score of 50, and to compare these scores at face value. However, it is necessary to note that without any treatment at all, the schizophrenics might have changed 5 and the neurotics 45; and thus, although the change in the schizophrenics was less, the impact of the treatment was greater for the schizophrenics. In other words, the cost-outcome figure for any particular group should be viewed as a function of two factors: first, the initial characteristics of the group, and second, the "treatment" the group receives. Thus, over time the neurotic depressives could change an average of 50 and the schizophrenics 30, but there would be no way of knowing whether the difference between the 30 and 50 was due to differences between the initial characteristics of the neurotic depressives and schizophrenics, or the difference between the reaction of these two groups to the treatment they received. The only way of assessing the degree of response to treatment is to equate the two groups on initial characteristics; then any changes over time can be ascribed to differences in treatments.

Let us return then to our original example of the cost-effectiveness comparison of a drug-therapy-only treatment versus a psychotherapy-only treatment with neurotic depressives. As mentioned earlier, we assume that a single cost-per-client figure can be derived; and from these figures, a mean and standard deviation can be derived for each group on cost-of-treatment per client. Likewise, via the decision-maker effectiveness matrix approach just described, a single outcome-per-client figure can be derived; and from these figures, a mean and standard deviation can be derived for each group on outcome-of-treatment per client. Cost-effectiveness analysis of the two treatment programs can then proceed by considering the logical possibilities in comparing the two treatment programs. Table 9-1 presents these logical possibilities for any two treatment programs, labelled A and B. The comparisons are shown by a two-dimensional matrix, involving: the mean patient *cost* of treatment (A is less costly, as costly, or more costly than B), and the mean patient *outcome* of treatment (A is less effective, as effective, or more effective than B). The determination of whether program A is more, less, or as costly (effective) as program B can be done in two ways: on the basis of the statistical significance level of *t*-tests comparing the relevant scores from program A and B.

As Table 9-1 shows, once the cost and effectiveness determinations are made, the comparison of A and B yields nine possibilities, one for each cell of the matrix. The decision to be made on the basis of cells 2 to 8 is quite straightforward and indicated in the exhibit. A "?" is placed in cells 1 and 9 because in these two cases the data do not dictate a decision. Specifically, in cell 1, A is less costly but also less effective than B. In cell 9, A is more costly but also more effective than B. The question facing the decision maker about cell 1 is, do the cost savings justify the reduced effectiveness of program A? Similarly, the question arising from cell 9 is, is the additional effectiveness of program A big enough to justify the additional cost?

There would appear to be three general types of approaches to the questions raised by cells 1 and 9. One solution is to consider cells 1 and 9 ambiguous and thus equivalent to cell 5, the "no difference" cell. In this case the decision as to whether to employ program A or B or both would depend upon considerations outside the scope of the analysis. A second solution to the questions raised by cells 1 and 9 is for the decision maker to try to get a good understanding of exactly what the difference in effectiveness involves so that its worth in dollars can be judged. One way to do this is to go back to the original items of the C*O*C*E adult interview and to do an item analysis between groups A and B. This is suggested over scale analysis since any scale summarizes items that are somewhat disparate in meaning, while each item refers to a particular kind of behavior, feeling, or judgment.

Table 9-1

Logical Possibilities in Comparing Two Treatment Programs, A and B

		Cost of A Relative to B		
		A is Less Costly	A is as Costly	A is More Costly
Effectiveness of A Relative to B	A is Less Effective	1 ?	4 Choose B	7 Choose B
	A is as Effective	2 Choose A	5 No Difference	8 Choose B
	A is More Effective	3 Choose A	6 Choose A	9 ?

A third solution to the questions raised by cells 1 and 9 is for the decision maker to examine the statistical magnitude of the cost and effectiveness differences. If the statistical level of significance of the cost difference were much less than that of the effectiveness difference, the decision maker would choose the program with the higher effectiveness. However, if the relationship were reversed, the decision maker would make the reverse decision.

While the above-described DEM method for making cost-effectiveness analysis can be utilized exactly as discussed, there are at least three ways in which it can be modified so as to adapt it to different evaluative situations:

Comparing Three or More Treatments

If three or more treatment programs are being compared, a matrix following the logic of Table 9-1 in which all of the programs are simultaneously compared is very complicated. One alternative approach is to generate a series of two-program comparisons, as illustrated in Table 9-1. For example, if three programs A, B, and C were being compared, the following separate comparisons would be made: A versus B; A versus C; and B versus C. Then, on the basis of these comparisons, the programs could be rank-ordered. For example, if A is more cost-effective than B or C, and C is more cost-effective than B, then A can be judged the most cost-effective program and B, the least.

Another alternative approach in dealing with a comparison of three or more treatments is simply to include cost-of-treatment as a 15th variable in the decision-maker effectiveness matrix discussed above. When this approach is used, the matrix yields a single score for each patient that reflects both the cost and outcome of that patient's treatment. By subjecting these scores to a one-way analysis of variance, the various programs can be compared in terms of whether there is a statistically significant difference among the various treatment programs taken as a group. If there is such a significant difference, the most cost-effective program(s) can be identified by t-test comparisons among all the different possible pairs of groups.

Modifying the Application of Weights

The presentation so far has assumed that a decision maker's values are to be translated into a particular weight for each cell in the decision-maker effectiveness matrix. Alternative translations are also possible, although the computation procedures are somewhat more complex. For example, a decision maker might want to build in the following "threshold effect": All programs with a mean consumer satisfaction score of less than 60 will be rejected from further analysis; if a program has a mean consumer satisfaction score of 60 or over, it will then be analyzed via the matrix weights on the other outcome variables. The level of complexity to which such analysis might go is illustrated in the research literature on profile analysis with the Minnesota Multiphasic Personality Inventory. For example, Paul Meehl has developed a complex series of logical and mathematical rules to convert a 13-variable MMPI profile into a single diagnostic variable with three values: "psychotic," "neurotic," and "indeterminate."

Comparing Decisions

The above-described procedures for reducing a large number of multiple outcome scores into one summary score in one step is obviously a radical reduction of multivariate data. An alternative approach would be first to reduce the large number of variables by conceptual or factor analysis to a much smaller number, perhaps around five, and then employ a decision maker effectiveness matrix based on those five variables. In any case, there is a very important empirical question as to whether, once a decision maker's values have been translated into weights so as to yield a single outcome score, to what extent the decision that is dictated by the single outcome score converges with the decision based upon presentation to the decision maker of multiple outcome scores. If such a convergence does not occur, two general possible explanations immediately present themselves. On one hand, it could be that analysis of the decision maker's thought process when presented with the multivariate data reveals that he is simply not dealing with the data in an explicit, systematic, and consistent manner, and thus that the single-variable approach is a better decision-making method. On the other hand, it could be that analysis of the decision maker's thought process when presented with multivariate data reveals that he is employing a set of logical and mathematical interrelationships among the multiple outcome measures that are different from those designed into his decision-maker effectiveness matrix. In this case, the decision process based upon presentation of multivariate data helps to improve the validity of the decision-maker effectiveness matrix—that is, to improve the correspondence between the decision maker's actual rational rules for decision making and the rules that are designed into that decision maker's DEM.

Treatment Cost in the C*O*C*E Methodology

The process of determining the cost of a particular patient's treatment is comprised of the following major steps:

1. Enumerate the different types of services of the CMHC.
2. Make a record every time a patient receives a particular service in such a way that these service records can be accumulated in two separate ways: by individual patient, and by the type of service.
3. Record each CMHC expense by the type of service for which it is used in such a way that these expense records can be accumulated by the type of service.
4. Over a certain period, perhaps one fiscal year, accumulate the service records of each service so that the total workload for each type of service is derived.
5. Over the same period as in the above step, accumulate the expense records of each type of service so that the total expenses for each type of service is derived. Call this total "Cost".
6. Divide Cost by Units of Workload to yield the average cost per unit of each type of workload. (This step is the process known as cost finding).[22]
7. Returning to the patient's data, accumulate all the patient's service records to yield total number of units of each type of service the patient has received. Then for each type of service the patient has received, multiply the number of units received by the cost per unit (as determined by the preceding cost-finding step). This yields the total cost of each type of service received by the patient. Finally, adding these different costs across service yields the total cost of treatment for that patient.

As can be seen from the above, an important prerequisite for performing cost-determination is to specify the different basic kinds of services provided by a CMHC. In the C*O*C*E methodology type of service is defined within a conceptualization of a CMHC as a collection of activities structured in terms of an organizational matrix generated by two dimensions: (a) NIMH service elements, and (b) center divisions. The NIMH service elements of a CMHC are based upon those generic services provided by a CMHC that have been defined on a nationwide basis by NIMH. The C*O*C*E version of these includes eleven basic elements, which have been derived to be consistent with the overall C*O*C*E methodology together with definitions of these elements by various NIMH sources.

The center divisions of a CMHC refer to the specific administrative organizational unity of that agency at a particular point in time. While the center divisions of some CMHCs closely follow the NIMH service elements, the center divisions of other CMHCs follow other categories, such as patient age, geographic regions within the catchment area, patient problem areas (for example, alcohol or retardation), and so forth.

The nature of the NIMH-service-element by center-division matrix is illustrated in Table 9-2 for a hypothetical community mental health center with ten organizational divisions. The cells generated by the matrix, including the marginal cells, are called "organizational cells." Since the matrix in Table 9-2 has ten center divisions and 11 NIMH service elements, this matrix has 110 nonmarginal organizational cells, that is there are 110 *possible* types of service that a CMHC with this number of center divisions can provide. In the example in Table 9-2, not all the possible organizational cells are assumed to actually exist. Those that are assumed to exist are indicated by an "X".

The pattern of X's in Table 9-2 represents the following CMHC organizational structure:

There are four geographic teams (Divisions 01-04), each of which provides partial, outpatient, and after-hours emergency care to all nonalcohol-abuse patients of all ages living in a specific quadrant of the CMHC's catchment area. Each of these teams also provides consultation and education services in their geographic quadrants.

All nonalcohol-abuse patients requiring inpatient care are handled by one of two centralized divisions: Division 05 if the patient is an adult or adolescent, and Division 06, if the patient is a child. All alcohol-abuse patients are served by Division 07, which provides comprehensive patient services. This division also provides consultation and education services in the area of alcohol abuse to the entire catchment area.

The Director's Office, Division 08, is involved with planning and development and administrative services. All research and evaluation activities are conducted by Division 09. This division is also involved with planning and development. The Business Office, Division 10, is involved with planning and development, general services, and administrative services. Finally, all the divisions participate in inservice training.

From Table 9-2 it can be seen that while each CMHC will probably have a different set of center divisions at any point in time (and even within the same CMHC, center divisions can change frequently over time), the services of every CMHC can be cross-categorized in terms of the NIMH service elements, thus

Table 9-2
Illustrative Organizational Matrix for a Hypothetical Community Mental Health Center

Center Divisions		NIMH Service Elements											
Div. No.	Name of Division	Inpatient Care 01	Partial Care 02	Outpatient Care 03	After-hours Emergency Care 04	Consultation Service 05	Education Service 06	In-service Training 07	Research & Evaluation 08	Planning & Development 09	General Services 10	Administrative Services 11	Total of All NIMH Serv. Elem. 00
01	Northeast Geographic Team		X	X	X	X	X	X					X
02	Northwest Geographic Team		X	X	X	X	X	X					X
03	Southwest Geographic Team		X	X	X	X	X	X					X
04	Southeast Geographic Team		X	X	X	X	X	X					X
05	Centralized Adult & Adolescent Inpatient Service	X						X					X
06	Centralized Child Inpatient Service	X						X					X
07	Alcohol-Abuse Services	X	X	X	X	X	X	X					X
08	Director's Office								X	X		X	X
09	Research and Evaluation Division							X	X	X		X	X
10	Business Office							X		X	X	X	X
00	Total of all divisions, 01-10	X	X	X	X	X	X	X	X	X	X	X	X

Note: The organizational cells that are assumed to exist at this hypothetical CMHC are indicated by an "X".

permitting each CMHC to be compared with any other CMHC. Specifically, the column marginal cells of the matrix will always be the same for any CMHC. In addition, the row marginals of the matrix yield information that is necessary for administration within the CMHC. From the matrix it can be seen that if data are collected by organizational cell, both the NIMH service element column marginals and the center division row marginals can be generated.

Notes

1. Baxter, R.B., Bannock, G., and Rees, R. *The Penguin Dictionary of Economics*, London: Penguin Books, Inc., 1972.
2. Rivlin, A.M. *Systematic Thinking for Social Action*, Washington D.C.: The Brookings Institute, 1971.
3. Walker, R.A. "The Ninth Panacea: Program Evaluation," *Evaluation, 1 (1)*, 1972, pp. 45-53.
4. Schultz, C. Testimony cited in R. Anthony et al.'s *Management Control Systems*, Homewood, Ill.: R.D. Irwin Publishing Company, 1970.
5. Suchman, E.A. *Evaluative Research*, New York: Russell Sage Foundation, 1967.
6. Rivlin *Systematic Thinking*.
7. Bergin, A.E. "The Evaluation of Therapeutic Outcomes," chapter 7 in Bergin, A.E. and Garfield, S.L. (Editors), *Handbook of Psychotherapy and Behavior Change*, New York: John Wiley, 1971. Reprinted by permission.
8. Ciarlo, J.A., Lin, S., Bigelow, D., and Biggerstaff, M. "A Multi-Dimensional Outcome Measure for Evaluation of Community Mental Health Programs," paper presented at the Annual Conference, American Psychological Association, Honolulu, Hawaii, 1972.
9. Kiresuk, T.J. "Goal Attainment Scaling at a County Mental Health Service," *Evaluation*, Special Monograph No. 1, 1973, pp. 12-18.
10. Dohrenwend, B.P. Personal communication, 1973.
11. Dohrenwend, B.P. "Social Status, Stress, and Psychological Symptoms," *American Journal of Public Health, 57*, 1967, pp. 625-632; Dohrenwend, B.P. and Dohrenwend, B.S. *Social and Psychological Disorder: A Causal Inquiry*, New York: John Wiley, 1969.
12. Leighton, D.C., Leighton, A.H., and Armstrong, R.A. "Community Psychiatry in a Rural Area: A social psychiatric approach," chapter in Bellak, L. (Editor), *Handbook of Community Psychiatry*, New York: Grune and Stratton, 1964.
13. Srole, L., Langner, T.S., Michael, S.T., Opler, M.K., and Rennie, T.A. *Mental Health in the Metropolis*, New York: McGraw-Hill, 1964.
14. Ciarlo, J.A. Personal communication, 1973.
15. Dohrenwend, Personal communication, 1973.
16. Warheit, G.J. and Holzer, C.E. Personal communication, 1973.

17. Buchanan, G., Horst, P., and Scanlon, J. "Federal Level Evaluation: Improving Federal Evaluation Planning," *Evaluation, 1 (2)*, 1973, pp. 86-90.
18. Davis, H.R. "Four ways to goal attainment," *Evaluation, 1 (2)*, 1973, pp. 43-48.
19. Suchman, *Evaluative Research.*
20. Walker, "The Ninth Panacea."
21. Ibid.
22. Sorensen, J.E. and Phipps, D.W. *Cost-Finding and Rate-Setting for Community Mental Health Centers*, National Institute of Mental Health, DHEW Publication No. (HSM) 72-9138, 1972.

10

Development of a Community Assessment Strategy for Program Evaluation in a Comprehensive Human Service Delivery System

B.J. Morrison and *Martin Sundel*

The relationship between man and his environment is critical to any definition of mental health or mental illness. Mental health has two components—an individual component and an environmental component.[1] The envrionmental component includes the other individuals in a person's social system as well as the settings in which interactions with these individuals take place.

Recently the association between environmental elements and quality of life has received attention on the macro level. The Office of Management and Budget (OMB) published a book entitled *Social Indicators, 1973* in February 1974. This compendium employs statistics on items such as crime, housing, birth rate, and job satisfaction to evaluate the progress of domestic programs.

A link has long been recognized between mental disorder and environment. Within the framework of an ecological model, mental disorder is defined as the failure of an individual to fit his environment.[2] This failure may be (1) *adaptive,* that is, the individual has adopted behavior patterns that are incompatible with societal norms, or (2) *coping failure,* that is, the individual is unable to deal effectively with immediate and transitory problem situations.[3]

Many studies have demonstrated a relationship between environment and mental disorders involving both adaptive and coping failures. Environmental characteristics operationally defined in terms of major sociodemographic characteristics have been related to such varied problems as juvenile delinquency, suicide, schizophrenia, family disorganization, alcoholism, drug abuse, and mental retardation.[4]

The link between mental disorders and socioenvironmental characteristics was given formal organizational recognition by the community mental health movement. The 1964 Federal Regulations, which followed the passage of the Community Mental Health Centers Act of 1963, required that needs assessment and priority setting precede construction of centers. Steps in the process included: (1) the division of territories into catchment areas with a population of between 75,000 and 200,000 persons, and (2) the ranking of areas according to relative need, as determined by incidence and prevalence of mental illness and emotional disorders. Indexes to be employed included the proportion of the population, as well as the total number of persons, who were in high-risk groups. The specified high-risk groups included persons in economic need, persons with mental health related problems such as delinquency, and persons in selected age groups, for example, those 65 years and over.

Much research regarding the mental health-environment relationship is aimed at developing sociodemographic *predictors* of mental health problems. The 1964 Community Mental Health Centers Regulations stressed sociodemographic characteristics as tools in *planning* for the extent and types of mental health services needed by a community.[5] Recently, however, attention has been given to the use of sociodemographic characteristics as a means of program evaluation. B.L. Bloom[6] views communitywide studies as an integral part of the evaluation of community mental health programs because they are aimed at reducing the incidence, prevalence, and severity of psychopathology in the total community. He suggests that evaluation of this objective can be accomplished by periodic monitoring of psychiatric disability in the community, and by observing changes in this pattern over time. M. Guttentag[7] stresses the utility of sociodemographic characteristics for comparing programs in different geographic areas, and in providing a direct measure of program effectiveness and community impact.

When the Research and Evaluation Department was established at River Region Mental Health-Mental Retardation Board in August 1972, an assessment of community needs and resources was incorporated into the basic evaluation plan. The assessment was to be based on a variety of environmental data, including census statistics, demographic characteristics of clients, surveys, field observations, and other agency statistics. The purpose of the Community Assessment Project was to provide relevant community information for program planning and evaluation to: (1) administrators; (2) staff involved in prevention efforts; and (3) clinical staff. There was, at this time, a particular need to develop a mechanism for measuring prevention efforts and community impact. A system had already been developed for monitoring direct services quantitatively through a standardized statistical reporting system and qualitatively through a process of peer case review.

This chapter describes the development of a community assessment strategy as an evaluation tool within the context of a community mental health program. The development of the Community Assessment Project is closely linked to the nature of the geographical area served by River Region Mental Health-Mental Retardation Board, and to its service delivery system.

The Region

River Region Mental Health-Mental Retardation Board is one of 15 regional mental health programs in Kentucky. Thirty-five citizen volunteers serve on a board that administers the River Region human services delivery system. This private, nonprofit corporation receives funds from a combination of federal, state, and local sources, including client fees.

River Region consists of seven counties in the north central area of Kentucky, bounded on the north and west by the Ohio River. Counties included in the region (Kentucky Department for Human Resources, Region VI) are Jefferson, Henry, Trimble, Oldham, Shelby, Spencer, and Bullitt.

The counties within the region are predominately rural except for one first-class city, Louisville, in Jefferson County. With a population of 361,472, Louisville is the largest city and also is the home of 47 percent of the 776,578 persons living in the River Region.

The region is divided into four catchment areas, each of which represents approximately 200,000 persons. Two of the four catchment areas, Area A and Area D, lie completely in Jefferson County. Area C lies partially within Jefferson County and includes Bullitt and Spencer Counties on the south. Area B also contains a segment of eastern Jefferson County, but the majority of its geographical area is composed of the counties of Oldham, Trimble, Henry, and Shelby.

The communities served by River Region are extremely heterogeneous. Within its boundaries live rural, suburban, and urban populations. Median family incomes for census tract populations range from $2,783 to $32,676 per year; percent of families below poverty level from 0 percent to 60.1 percent. River Region's population varies greatly in ethnic content with the percentage of black residents ranging from 0 percent to 99.7 percent between census tracts. Family composition indicators such as youth dependency ratios vary from four children under 18 per 100 persons 18-64, to 121 children per 100 adults.

The River Region service delivery system was designed to accommodate this highly heterogeneous population. Committed to serving people in their own communities, the board developed and implemented a plan for a network of 16 mental health centers (and five "outposts" in the rural counties) that would deliver the basic services required by the Community Mental Health Centers Act of 1963. There are currently four centers, each serving 50,000 persons, within every catchment area. The four catchment areas are responsible fiscally and programmatically to a centralized regional administration. A regional research and evaluation staff provides consultation and direct assistance to all centers, as well as to regional program and planning staff.

Within each center, services in the areas of mental health, drugs, alcohol, and mental retardation, as well as consultation and community education programs, are available. Programs are implemented by multidisciplinary teams of mental health professionals.

The preventive services team within each center is responsible for outreach, consultation, and community education. This team has been given the mandate to develop and evaluate prevention efforts based on objective data. Consequently, community assessment has been formalized as a responsibility of the preventive services team within each center. In fact, centers are evaluated on the extent to which they have assessed community needs and resources and have developed objectives based on these data.

Community Assessment Data Sources

Community Assessment Profile (CAP)

Research and evaluation staff began by offering relevant census data to prevention teams on a request basis. As contact with more centers was established,
and as the demands for information increased, a decision was made to develop a
standardized format for presenting relevant census data for: (1) familarizing new
staff with the community; (2) providing input for planning and priority setting;
and (3) providing a mechanism for evaluation of impact.

Major considerations in designing the profile were the size of the geographical unit for which information would be provided, that is, census tract, center,
area or region, and which sociodemographic items to report. An examination
of literature in the areas of epidemiology, sociology, mental health, and urban
ecology strongly suggested that areas within communities vary greatly on such
dimensions as communication behavior, family life cycle, social rank, and political participation.[8] In addition, great variations in data for census tracts within
the same mental health center area indicated that even the populations served
by individual centers were highly heterogeneous. For example, within one center,
median family income ranged from $6,359 to $32,676 per year. These findings
corroborated the decision to use census tracts as the primary unit for analysis,
especially since many other data sources recorded information in a similar manner, for example, crime statistics, health statistics.

The community assessment profile was constructed to yield information
in the following areas: general population characteristics, family/nonfamily
characteristics, social characteristics, economic characteristics, and housing characteristics. Social and economic characteristics were recorded separately, rather
than as a single indicator of social rank, in accordance with recent evidence sub-
stantiating the earlier finding that the two factors are distinct.[9]

Items to be included within each major category of the community assessment profile were chosen on the basis of their usefulness either as predictors
of potential need for human health services, or on their comparability to client
data routinely collected. For example, the number of recipients of public welfare has been found to be significantly related to social pathology, such as
alcoholism and drug addiction.[10] Accordingly, one item included in the profile
is number and percent of persons in each census tract on public assistance rolls.

The profile also includes various statistics that reflect the major constructs
used in social area analysis, for example, social rank, urbanization, and segre-
gation.[11] These items were included to provide a data base for proposed social
area research relating to patterns of mental disorder.

Outline for CA Profile

I.   Population characteristics

1. Total population (1)
2. Ethnicity:
      White (2)
      Black (3)
          % black (4)
      Other/unknown (5)
3. Age:
      % of population under 6 (6)
      % of population under 18 (7)
      % of population 65 and over (8)
4. Sex:
      Male (9)
          % male (10)
      Female (11)
          % female (12)

II. Family/nonfamily characteristics
    1. Household size:
          Persons per household (13)
          % small households (one person) (14)
          % large households (six or more persons) (15)
    2. Normal family life index:
          % husband-wife households (16)
          % children under 18 living with both parents (17)
    3. Matriarchy index:
          % families with female head (18)
          % children under 18 living with female family head (19)
    4. Marital status:
          % males, single, 14 and over (20)
          % female, single, 14 and over (21)
          % married (22)
          % divorced (23)
          % widowed (24)
    5. Family life cycle:
          Youth dependency ratio (persons under 18 per 100 persons
              18-64 in households) (25)
          Aged dependency ratio (persons 65 and over per 100 persons
              18-64 in households) (26)
    6. Persons not in families:
          % of population in group quarters (27)
          % persons in households who are primary individual heads (28)
          % persons in households who are unrelated to head (29)

III. Social characteristics

   1. Education:
        % age 16-21 not high school grads, not in school (30)
        Median school years completed, persons 25 and over (31)
        % high school grads, persons 25 and over (32)
   2. Job:
        % employed population, 16 and over, in low-status occupations
              (operatives, service, laborers) (33)
        % employed population, 16 and over, in high-status occupations
              (professional, technical, managers) (34)

IV. Economic characteristics
   1. Employment:
        % males in civilian labor force, 16 and over unemployed (35)
        % females in civilian labor force, 16 and over, unemployed (36)
        % females, 16 and over, in labor force (37)
        % married women, husband present, in labor force (38)
        % married women, husband present, with children under 6, who
              are in the labor force (39)
   2. Family income:
        Median (40)
        Mean (41)
        % with social security income (42)
        Mean social security income (43)
        % with public assistance income (44)
        Mean public assistance income (45)
   3. Familes below poverty level:
        Number (46)
        % of all families (47)
        Mean income (48)
        % with female head (49)
   4. Persons below poverty level:
        % of all persons (50)
        % of persons below poverty level 65 and over (51)
        % of children under 18 living in poverty (52)

V. Housing characteristics
   1. Value:
        Median value, owner occupied units (53)
        % owner occupied, less than $10,000 (54)
        Median Monthly rent (55)
        % renter occupied, less than $80/mo. (56)
   2. Characteristics:
        % year-round units owner occupied (57)

% year-round units renter occupied (58)
% total year-round housing units vacant (59)
3. Mobility:
% persons, 5 years and over, in different house in 1965 (60)
4. Condition:
% occupied units that are overcrowded (1.01 to 1.50 persons
per room) (61)
% occupied units that are highly overcrowded (1.51 or more
persons per room) (62)

Finally, many items were based on those included in the Mental Health Demographic Profile System being developed by the National Institute of Mental Health.[12] This would allow for comparisons of each tract statistic with NIMH statistics for catchment area, county, state, and United States. After the 62-item community assessment profile was finalized, profiles were constructed for each of the 16 centers. Each profile item was reported by census tract, and for the entire center area.

Plans have been made to provide each center with a booklet containing community assessment profiles for all centers in the region, along with area and regional statistics, by June 1974.

Client Data

A system for collecting client data was devised to allow for comparisons between the characteristics of the total population and those of clients, and for observation of the patterns of client characteristics over time. Many items relating to clients were already being collected on the "application and intake" form completed by each person making contact with a River Region facility. The information was reported by catchment area rather than by center or by census tract, and was limited to frequency counts for each item.

A pilot project was set up to determine the usefulness of client data in program planning and evaluation, and to experiment with data displays that would prove best suited to these functions. Constraints placed on the pilot project were: (1) that demographic items selected be in the same format as general population data collected; (2) that the data be easy for center personnel to collect and code; and (3) that the system utilize the standard coding categories already in use, to allow for the transition of all data to this system if the project could be demonstrated to be worthwhile.

Items of client data selected for the project were: (1) month of entry; (2) year of entry; (3) client status: that is, contact, intake, terminated; (4) program: for example, mental health or drugs; (5) marital status; (6) sex; (7) ethnicity; (8) census tract; (9) age; (10) education; (11) religion;

(12) occupation; (13) income; (14) number of dependents; (15) source of referral; and (16-18) up to three presenting problems.

Information in all categories is recorded for all new contacts by the medical records librarian and reported monthly to Research and Evaluation. New information is then added to the data file, as are any updates on information already in the data file, for example, status changes. Data are tabulated by using a survey sort program called SURVE8. The program tabulates the number and percentage of persons in each category, on any given variable, and can present cross tabulations on up to five different variables simultaneously.

Other Data

In addition to census and client statistics, information from other agencies and community institutions has proven to be a valuable source of assessment data. Types of data collected and disseminated to centers include: (1) police statistics reported by census tract; (2) profiles and reason for referral for juvenile offenders and dependent children, by census tract; (3) information on births (legitimate/illegitimate) and deaths, by census tract; and (4) information on new apartments and new homes, by zip code, as well as zoning changes by planning district.

Transmitting Community Assessment Data

In order to insure maximum utilization of community assessment information, several procedures have been implemented. First, profiles are sent to the center's preventive services team leader. Second, a meeting is set up with the team to review available data, to compare statistical data with observation data obtained through field investigation in the community, and to discuss possible applications. At this meeting patterns are pointed out that give the team a feel for using the statistical data. For example, it has been found that where the percentage of persons 65 years and older is high; the percentage of one person households, widows, and females also is frequently high. The identification of patterns and relationships helps team members isolate characteristics that are potentially helpful in locating high-risk client populations, and in deciding where to focus preventive efforts, such as providing educational programs for the elderly.

In-service training sessions with the entire staff are often jointly conducted by research and evaluation staff and center preventive services teams. Staff members are familiarized with the area via maps and presentations of both statistical and observational data. These sessions also provide clinical staff with a broader perspective of the interface between mental health and environment.

Uses of Community Assessment Data

Administration

Community assessment data is being utilized by center supervisors in a variety of ways, including:

1. To characterize the population of their communities, as well as their client population
2. To determine the needs, actual and predicted, of the community so that sufficient numbers of appropriate staff may be available in areas of greatest need. For example, one supervisor assigned additional personnel to personal care homes after tallying the number of clients, including ex-hospital patients, living in these residences.
3. To locate high-risk populations in order that primary and secondary prevention programs might be available and accessible. For example, one center located a program for geriatric clients in a housing project after discovering a quarter of people in that census tract were 65 and over.
4. To characterize clients in particular programs so that programs can be tailored to meet their needs. For example: Is the alcohol program composed of middle class housewives or middle-aged, unemployed males?
5. To determine average length of treatment by program, and over all programs, so that reasonable caseloads can be assigned
6. To determine number of new clients per month, total number of cases within programs, and total number across programs.

Tables 10-1 and 10-2 show examples of the types of information that might be compiled by a center supervisor to determine the need for in-service training in the area of family therapy.

Prevention

One asset of the Community Assessment Project is that it provides an approach to evaluation that is simple and not time consuming; furthermore, it can be implemented by teams in each center. Second, it is applicable for both planning and evaluating a broad range of prevention activities, for example, outreach, consultation, and community education.

Outreach. Community assessment can be useful in planning outreach activities and setting priorities, because it allows for pinpointing areas of predicted need geographically,[13] as well as areas of actual need based on client data.

Table 10-1
Marital Status of Persons 14 Years Old and Over

		Total Population (1970)	Client Population (May 73 - Jan. 74)
Married	N	26,810	127
	%	69.9%	40.4%
Divorced	N	912	22
	%	2.4%	7.0%

Table 10-2
Primary Presenting Problems Related to Disturbances of Social Behavior with
Spouse May 1973 - January 1974

		N	% of Total
1973	May	— —	— —
	June	4	13.8
	July	9	23.7
	August	5	20.0
	September	10	27.0
	October	6	12.8
	November	2	14.3
	December	2	5.9
1974	January	10	20.4
	Total	48	16.2

For example, some centers are locating their clients on large street maps, using color codes for diagnosis. The maps provide an immediate visual assessment of geographical clusters of social pathology and emotional disorders. Furthermore, such representation has stimulated additional investigations into the socio-demographic characteristics of the area where pathology appears.

Evaluation of outreach can be carried out in two ways: First, an assessment can be made of which census tracts new clients are coming from, by month, to determine if increases are greater for areas in which outreach activities have been focused. Second a comparison can be made between the proportion of the total population and the proportion of the client population representing any given geographical area or any demographic group.

Consultation. Consultees can provide valuable input to the preventive services team by making them aware of actual need and the existence of high-risk populations, and by validating assumptions of need based on statistics.

Furthermore, client data regarding source of referral can be utilized in a multivariate evaluation of consultation. Source of referral may be monitored since direct referrals are often a spin-off measure of consultation services.

Community Education.   A mass media preventive education program is currently being carried out by River Region Mental Health-Mental Retardation Board. The project involves the presentation of mental health messages via television, radio, newspapers, billboards, and bus cards. The program is being evaluated by two major methods: (1) a series of four surveys being conducted by an independent marketing research firm with independent samples of over 500 respondents from throughout the area; and (2) an analysis of calls to a 24-hour Crisis and Information Center. The survey has two dimensions: to measure the respondent's awareness of mental health services, and his attitudes regarding mental health issues as related specifically to messages presented on the media.

All questions in the survey are being cross-referenced by selected socio-demographic characteristics of the respondents; analyses are being carried out to determine which variables are significant.

Treatment

While the major use of the Community Assessment Project has been to evaluate prevention efforts, data have been creatively utilized by center treatment teams, such as children's teams, drug teams, and alcohol teams. For example, children's teams in two centers have recognized the important interface between mental health and environment, as indicated in major studies of children's mental health.[14] These teams have designed and initiated an assessment of the needs of persons under 18 years of age residing within their center boundaries. Components of the assessment in one center are: (1) collection of all relevant census data; (2) analysis of client data including demographics, source of referral, presenting problem, and length of treatment; (3) juvenile court data for offenders and dependent children living in their census tracts; and (4) school data, including statistics and information obtained from interviews with school personnel. Relationships determined from these data are then presented graphically and the team formulates objectives based on this assessment, and an evaluation is planned that will determine whether the child component of the caseload is increasing relative to the proportion of children in the total population of the area.

Similar activities have been initiated by staff responsible for precare and aftercare of clients requiring inpatient services. In-service admission data are being collected that include: demographics, source of referral, number of previous admissions, length of last admission, and diagnosis. The SURVE8 program will be used to sort and present this information so that the relationships between relevant dimensions can be observed and analyzed.

Research

In 1973 River Region provided over 216,395 direct services to nearly 12,000 persons in the seven-county area. There were 39,876 more that made contact with the Crisis and Information Center. Because such a large number of persons are touched by River Region's clinical services, the collection of data on these persons can yield valuable information on the incidence and prevalence of various mental health problems in the Louisville area.

Studies are being planned to examine the relationship between selected sociodemographic characteristics and types of mental health problems. B.L. Bloom[15] has carried out similar studies in Pueblo, Colorado to determine the relationship between selected environmental characteristics and hospitalization rate by diagnosis and by type of facility. Using a cluster analysis he found three major clusters that account for a majority of the observed variance. These are social rank, young married (which contains statistics relating to lifestyle), and social isolation. It is interesting to note the similarity between these dimensions and those proposed by social area analysis (e.g., Shevky and Bell[16]).

Further investigation may determine whether similar patterns exist for admissions to outpatient community mental health services.

Conclusion

This chapter describes the evolution of a Community Assessment Project in a regional community mental health program serving a seven-county area composed of nearly 800,000 persons. The evolution of the project within the agency is discussed. Major components of the project include collection of census data, client data, and other relevant community statistics.

The project results are being utilized by administrators, prevention and treatment teams in 16 mental health centers to guide planning and aid in the evaluation of program effectiveness and community inpact.

Notes

1. Newbrough, J.R. Community Mental Health Epidemiology: A Collaborative

Study of Depressed Mood. Paper presented in a session on "Definition and Measurement of Mental Health," the Public Health Conference on Records and Statistics meeting jointly with the National Conference on Mental Health Statistics, Washington, D.C., June 1972.

2. Meyer, A. *Psychobiology*. Springfield, Illinois: Charles C. Thomas, 1957.

3. Newbrough, J.R. Community Mental Health Epidemiology.

4. Dunham, W.H. *Community and Schizophrenia*. Detroit: Wayne State University Press, 1965; Faris, R.E.L., and Dunham, H.W. *Mental Disorders in Urban Areas*. Chicago: University of Chicago Press, 1939; Hollingshead, B., and Redlich, F.C. *Social Class and Mental Illness*. New York: John Wiley, 1958; Klee, G.D.; Spiro, Evelyn; Bahn, Anita K.; and Gorwitz, K. An Ecological Analysis of Diagnosed Mental Illness in Baltimore. In Russell R. Monroe, Gerald D. Klee, and Eugene B. Brody (eds.) *Psychiatric Epidemiology and Mental Health Planning*. American Psychiatric Association, Psychiatric Research Report #22, April 1967; Knobloch, H., and Pasamanick, B. Environmental Factors Affecting Human Development Before and After Birth. *Pediatrics*, 1960, 26, 210-218; Langner, T.S., and Michael, S.T. *Life Stress and Mental Health*. New York: Basic Books, 1963; Leighton, Dorothea C.; Harding, J.S.; Macklin, D.B.; Hughes, C.C.; and Leighton, A.H. Psychiatric Findings of the Sterling County Study. *American Journal of Psychiatry*, May 1963, 119, 1021-1026; Mowrer, E.R. *Family Disorganization*. Chicago: University Chicago Press, 1927; Pfautz, H.W., and Hyde, R.W. The Ecology of Alcohol in the Local Community. *Quarterly Journal of Studies on Alcohol*, September 1960, 21, 447-456; Porterfield, A.L. Suicide and Crime in the Social Structure of an Urban Setting: Fort Worth, 1930-1950. *American Sociological Review*, June 1952, 17, 341-349; Schwab, J.J.; Warheit, G.J.; and Holzer, C.E., III. Suicidal Ideation and Behavior in a General Population. *Diseases of the Nervous System*, 1972, 33, 745-748; Shaw, C.R., and McKay, H.D. *Juvenile Delinquency and Urban Areas*. Chicago: University of Chicago Press, 1942; Srole, L. et al. *Mental Health in the Metropolis. The Midtown Manhattan Study*. New York: McGraw-Hill, 1962; Wechsler, H., and Pugh, T.F. Fit of Individual and Community Characteristics and Rates of Psychiatric Hospitalization. *American Journal of Sociology*, November 1967, 73, 331-338.

5. Andrew, G. Uses of Data in Planning Community Psychiatric Services. *American Journal of Public Health*, 1965, 55, 1925-1935; Kramer, M. Some Implications of Trends in the Usage of Psychiatric Facilities for Community Mental Health Programs and Related Research. Paper presented at Annual Meeting of American College of Neuropsychopharmacology, San Juan, December 1965.

6. Bloom, B.L. Mental Health Program Evaluation. In Golann, S.E., and Eisdorfer, C., eds. *Handbook of Community Mental Health*. New York: Appleton-Century-Crofts, 819-839, 1972.

7. Guttentag, M. Models and Methods in Evaluation Research. *Journal for the Theory of Social Behavior*, 1971, 1 (1), 75-95.
8. Charde, P.M. Some Effects of Differential Social Structure Upon Communication Behavior in a Metropolis. Paper presented to the American Sociological Association, 1971; Goldsmith, H.F., and Unger, E.L. Social Areas: Identification Procedures Using 1970 Census Data. Mental Health Study Center, National Institute of Mental Health, Laboratory Paper No. 37, May 1972; Green, B.S.R. Social Area Analysis and Structural Effects, *Sociology*, January 1971, 5 (1), 1-20.
9. Goldsmith, H.F., and Unger, E.L. Social Rank and Family Life Cycle: An Ecological Analysis. Mental Health Study Center. National Institute of Mental Health, Laboratory Paper No. 43, May 1972.
10. Schulberg, Herbert C., and Weschler, Henry. The Uses and Misuses of Data in Assessing Mental Health Needs, *Community Mental Health Journal*, Winter 1967, 3 (4), 389-395.
11. Abu-Lughod, Janet L. Testing the Theory of Social Area Analysis: The Ecology of Cairo, Egypt. *American Sociological Review*, April 1969, 34, 198-212; Anderson, T.R., and Bean, L.L. The Shevky-Bell Social Areas: Confirmation of Results and a Reinterpretation. *Social Forces*, December 1961, 40, 119-124; Shevky, E., and Bell, W. *Social Area Analysis*. Stanford: Stanford University Press, 1955.
12. Redlick, R.W.; Goldsmith, H.F.; and Unger, E.L. 1970 Census Data Used to Indicate Areas with Different Potentials for Mental Health and Related Problems. National Institute of Mental Health, *Mental Health Statistics*, Series C, No. 3, 1971.
13. Rosen, B.M. A Model for Estimating Mental Health Needs Using 1970 Census Socioeconomic Data. Paper presented to the Southeastern Psychological Association Meeting, New Orleans, April 1973.
14. Joint Commission on Mental Health of Children. *Mental Health of Children: Services, Research and Manpower*. New York: Harper and Row, in press; Kantor, Mildred B. Some Consequences of Residential and Social Mobility for the Adjustment of Children. In Mildred B. Kantor (ed.) *Mobility and Mental Health*. Springfield, Illinois: Charles C. Thomas, 1965.
15. Bloom, B.L. A Census Tract Analysis of Socially Deviant Behaviors. *Multivariate Behavioral Research*, 1966, 1, 307-320; An Ecologic Analysis of Psychiatric Hospitalizations. *Multivariate Behavioral Research*, 1968, 3, 423-463.
16. Shevky, E. and Bell, W., *Social Area Analysis*.

Comment

William G. Smith

Ms. Morrison, describing a strategy for evaluation of a comprehensive human services system, outlines with considerable clarity the use of sociodemographic data to describe a population and identify areas of need for human services. Any large community mental health service will have continuing need for some of this kind of data to plan the distribution of health services. Beyond this worthy purpose, however, there are genuine problems with relying upon a broad-gauge population approach in mental health program evaluation. I appreciate the opportunity to comment on these problems from the perspective of similar work that we carried out over the past decade at a regional mental health center in northern Illinois.

At a very general level there can be little argument that there is a relationship between mental health and sociodemographic factors. The details concerning this relationship, however, are still quite unclear and it has, therefore, been difficult to link this data with useful clinical and preventive programming.

As I see it, there are a number of reasons to question the usefulness of sociodemographic variables in program evaluation:

1. The definition of mental illness varies widely among professionals. Some would include only clearly defined psychoses and unequivocal neurotic behavior; others include all grades of emotional upset (e.g., grief reactions) and behavior deviation (e.g., crime and delinquency). As a result, estimates of prevalence and risk vary from 3 to 80 percent of the population. With so much variation, it is hard to intelligently deploy limited resources in a better than random or intuitive manner.

2. Even in specified "high-risk" populations, the proportion of persons who manifest frank disturbance is low. For instance, in our studies divorce occurred within a year prior to mental hospital admission in 11 percent of cases; the annual divorce rate was about 2 percent. This leaves a rather small group of divorcees who require formal mental health care. In addition, there is no efficient way to identify which of the divorcees at risk actually need assistance.

3. The mental health professions do not have a proven technology for intervention in many disturbances of human behavior. If racial discrimination or criminality are viewed as psychological disturbances, how can mental health professionals practically intervene in these phenomena.

4. Even when there is a known correlation between mental illness and a sociodemographic factor, the relationship between the two is often complex.

For instance, while divorce may be a stress leading to emotional upset, it can equally be the result of characterlogic deficits. Divorce can also provide the resolution of a serious personal or familial crisis state. Facetiously since there is a correlation between never being married and schizophrenia, are we to recommend marriage for all single persons?

5. In another investigation we applied a wide array of demographic variables in an attempt to discriminate between good prognosis patients and those who went on to chronicity. Even using multivariate analyses, we were unable to discover reliable predictors.

All of these difficulties raise important questions for mental health planners and clinical staff:

1. How is it possible to intervene in a human disturbance for which mental health does not have a demonstrated technology, for example, racial discrimination, crime, or high divorce rates.
2. How does a mental health program identify the small proportion of persons with a high-risk characteristics who could profit by its intervention?
3. How do mental health professionals get high-risk persons who may need their services to actually use them?
4. How do mental health programs affect large population groups? Do they really have special expertise or sanction to do so?
5. Is it not plausible that making recommendations with such sketchy knowledge may have unforseen and damaging effects?
6. How, in face of all these problems, can broad population statistics be used to monitor program effectiveness?

At this point it appears to me that there are no favorable answers. Mental health technology is in danger of being oversold. We simply do not know how to eliminate all the social and psychological ills afflicting mankind. Such grandiose plans can even lead to disillusionment and withdrawal of support for programs that mental health professionals can in fact deliver, viz, medication management, support, social services, and rehabilitation programs for the seriously disturbed, and counseling for persons experiencing distress and who want this kind of help.

Hence, it appears to me that demographic studies are still largely in the realm of basic science. They can be applied in describing the population to be served and in distributing facilities and staff to poverty areas. But for the most part evaluation systems should be more precisely focused upon therapeutic interventions and their clinical outcome and upon assuring quality of care. In light of current experience, it seems premature to assess program effectiveness by wide-based sociodemographic indicators that have doubtful applicability to what mental health professionals can accomplish with their limited skills and manpower resources.

Response

B.J. Morrison and *Martin Sundel*

In response to Dr. William G. Smith's preceding comments about this chapter, we would like to clarify some issues basic to the approach described. A primary point of clarification involves the distinction between the evaluation of social programs and the assessment of community needs. A comprehensive evaluation of community mental health programs requires a multidimensional approach that encompasses measures of effort, effectiveness, and efficiency. Furthermore, since community mental health programs are both legally and philosophically committed to serving consumers within circumscribed population areas, a major component of evaluation should include a measure of the extent to which services are reaching persons in need of those services. Such an approach requires measures of availability, accessibility, and utilization.

A needs assessment strategy based on objective data is fundamental to evaluating the impact of a community mental health program. Needs assessment, in its various forms, provides (1) data for program planning and distribution of services, and (2) baseline data for setting measurable objectives and evaluating outcome. We did not intent to convey, however, that needs assessment is a substitute for evaluative measures of program effort, effectiveness, or efficiency.

The technologies available for determining community needs accurately are far from perfect; however, probabilistic estimates of the prevalence of various mental disorders can be made through the use of field surveys conducted on appropriate samples of the population. Demographic approaches such as the one we have described are not intended to provide a statistical estimate of the need for mental health services. What does emerge are patterns of relative need for human services within and among communities. Thus, if areas with a greater predicted need for assistance in dealing with problems of living can be identified, then efforts can be made to provide services to these areas on a top priority basis.

Dr. Smith points out that even if such high-risk groups can be identified, the proportion of persons with disabling disturbances within these groups is still low. While it is true that only a small percentage of persons are admitted to mental hospitals, there is evidence to indicate that a large percentage of the population will need help at some time with various problems of living. It is especially with this group that community mental health centers, which encompass both inpatient and outpatient programs, must be concerned.

The relationship between selected demographic characteristics and mental and/or emotional problems has been well documented in the literature. The

177

importance of this relationship lies primarily in the fact of association, not necessarily causation. A demographic community assessment approach need not be based on the assumptions that (1) selected demographic factors lead to mental and/or emotional problems, and (2) by eliminating certain social conditions mental and/or emotional problems can be completely averted.

In summary, the study of demographic characteristics of the community is one component of a systematic, multidimensional evaluation of a community mental health program. The utilization of such an approach in no way obviates the need for evaluation of clinical outcomes based on controlled experimental studies or an applied goal-oriented clinical evaluation system.

Part III

Evaluation Techniques Applied to Individual Fields

11

Current Applications of Evaluation

William A. Hargreaves,
C. Clifford Attkisson,
Marguerite H. McIntyre and
Larry M. Siegel

To assess current practices in mental health program evaluation, the authors visited a variety of human service centers in 1972 and 1973, under a contract with the NIMH Office of Program Planning and Evaluation. Our task was to assess the current level of program evaluation capability in community-based facilities, and to identify or develop resource materials that might help these organizations to improve their program evaluation capability.[1] Within a four-state region we visited facilities in 40 different catchment areas, and also talked to evaluators and administrators who were concerned with multiple catchment areas, such as in larger urban counties. In addition we visited state-level evaluators and a few well-known programs outside of the region, so that altogether our travels took us to about 70 facilities. Our attention during these visits was upon the management of community-based mental health organizations. We looked for ways in which program evaluation provided, or could provide, useful tools for program managers, or what Carol Weiss[2] has labeled the "administrative" use of evaluation.

While we found a great deal of interest in program evaluation in a majority of the programs we visited, the level of actual capability in many centers remains minimal. We identified many obstacles that currently impede effective program evaluation. To clarify these obstacles further and to validate our own perceptions, we queried a group of 80 Northern California program managers, evaluators, and clinicians, using the nominal group method, a structured group problem identification and planning process.[3] They identified five major areas of concern relevant to enhancing a program's capability for evaluation:

1. Lack of well-defined program goals
2. Lack of clarity about the roles of evaluation, or of an evaluator
3. Difficulty in making evaluation data relevant to specific management decisions
4. Technical problems in developing and maintaining a useful management information data base
5. Lack of established methods for evaluating the effects of specific service techniques

As can be seen, there is a mixture of organizational and technical problems.

Preparation of this chapter was supported by NIMH Contract N01-MH-2-0105(OP).

181

Both must be solved in order to develop evaluation capability in a center. We visited centers in which staff had good technical skills but evaluation was not adequately related to other management functions. In other programs a well integrated management group was stymied by the lack of technical resources. In other publications[4] we have summarized the conceptual areas of evaluation in a model of program evaluation capability. The model describes three aspects, or dimensions, of this capability: the level of evaluation activity, the level of technical informational capability, and the degree of integration of evaluation into management. This conceptual model conveys our views about how program evaluation can be organized most usefully. The focus of this chapter, however, is the process of development through which organizations go on their way to effective program evaluation.

Developmental Stages

Program evaluation capability is one aspect of management skill. It is clear that this capability must be intentionally nurtured by the organization, and mature over a period along with other aspects of management. It cannot be ordered out of the catalog as an easy-to-assemble kit. We have come to think of four general stages in the development of the program evaluation aspect of center management: rudimentary monitoring; integrated monitoring; optimizing outcomes; and optimizing community impact.

Rudimentary Monitoring

The lowest level of evaluation capability can only be described as a state of "rudimentary monitoring." This level includes the initial establishment of the scope and direction of the organization. There is usually some responsiveness to community pressures, which might be considered a rudimentary assessment of community need, but the tasks of assessing community needs and establishing program priorities and goals are inadequately addressed. A fiscal bookkeeping system and a process for collecting basic statistics on clients are functions required by external reporting demands. These activities satisfy the minimal accountability requirements of funding agencies, but in the absence of any local planning initiative they rarely provide useful guides to internal management decision making. Management attention at this stage often must be restricted to the short-range perspective of handling day-to-day problems while trying to avoid an atmosphere of continual crisis. Newly formed organizations frequently go through this hectic stage, and many that we visited had not progressed beyond it.

Integrated Monitoring

Some organizations were on the road to the second level of "integrated monitoring." The middle ground between rudimentary management and integrated monitoring encompasses virtually all of the remaining centers we visited, although there are a few programs that do a good job of integrated monitoring. A variety of monitoring activities are initiated along the way, but the crucial development is not so much the specific activities, but the program leaders' increased attention to, and skill in, using program information for long-range planning. Only in this context do the pieces of program evaluation begin to come together in the service of local management.

The statistical system is developed to answer recurring management questions about the functioning of the program. Statistical and accounting systems are integrated so that meaningful cost finding is possible. The program leaders take the initiative in assessing community needs, aided by census data and a variety of simple assessment and goal-setting activities. At budget time, or when a new or expanded program is being considered, the program planners ask questions such as: "Are we serving the clients we intend to serve?" "Are services accessible to clients regardless of income or location within the catchment area?" "Do clients who need services get lost due to inadequate continuity of care?" "Do the costs of specific services, and the overall allocation of the budget, reflect the service priorities that we espouse?"

A program that has reached this second level of evaluation activity is likely to be very well managed by today's standards. In spite of the concern we all have about the ultimate effectiveness of programs, these descriptive monitoring and needs assessment activities are the first applications of program evaluation in most programs. We feel that this is an entirely appropriate order of development, and others have suggested this also.[5] Systematic planning and goal-setting activities, statistical monitoring, and routine cost finding allow the kind of stable program management within which program effectiveness can begin to be examined.

Optimizing Outcomes

At the third level program staff are ready to begin answering questions such as: "Which clients are least satisfied with the services they receive?" "Do our aftercare services for schizophrenic clients successfully prevent unnecessary rehospitalization?" "Did last year's consultation efforts with the schools accomplish the goals that we and the school people agreed upon?" "Would a new program for suicidal patients help these clients to survive more frequently than they do at present?" A thoughtful approach to outcome questions such as these requires skilled center management and well developed program evaluation capability. Most organizations lack the management skill to operate at this level. A few centers have demonstrated that they have this skill in utilizing outcome evaluation and are, deservedly, highly visible on the program evaluation scene.[6] We have elsewhere discussed various approaches to this level of evaluation[7] and outcome measuring tools that may be useful.[8]

In contrast to the success of a few programs utilizing outcome evaluation, we have yet to see any effective evaluation at the fourth level, "optimizing community impact." Goals of improving the "quality of life" and "average mental health" of a community are more properly goals for the entire human services network of a community, and involve questions about the optimum components and linkages in this network. It seems to us that a good bit of basic research will be needed before communities will have the conceptual and methodological tools to evaluate the effectiveness of a human service delivery system at this level. In a more modest way, of course, the periodic review of community needs[9] is also an opportunity for an informal common-sense estimate of the program's relevance to the community it serves. Unfortunately, even this simple review is not attempted by many programs.

How does an alcoholism, drug abuse, or mental health program move along this road of increasing evaluation capability? Our observations suggest that there is both a technical tool-building development and an organizational role-relationship factor that limit or facilitate effective evaluation.

Informational Capability

The "natural data systems" of most programs are of little use for evaluation. Case records, financial records, and personnel records are generally uncoordinated and dispersed, and therefore not accessible in a form that can provide the necessary program overview the manager needs. In developing better information capability, a central integration of various data handling tasks is needed. The first product of this effort is a minimum set of routine management reports. As the informational capability develops, greater flexibility in data analysis is acquired in order to keep pace with changing management concerns, changing external reporting requirements, and increasing management skill in using program data in decision making. Developing these information procedures often absorbs much of the technical program evaluation leadership available in a program for a period of several years. The wealth of new materials on management information systems[10] should help centers to shorten the time needed to acquire these information tools, so that they can concentrate more quickly on the task of learning to use the tools to improve management effectiveness. As these tools become available in a program, the program evaluation leadership is then able to focus more on time-limited special studies related to emerging management issues. Such studies may gather new data, such as posttreatment follow-up outcome, but will also take advantage of the routine information now available in the program.

Role of Evaluation

The organizational role of evaluation is the other major factor that seems to determine how quickly and how effectively management learns to utilize evaluation methods. There are excellent examples of small, new programs where crucial evaluation functions were optimally located: inside the head of the program director.[11] Many larger and older organizations also are blessed with a director who has these skills. In both situations, when evaluation activities are then delegated to other members of the staff, the manager can insure that the relationship of program evaluation to other management functions remains clear. This allows the essential mutual learning to continue. This learning can take place only if the key program evaluation person is a participant in the management process along with the other clinical and administrative leaders. In organizations where this is not the case, it is common to recruit a program evaluator, or to rechristen a slightly used chief psychologist, without any clear conception of how this newly labeled function fits into the existing management process. As a result the evaluation functions become encapsulated in ways that limit their utility for the program. One such limited role might be described as the "statistical" staff person, who is often the first staff hired for evaluation as a stop-gap measure to meet funder data collection requirements, with little thought given to their relationship to management. "Clinical-experimental" staff are usually trained in clinical psychology and have specialized research skills and interests. They may undertake special research projects, but are otherwise unrelated to management, and their research has little local relevance or impact. Technical-evaluative specialists have some training or experience in program evaluation, and provide technical analyses of center operations. But these persons often lack sufficient management perspectives or skill to undertake competent *policy analyses*, weighing the broadly political aspects of the decision process.

Thus, each of these three roles falls short of the degree of direct participation in management that is essential. Without assuming a real part of the coordinative and decision-making responsibility of management, the program evaluator may never learn how to shape his work to be adequately relevant. At the same time the other management people are not getting the long practice in utilization of evaluation that they need, and that can best come from extended day-to-day collaboration with the evaluator.

A Snapshot of Current Applications

With this conceptual view as a background, we will try to portray in more detail the level of program evaluation applications as of early 1973. To do this we made three global judgments of each of 51 care provider organizations we visited within California, Nevada, Arizona, and Hawaii. Of the 51 organizations, 25 were federally funded community mental health centers. Table 11-1 shows our judgments about the overall level of utilization of evaluation in these programs. Fourteen centers made negligible use of any systematic program information, and were judged to be functioning on the level of "rudimentary monitoring." Eighteen had begun to do a little something, while 17 were engaged in thoughtful monitoring and planning. However, none of these facilities carried out "integrated monitoring" as we have described it, even the two that had begun to utilize outcome studies in program planning. For example, none of these centers could do meaningful cost-finding at the time of our survey.

Table 11-1

Ratings of 51 Community-based Programs on "Level of Evaluation Activity"

Level of Evaluation Activity	Number of Programs
1. Negligible use of program information in local management	14
2. Minimal but regular collection and summary of information for management use	18
3. Good monitoring of client characteristics and service activities; no serious look at outcome	17
4. Regular outcome assessment or planned treatment comparison studies	2
5. Assessment of outcome of direct and indirect services, and one or more community impact studies	0

Table 11-2 shows informational capability. The most common level of development corresponds to those 18 programs where at least some consistent set of admission characteristics were recorded for all clients, but no routine procedure had been developed to produce summary reports. That is obviously not a very impressive informational capability. Twelve sites did have procedures for centrally analyzing and reporting at least a few statistical characteristics of their clients. Only six of the centers had reached a level where they had really usable information tools, with, for example, a computer system that could provide fairly quick response regarding unanticipated descriptive questions. Just two programs had all of the foregoing capability plus some staff time allocated for follow-up interviewing or other special data collection.

Table 11-2
Ratings of 51 Community-based Programs on "Level of Informational Capability"

Level of Informational Capability	Number of Programs
1. Nonuniform raw records must be abstracted by hand	15
2. Planned uniform minimal content and format of records, but still inaccessible	18
3. Centrally collected information reasonably accessible for routine statistical summaries	12
4. "Quick response" capability for unanticipated summaries of already collected data	4
5. Special data collection capacity such as staff available for follow-up assessment	2

The organizational role of evaluation presented a similar picture of very limited development (Table 11-3). The first two levels are euphemistic descriptions of programs where we could discern no real role of evaluation at all. At the other extreme, about one-fifth of the centers had developed an evaluation function that seemed to be reasonably well integrated into the overall management of the organization. The remainder of the programs had developed one of the three suboptimal evaluation roles that were described above, the "statistical," "research," or "technical" roles.

Table 11-3
Ratings of 51 Community-based Programs on "Level of Integration (of Evaluation) into Management"

Level of Integration into Management	Number of Programs
1. Clerical work, little attention by management	8
2. Isolated "studies" of marginal relevance or incidental data review by clinician or manager	12
3. Evaluator with some skills but who participates minimally in management decision making	10
4. Professional evaluator with at least moderate technical or clinical research skills, but communication between evaluation and other management functions is ineffective	11
5. Professional evaluator communicates effectively with management; clinicians and managers effective utilizers of evaluation.	10

Recommendations

Altogether, we found a very unimpressive program evaluation capability in these organizations. If this four-state sample is representative of what is happening across the country, then one could say with some confidence that there are clear opportunities for improvement. The initiative for this improvement must come primarily from within the local organizations.

Many local programs are now actively seeking outside assistance in developing their evaluation capability. In a survey by *Evaluation* magazine,[12] four preferred forms of technical assistance were emphasized: (1) outside expertise, (2) written information, (3) conferences, and (4) NIMH central or regional consultants. Outside expertise in the form of a knowledgeable consultant who works with an individual program is often seen as the most useful type of technical assistance. However, it requires considerable initiative from within a program to locate a potential consultant and determine whether the person can actually be useful in that setting. We can see two ways to help this process along. The first is to promote exchange of information about potential consultants. Since nationally visible program evaluation consultants are in short supply, information about locally available effective consultants would be especially useful. Second, programs should look to each other for mutual aid. In a number of locations informal organizations of program evaluators and program managers are springing up, and seem to be helpful.

A wealth of written materials related to program evaluation has recently become available. The information systems area is currently the best developed, with two major new books: one is *Guidelines for a Minimal Statistical and Accounting System for Community Mental Health Centers*, by E. Myles Cooper, and the other is *Integrated Management Information Systems for Community Mental Health Centers*, edited by Todd Smith and James Sorensen.[13] The multistate information system is now also well documented and seems to be functioning adequately as a service bureau data system operated by remote terminal.[14] Programs ready to invest in a major computer system may find that the multistate system is competitive with other approaches in terms of its cost, performance, and relevance to local needs.

There is also new material related to needs assessment and planning, and to the evaluation of client outcomes and program effectiveness. There is less consensus about how to proceed in these tasks, however. We have prepared a set of "Resource Materials for Community Mental Health Program Evaluation"[15] that we hope will be useful to program managers and evaluators. The set contains a wide variety of papers on the organization of program evaluation and on techniques for specific evaluation tasks.

Two areas of evaluation methods seem particularly to need research attention. The first involves management utilization of brief outcome experiments and other time-limited studies. Experience in this area is fragmentary. Research methods for comparative treatment experiments, including the measurement of treatment outcome, have seen considerable development in the past decade, but traditional clinical experiments are too unwieldy for effective integration into the management process. Experience is needed in executing brief, simple study designs in relation to specific management issues, in a context where the management utility of such experiments can be compared to other program evaluation approaches.

The second area needing developmental research is the study of community impact, at the level of the total network of health and human service efforts in a community. We feel this is the least developed area of program evaluation, but that there are a number of possible approaches to explore. It would seem useful to support efforts in a few communities to monitor client flow, service cost, and limited aspects of outcome simultaneously across a range of different human service systems. The development of feasible monitoring methods could be followed by attempts through simulation to anticipate the effects of the removal or addition of specific programs, and of changes in admission screening and referral patterns among the programs. This would then provide hypotheses to be tested during the quasi-experimental evaluation of subsequent modifications aimed at improving the system.

These long-range fantasies need to be encouraged. Meanwhile, we must attend to the current realities of strengthening technical assistance to local program management. We think that a case can be made that strengthening the management capability (including the evaluation capability) of care provider organizations will give an excellent return in greater program effectiveness. We argue for greater attention at both state and federal levels to technical assistance to local programs, and for funding of technical assistance at least equal to the funding that state and federal agencies devote to their own program evaluation needs.

Notes

1. Hargreaves, W.A.; Attkisson, C.C.; Siegel, L.M.; McIntyre, M.H.; and Sorensen, J.E. (Eds.) *Resource materials for community mental health program evaluation*, San Francisco: NIMH, 1974.
2. Weiss, C. "Evaluation in relation to policy and administration." (Chapter 16, this volume.)
3. Delbecq, A.L., and Van de Ven, A.H. "A group process model for problem identification and program planning," *The Journal of Applied Behavioral Science*, 1971, 7, 466-492.
4. Attkisson, C.C.; McIntyre, M.H.; Hargreaves, W.A.; Harris, M.R.; and Ochberg, F.M. "A working model for mental health program evaluation," *American Journal of Orthopsychiatry*, 1974, in press; McIntyre, M.H.;

Attkisson, C.C.; and Keller, T.W. "Components of program evaluation capability in community mental health centers." In: Hargreaves et al. (Eds.) *Resource materials.*

5. Cooper, E.M. *Guidelines for a minimal statistical and accounting system for community mental health centers,* Washington, D.C.: DHEW Publication No. (ADM) 74-14, 1973; Smith, T.S., and Sorensen, J.E. (Eds.) *Integrated management information systems for community mental health centers.* Rockville, Md.: NIMH, 1974; Sorensen, J.E., and Phipps, D.W. *Cost finding and rate setting for community mental health centers.* Rockville, Md.: NIMH, 1972.

6. Kiresuk, T.J., and Lund, Sander H. "Process and outcome measurement using goal attainment scaling (chapter 14, this volume); Smith, W. "The ideal and the real: Practical approaches and techniques in evaluation" (chapter 7, this volume).

7. Hargreaves, W.A.; Attkisson, C.C.; and Ochberg, F.M. "Outcome studies in mental health program evaluation." In: Hargreaves et al. *Resource materials.*

8. Hargreaves, W.A.; McIntyre, M.H.; Attkisson, C.C.; and Siegel, L.M. "Outcome measurement instruments for use in community mental health program evaluation." In: Hargreaves et al. *Resource materials.*

9. Siegel, L.M.; Attkisson, C.C.; and Cohn, A.H. "Mental health needs assessment: stategies and techniques." In: Hargreaves et al. *Resource materials.*

10. Crawford, J.L.; Morgan, D.W.; and Gianturco, D.T. (Eds.) *Progress in mental health information systems: computer applications.* Cambridge, Mass.: Ballinger, 1974; Cooper, *Guidelines for a minimal statistical and accounting system;* Smith and Sorensen, *Integrated management information systems.*

11. Biegel, A. "Evaluation on a shoestring: A suggested methodology for the evaluation of community mental health services without budgetary and staffing support." In: Hargreaves et al. *Resource materials;* Lombillo, J.R.; Kiresuk, T.J.; and Sherman, R.E. "Contract fufillment analysis: evaluating a community mental health program." *Hospital and Community Psychiatry,* 1973, *24,* 760-762.

12. Davis, H. "To the reader," *Evaluation,* 1973, 1 (no. 3), 25.

13. Cooper, E. Miles. *Guidelines for a Minimal Statistical and Accounting System for Community Mental Health Centers,* Washington, D.C.: NIMH, 1973; Smith, Todd, and Sorenson, James, (eds.), *Integrated Management Information Systems for Community Mental Health Centers ,* Washington, D.C.: NIMH, 1974.

14. Laska, E.M. "The multi-state information system," In: Crawford, Morgan, and Gianturco, *Progress in mental health information systems.*

15. Hargreaves et al. *Resource materials.*

12 Alcoholism Evaluation Overview
Donald G. Patterson

Evaluation joins the other basic management functions of planning, organizing, staffing, and execution in health service delivery as in any other setting. Evaluation is a vital input to the planning and execution functions and without appropriate evaluation those functions are seriously impaired. Evaluation activities, however, often are devoted solely to research questions rather than to the needs of ongoing programs.

As the entire problem of alcoholism has received more national attention in the early seventies, so a major increase of emphasis in evaluation of all areas of alcoholism program activity has occurred. Prior work by individual researchers and organizations has provided a significant background of evaluative information, and specific measures of alcoholism and alcohol abuse have been derived.

A large-scale evaluative effort spearheaded by the National Institute on Alcohol Abuse and Alcoholism (NIAAA) within the Department of Health, Education, and Welfare began at the federal level in 1971. The public law that established the institute contained an evaluation requirement that supported the strong emphasis placed by Dr. Morris E. Hafetz, institute director, on the evaluation function.

Evaluations of alcoholism-related programs by other federal agencies have also been undertaken in the late sixties and early seventies; for example, the Department of Transportation is involved in nationwide drinking driver programs in which evaluative elements are established. Individual states have developed monitoring and evaluation programs in some instances, and many others are preparing to develop such programs. The NIAAA is providing assistance to the individual states in order to facilitate standardization of data elements and of definitions used in alcoholism evaluation efforts across the nation and to help states establish data systems for use in their own evaluation programs.

The federal alcoholism treatment program monitoring and evaluation effort varies in some important ways from the individual evaluations performed by local projects and by researchers. The purpose of the monitoring and evaluation of federally funded alcoholism treatment programs by NIAAA is to determine the treatment effectiveness and efficiency of those programs, to monitor program progress toward stated objectives, and to assist programs to improve their services to persons suffering from alcoholism. Information from the system is useful to the individual project as well as at the national level.

Local evaluative efforts mainly are directed either toward the general management of the individual project or toward specific case evaluation of individual

191

clients. Some monitoring and evaluation needs are common at both the local and federal levels and a monitoring system was developed for the purpose of serving those dual needs.

Because of the difference between local treatment project needs and those of the federal and state agencies, two levels of evaluation have emerged and are mutually supportive. Although project directors may rely only on those data and analyses provided by the national-level system, additional information is required by the treatment agency, and should be collected in order to make detailed management decisions and to track client progress in a timely way at the local level.

Because of the number of projects involved, their geographic span, and the apparent trend towards increased data commonality at the federal and state levels, the federal system is emphasized here. Aspects of some of the variety of local-level evaluation schema are noted briefly later.

Alcoholism Treatment Program Monitoring System

There are more than 400 alcoholism treatment programs funded, at least in part, by the National Institute on Alcohol Abuse and Alcoholism. Although these programs represent only a small segment of the total universe of alcoholism treatment facilities in the United States, they represent the largest data base currently in existence for alcoholism program monitoring and evaluation. At this writing, almost 100 of the projects routinely provide data into a uniform data collection and monitoring system, with the remaining projects to be included within the system in the near future.

The specific target populations being monitored include: alcoholism treatment centers (ATCs) oriented toward the general population; public inebriate projects; drinking driver programs; American Indian alcoholism projects; industrial employee alcoholism programs, and poverty projects.

The NIAAA alcoholism program monitoring and evaluation system is action-oriented and designed to provide information to local, state, and federal levels. The NIAAA system was designed to support decision making at all levels regarding program and project management and to measure the effectiveness of alcoholism programs in terms of meeting their objectives. The system provides computerized routine feedback information monthly, in summary form, to all Systems users. The reports, for example, show how well outreach and follow-up are performed, client outcome from treatment, cost of treatment, the amount of staffing effort expended on direct and indirect services, and client characteristics.

The feedback report format is designed to provide comparison among projects of each group. Routine reports, such as that shown in Table 12-1, also allow for trending of specified information, by month, over the past one-year period.

TABLE 12-1
NIAAA Alcoholism Treatment Monitoring System, Report IIIA—Client Intake Characteristics, Period Ending September 1974

TREATMENT CENTER—SAN JOSE
STATE—CALIFORNIA
REGION—09

CHARACTERISTIC	CATCHMENT AREA	4TH QTR 1973	1ST QTR 1974	2ND QTR 1974	3RD QTR 1974	TWELVE MONTH	ALL ATC CENTERS
NUMBER OF INTAKES		262	279	437	414	1,392	14,893
MEAN AGE		39.4	38.5	39.0	37.9	38.7	41.0
PERCENT MALE		78.6%	77.4%	80.5%	82.9%	80.2%	82.9%
ETHNICITY							
WHITE	94.3%	77.6%	76.0%	72.6%	68.1%	72.9%	77.4%
BLACK	1.7%	5.5%	6.6%	4.7%	3.7%	4.9%	11.4%
SPANISH DESCENT		14.1%	13.3%	20.2%	25.2%	19.2%	6.9%
AMERICAN INDIAN	.4%	1.6%	2.6%	.5%	2.0%	1.5%	2.8%
ALASKAN NATIVE	.0%	.0%	.0%	.2%	.2%	.1%	.3%
ASIAN DESCENT	2.3%	.4%	1.1%	.5%	.5%	.6%	.2%
OTHER	1.3%	.8%	.4%	1.4%	.2%	.7%	1.1%
MEDIAN SCHOOL YEARS	12.8	12.4	12.5	12.5	12.3	12.4	12.2
MARITAL STATUS							
MARRIED	63.3%	35.2%	35.5%	38.7%	37.3%	37.0%	37.4%
DIVORCED/SEPARATED	6.2%	34.9%	38.4%	37.8%	36.3%	36.9%	38.3%
SINGLE/WIDOWED	30.5%	29.9%	26.2%	23.6%	26.4%	26.1%	24.3%
PERCENT UNEMPLOYED	5.2%	39.5%	29.0%	33.6%	34.4%	34.0%	36.6%
PERCENT IN WORK FORCE	79.2%	86.4%	87.7%	85.8%	83.8%	85.6%	82.4%
PERCENT HAD PRIOR TREATMENT		33.5%	21.5%	28.7%	18.7%	25.2%	29.6%
MEAN INCOME LAST YEAR	$13,644	$8,072	$8,434	$8,344	$7,167	$7,917	$7,467
YEARS HEAVY DRINKING		13.6	12.8	11.6	11.1	12.1	13.3
YEARS LIVING IN COMMUNITY		6.7	6.3	7.8	8.6	7.5	9.8
ALCOHOL CONSUMED/DAY (OZS.)		4.4	3.6	3.4	3.5	3.7	6.0
OCCUPATION							
PROFESSIONAL	28.7%	14.5%	17.9%	14.0%	10.9%	14.0%	9.9%
SALES AND CLERICAL	11.3%	11.5%	12.2%	12.8%	9.2%	11.4%	9.7%
CRAFTSMAN	24.7%	21.8%	29.4%	31.6%	30.1%	28.8%	31.0%
LABORERS	4.6%	16.0%	15.4%	13.0%	21.4%	16.5%	20.2%
SERVICE	5.9%	17.2%	11.1%	12.4%	13.6%	13.4%	12.2%
STUDENT / HOUSEWIFE	14.2%	7.3%	7.2%	8.0%	8.7%	7.9%	6.6%
NONE	10.6%	11.8%	6.8%	8.2%	6.1%	8.0%	10.4%

Participating in the NIAAA monitoring system development were Leland Towle, Stanford Research Institute; Dr. Howard Blane and Dr. David Armor, consultants to NIAAA; and John Deering and Donald Patterson of the NIAAA staff. Alcoholism treatment project staffs also were involved.

Data Collection

Data input elements to the NIAAA alcoholism treatment program monitoring system are determined by the needs for evaluative measures related to program objectives. Data are both management- and client-oriented and may be combined to provide a number of effectiveness and efficiency measures. Information is collected on basic patient characteristics such as age, sex, ethnicity, marital status, occupation, employment status, income, education, condition on admission, and source of referral.

The primary means of collecting data for use in measuring client change is through client interview and observation. Client interviews are scheduled at client intake, at 60 days and at 180 days after intake. Each of the alcoholism projects funded by the institute provides client-oriented data on specified data collection instruments. Completed forms are submitted weekly for centralized processing. Additional information regarding staff use and project financial data are provided in accordance with an established schedule.

The data collection forms used by the monitoring system are:

Initial Contact Form – completed by an ATC staff member the first time a potential client is seen.

Client Intake and Follow-up Form – Administered to clients upon intake and at 60 and 180 days later. It records demographic/socioeconomic background information about the client, drinking patterns, and other pertinent characteristics that can measure client change.

Client Services Report – A summary of the various types and amounts of treatments and services administered to each client and family member over a one-month period.

The resource-oriented forms consist of:

Monthly Activities Report – A profile of the staffing patterns and time devoted by each discipline in performing agency functions.

Quarterly Inventory Report – A report of agency and affiliate staff numbers, expenditures of the agency for the quarter, and all sources and amounts of revenue.

Data entries are reviewed and edited prior to processing. Validity checks are performed within the data processing cycle.

Effectiveness Measures

Although there is no single client outcome measure identifiable as the sole indicator of success in alcoholism treatment programs, there are several outcomes viewed as desirable by NIAAA and program directors. Abstinence from use of alcohol, reduction in the amount of alcohol ingested, and improvement in behavior and in physical health are all factors reflecting positive change in the individual. Improvements in employment, increased income, and improved family situation are other indications of program success. Criteria for use in evaluation also are being developed.

Multiitem scales to show the quantity and frequency of drinking and client behavioral impairment are utilized to yield scores to indicate improvement or deterioration in client condition. These indexes are designed to reflect client changes from one report period to another. The measures are complemented by the other indicators mentioned.

Indexes of client outcome provided by the system and used in the evaluation of effectiveness include:

Quantity-Frequency Index

The *quantity-frequency (Q-F) index* is a measure of the rate and consumption of alcoholic beverages over the past month (in units of the average ounces of pure ethanol ingested per day). The total Q-F index is a composite of client Q-F indexes calculated individually for beer, wine, and liquor. The scoring mechanism is based on R. Jessor's index.[1] The rationale behind this index is that particular threshold values of absolute alcohol intake into the blood stream result in varying degrees of impairment. Comparisons are made of Q-F indexes calculated at intake into an alcoholism program and at various points during and after treatment; such comparisons reveal changes in the alcohol consumption pattern of the individual or group. Comparisons of Q-F indexes between treatment programs provide insights into variations in consumption among the client populations being treated by these programs. The calculation of the index involves the amount of alcoholic beverage reported consumed, the frequency of consumption during the past 30 days, and the alcohol content of the beverages consumed.

Very simply, the individual Q-F index score for beer, wine, or liquor is equal to the ounces consumed per typical day of drinking, multiplied by the absolute alcohol content of the beverage and by the frequency of consumption. The total Q-F index for an individual is equal to the sum of the individual beverage Q-F index scores.

Impairment Index

This indicator is a composite of scores provided by responses to 12 questions asked of the client. The questions are designed to measure the behavioral effects of excessive alcohol use.[2] The index can be used to measure changes as a result of treatments provided and for comparison among various client groups.

These two indexes have been used in conjunction with self-perception, self-esteem, and others. Only the two described here are calculated on a regular basis due to the high correlation in results obtained during a pilot study. It is through the use and interpretation of a number of key indicators, however, that conclusions are drawn regarding the progress of alcoholism treatment programs toward their objectives.

A comparison of client change data from various programs is shown in Table 12-2.

Validity of Outcome Measures

Reliability and validity of client outcome indexes are under study, and preliminary investigation reveals significant reliability, and probable validity of the quantity-frequency index as applied to client groups and to the general population through data acquired in a series of nationwide surveys by the Louis Harris organization.

The apparent validity of the quantity-frequency index applies only to grouped data. Individual as well as group data were being investigated in the 1974 study. Findings should contribute significantly to evaluation of client outcome and to program effectiveness. The researchers were addressing possible alternative effectiveness measures in addition to the indexes described earlier.

Problems

The development of the monitoring system has not been without problems. In particular there is no universally accepted definition of recovery from alcoholism. The vagaries of the concept of rehabilitation as recognized by those involved in treatment programs contribute significantly to the evaluation problem.

For example, a number of possible client changes are viewed as desirable. The complete abstinence from drinking is considered as the sole measure of client improvement by some, whereas others strive for a reduced level of alcohol consumption, improvement in client behavior, employment, and family situation, or other indicators of return to normal functioning.

The monitoring system used accommodates the varied definitions of treatment success by providing several client outcome measures.

Client Follow-up Studies

Further work at the federal level includes the study of clients over a period

Table 12-2
NIAAA Alcoholism Treatment Monitoring System, Report III/M – Client Changes, Period Ending September 1974

TREATMENT CENTER–ALL CENTERS
STATE–ALL STATES
REGION–000

PAGE NO. 45

	NUMBER OF CLIENTS	AT INTAKE	60 DAYS AFTER INTAKE	180 DAYS AFTER INTAKE
ABSOLUTE ALCOHOL CONSUMED / DAY (OZS.)	2,451	5.3	.8	1.2
IMPAIRMENT (0–33)	2,412	11.3	2.9	3.4
DAYS DRANK LAST MONTH	2,434	13.6	3.5	4.8
DAYS WORKED LAST MONTH	2,442	12.1	11.4	13.6
INCOME EARNED LAST MONTH	2,322	$ 378	$ 352	$ 422
UNEMPLOYED (PERCENT)	2,003	35.6%	29.2%	20.9%
ABSTAINED (PERCENT)	2,434	15.7%	66.2%	57.4%

in order to determine their condition following various treatment services. Specifically, the National Institute on Alcohol Abuse and Alcoholism has sponsored a research project to contact a selected sample of over 2,000 persons from the group served by ATCs one year previously. Individuals treated, including dropouts, are being sought out and interviewed by the local projects under supervision of professional interviewers. Resultant findings should provide the basis for program and policy direction. Information regarding treatment outcome for clients with varied characteristics and lengths of stay in the program are being sought. Additionally, information regarding the types of treatment received and the staff disciplines involved in client service will be determined from the current data base. Factual information regarding optimum program structure and costs to serve the various client types is expected as a study outcome.

A second objective of this study is to provide more information regarding the reasons clients drop out of treatment programs and perhaps to derive better means for their retention.

The state of Texas is conducting a follow-up study of clients treated for alcoholism in state hospitals. It involves interviewing samples of 900 persons released from hospitals in 1971 and 900 released in 1973. The 1973 group receive an interview on release and another one a year later. The major purpose of the study is to determine the effectiveness of the state aftercare program.

Other states including Washington and Iowa have recently performed longitudinal studies of client treatment effects.

State Data Systems

Many of the states are involved in the development of data systems for alcoholism data gathering and evaluation. The National Institute on Alcohol Abuse and Alcoholism is working through the Council of State and Territorial Alcoholism Authorities to provide needed technical assistance and other resources to help and to coordinate the effort nationally.

The use of common data elements and definitions regarding alcoholism treatment programs throughout the nation is one goal of the assistance program. The potential for greater exchange of evaluative information, expansion of data bases, and reduction of duplication in reporting are other benefits to be expected.

Prevention

The prevention function is receiving an increasing emphasis among those concerned with alcoholism. Prevention, of course, provides the greatest hope for success in solving the alcoholism problem. Among the evaluative programs in action, nationwide surveys conducted by NIAAA are providing significant information regarding the prevalence of drinking and the patterns of drinking among the different segments of society. The changes in attitudes of the public as a result of prevention activities has been discernible. Changes have been initiated in NIAAA prevention programs and the NIAAA media campaign has been improved due to survey findings.

State and Local Evaluation

The numbers of systems devoted to evaluation related to alcoholism at the nonfederal level are too numerous to list. Many of these systems have provided a wealth of client-oriented data directly pertaining to alcoholism problems, while others also cover mental health and sometimes other drug problems.

Specific ongoing systems directed to the local management and treatment scene include the "multistate information system" implemented in a number of states; the states of Iowa, Kentucky, Texas, Florida, Minnesota, California, and others have developed individual state systems.

NIAAA has initiated a study of the impact of Formula Grant funds provided to states under Public Law 91-616. That study should result in a system design that will provide monitoring of state alcoholism programs in terms of Formula Grant impact over time. The immediate work includes a pretest of monitoring system data collection in three pilot states.

There are numerous local evaluation systems, ranging in scope from single project, in-house studies, to centralized, on-line, computerized evaluation systems. One major factor differentiating these evaluation efforts from those at a higher organizational level is their invariable devotion to individual case study and the timeliness of data availability. The detail of data and its applicability to local objectives also are prime considerations.

Conclusions

Only a brief overview of the current state of evaluation efforts in the study of alcoholism and in the evaluation of alcoholism programs is presented here. The number and quality of those efforts, however, lend optimism to those searching for improved means of meeting the alcoholism problem in this country.

The fact that there are several levels of evaluative activity with different objectives at each level provides greater support to the evaluation function as a management entity. It is expected that the current emphasis in treatment evaluation will be expanded into personnel training and will be increased in the areas of prevention and research. A concerted effort by NIAAA and by state authorities should provide an added thrust to evaluation of alcoholism programs and contribute to program improvement.

Notes

1. Jessor, R. et al., *Society, Personality, and Deviant Behavior*, Holt, Rinehart, and Winston, New York, 1968, pp. 166-170, 483-486.
2. Shelton, J.; Hollister, L.; and Gocka, E., "Quantifying Alcoholic Impairment," *Modern Medicine*, pp. 188-189 (Nov. 17, 1969).

13

Federal Evaluation and Project Performance

Selma J. Mushkin

Two things are considered in this chapter: (1) methods of slowing down applications of evaluations on basic resource allocation policies, and (2) methods of accelerating project evaluations that can provide in substance an experimental base for better understanding of methods and processes on specific drug projects.

Military Mission Evaluations and Civilian Policies

Is it possible simultaneously to accelerate efforts to evaluate projects and yet slow down application of evaluative studies of broad policy issues? In pursuit of this question differences between general military evaluative efforts and those in the civilian sector appear to offer some guidance. The comparison, it should be noted, is not between military drug evaluation studies and those in the civilian sector but between evaluation of military missions and methods of defense and federal social program evaluations. Earlier, in an article for *Evaluation* magazine, I noted a number of reasons why I believe it is necessary to slow down policy applications of civilian sector evaluations.[1] Among those reasons was the lack of basic knowledge about the cause of program interactions, about methods of dealing with programs that have interlocked and interdependent benefits and deficiencies in analytical methodology. Improvements are indicated in factor analysis and regression analysis when applied to evaluation.

One process suggested was an independent review panel of experts to pass on the validity of evaluation. It is not a new process. It was used in connection with the Coleman report.[2] F. Mosteller and D.P. Moynihan brought together a distinguished group to assess and publicly comment on the Coleman report on inequality.[3]

In its report that group sought to further the analysis in the Coleman study and to make the findings available to others concerned with achievement of equality of educational opportunity. Commenting on the task force undertaking, Mosteller and Moynihan noted: "What had been expected to be rather a specialized undertaking soon attracted widespread interest . . . . Here was a subject of such inherent intellectual and social interest as to challenge the best of minds." In their professional judgments the review supported the work that had been done. "On reexamination we find [the Coleman study] does not confirm all of the reported findings . . . but they confirm many of them and just as importantly they establish new parameters of what is likely to be true about education . . . ."

An independent review panel is one method, but it also has its drawbacks. It is essentially an outside process apart from decision making. It provides a study rather than a course for action. Given the state of the art, it is more likely to result as did the Mosteller-Moynihan review in a recommendation for more study, a process that leads the policy official essentially to question the usefulness of evaluation and reevaluation to his own decision-making processes.

The National Science Foundation, through its Research Applied to National Needs (RANN) program, followed a similar process in meeting what it identified as a need for a study of the kind produced by Harvey Averch and others for the Commission on School Finance.[4] In that case it was an evaluation of elementary and secondary school evaluations.

The RANN support of evaluations for a series of designated areas of public concern represents a step toward a process of outside review. RANN called uniformly for assessment of work done in terms of scientific validity, external uniformity of findings, and policy relevance. The studies announced initially in 1973 will be a review of the state of the evaluation art on selected topics that bear on policy. But again the evaluations will be apart from government, without the involvement of the government, and in the strength of its isolation from government it may also find it is removed from the realities of governments, or even, in its isolation, produce an environment hostile to change.

A different model is provided by evaluation in the Department of Defense of military issues. It is a model that yields much dialogue, testing, research, reassessment, and multiple reviews prior to application. Yet, it is of government, produced both in-house and out without the fanfare that has accompanied some civilian sector reports such as the Jencks study.[5] Surprisingly there appears to be more scientific prodding and questioning in the military system than is currently built into the civilian sector evaluations.

May I hasten to add that I am not an expert on military evaluation. The brief exposure that I have had to discussions about military program evaluations suggests, however, that it may prove useful to examine this model. Some of the differences between the military effort and the civilian one are these:

1.   Evaluation appears to be built into operations and budget decision at each of many administrative levels. Some evaluation at the military base feeds up through the chain of command to the secretary's office of each of the forces and in addition there is the overseeing role of the secretary of defense's office. Some examples exist of multilayer evaluations in civilian activities, but these are few. Perhaps the drug abuse prevention evaluations of individual projects and treatment modalities come closest to the military command post study. Such examples in the civilian sector are few in number. Generally, the evaluation done is of the single study type. The notion of a hierarchy of evaluative efforts is not adopted as an operational procedure.

2. Evaluation and analysis are by now so imbedded into the practices of military administrative structures that it would be difficult to sort out the analytical resources applied. In the civilian sector each evaluation is a precious thing, or nearly so. In the case of evaluation studies on drug treatment rehabilitation and education, it is possible to count up evaluation projects and dollars as if these studies were separate and apart and not a piece of ongoing administrative action. Some 29 evaluation projects are funded by nine agencies in amounts from $5,000 to $1.2 million. Some $5.7 million is being devoted federally to drug evaluations and this is probably the total sum for the nation. Much of this expenditure is isolated as it were from costing of activities, selection of processes and program methods, and making budget decisions. The role of the Special Action Office for Drug Abuse Prevention as a temporary agency in fostering and funding research and the current redesign even prior to 1975 with its greater measure of responsibility for the National Institute of Drug Abuse (NIDA) perhaps contributed to some of the isolation of evaluation from administration.

3. Evaluation outlays appear to be relatively high in the military. Given the many layers and kinds of activities involved—for example, training on campuses, on-the-job instruction—it is hard to identify the full range of costs for evaluation and analysis. In the civilian sector, estimates have been made that suggest evaluation expenditures of approximately $120 million—some of which is obtained from earmarked funds of one percent of appropriations authorized by statute for selected DHEW programs such as elementary and secondary education. This $120 million for evaluation is the equivalent of less than one-tenth of one percent of civilian sector expenditures. By way of contrast the evaluation effort for drug prevention and control is larger, deficient as it is. The $5.9 million reported as the amount set aside for drug evaluation studies is the equivalent of nine-tenths of one percent of the $690 million outlays in 1974 for drug control and drug prevention.

4. Perhaps the most important difference between military and civilian evaluations is the recognition given in military evaluations to the many components of evaluation as separate parts, each to be assessed and reviewed. In place of a single composite evaluation of evaluations that is characteristic of those few civilian efforts that have been subject to reassessment, in the military case it is not unusual to examine components separately or even part of components of assessment. For example, reexamination of statements of mission or of purpose might be the subject of one assessment, adequacy of criteria and comprehensiveness of coverage of those criteria might be still another. Cost analysis—its methods, data base, coverage of cost components, discount rates—is subject to review in the detail of one or another of the topics that necessarily are part of the analysis. The concern in cost reassessment is for adequacy of documentation of information elements, method of calculation, adequacy of samples, and statistical significance of the data. Review again need not encompass all the cost components, it is sufficient to reexamine a component

and, if need be, question that component. Similarly, benefit or effectiveness measurements are not simple "facts." The measurements have a conceptual framework, depend upon different methods of fact gathering, and are grouped and priced under a variety of assumed conditions and projected by use of different techniques. Again, each of these may be subject to assessment, not as part of an overall evaluation but as a segment of an evaluative activity. Uncertainty further requires quantification and again a variety of assumptions and methods can be used and review may be restricted to some phase of the evaluation rather than to the whole of it. Consequences of recognizing components of evaluation, and, if need be, limiting evaluation to components or parts of such components are: (a) in-depth examination of some part of the program or activity, and (b) encouragement of a dialogue on evaluation and, where feasible, testing of results.

5. The encouragement to dialogue and restudy is that part of the model of the military assessment that warrants full consideration. When evaluations are done and reassessed, the conversation about mission, criteria, cost, methods of assessing effectiveness, and quantification of uncertainties all become possible steps for discussion. The more each of these phases of evaluation are worked on, the more specific and technical in a sense becomes the conversation; factors determining the operation of the activity or program come to be understood more fully and, importantly, questions that are not already answered come to be identified. In the civilian sector the conversation is often shallow, the basis for judgment weak, and many questions important to understanding an activity or policy are not raised.

6. In the military evaluation and analysis have had top support over a substantial period. Former Secretary of Defense McNamara's enthusiasm for quantification and analysis clearly left its imprint, an imprint that was reenforced by the support given to the Rand Corporation by the Air Force. While the bureaucracy of the armed forces hardly was enthusiastic for the new look injected by the analysts at the outset, over the years there has developed a routine of evaluation that is now paying off in new support both from the systems analyst who is now Secretary of Defense as well as from some of the "old liners."

There are other differences, some of which make it simpler to perform evaluations in the military sector. Many of the questions are essentially restricted to relevant costs on methods of providing, for example, a helioport; the cost analyses involve fairly straightforward engineering problems; human behavior and human reaction and responses are not critical to the analytical effort. In the civilian programs, however, many of the questions concern human response, personal behavior, and methods of identifying and determining response. The basic data required have been lacking; part of what evaluation is engaged in is conversion of experience hopefully in a controlled experiment. A basis is set for learning about some of those responses for which science now has a few answers.

There have been new questions raised in the military process as a consequence of analysis but the extent of this is far more restricted in many ways than it is in the civilian area; it becomes clear that we need to know even about biological and physiological processes. A start must be made in understanding those basic scientific questions for which scientific research methods are more readily available. The way in which a drug works on brain cells or cell membranes is an example of a research question whose answer could contribute greatly to the way in which programs are formulated and pursued. Do heroin addicts have some abnormal function in their brain cells? Are these abnormalities caused by heroin use, or do they contribute to use of heroin? Such problems over the gamut of civilian issues raise thousands of questions for which ready answers are not at hand. Yet, the issues are highly relevant to policy formulation in the civilian sector.

The military is not without its difficulties, as the body count problem with its impact on the Viet Nam war and public reaction illustrates. In commenting on the McNamara effort, Donald Campbell noted, "We want to avoid the mistakes he made, and we want to recognize that whenever we set up an official indicator, we may be doing evil things to the social process."[6] He illuminated the problem by referring to the reports of enemy casualties out of South Viet Nam. The introduction of the body count, Campbell noted, created a goal in addition to or instead of holding territory. There was now a goal of having bodies to count. As Campbell put it, "Poor Lt. Calley was engaged in getting bodies to count for the weekly brag sheet."

The Drug Evaluation Case

Compared to other programs, drug abuse has received more attention in evaluation studies. Great emphasis has been placed on evaluation, however, only over the past several years. Evaluation is sought for the following reasons:

1. To define the needs for and size of resource commitment
2. To provide guidance on selection of methods of treatment
3. To facilitate choices between prevention, treatment, and control
4. To assist in determining division of responsibilities among governments

Evaluation, as the term is used here, is intended to be an assessment of program and policy impacts for those policies or programs already in operation. It is distinguished from the term policy or program analysis in that it is after the fact rather than ex ante. Evaluation in this definitive framework becomes a potential datum for policy analysis.

The importance given to evaluation originates in the conclusion reached earlier that traditional methods and programs of the past for preventing individuals from becoming heroin addicts and treating the known addict were noteworthy mainly for their lack of success. When the Special Action Office for Drug Abuse Prevention (SAODAP) was established in 1972, the expectation was stepped up for an improved evaluation structure through which specific modalities would be assessed as a component of a policy research design. On the one hand, the new law called for the development by SAODAP of a national strategy for drug abuse prevention; on the other, it set the stage for the monitoring of on-going programs and the collection of information on (1) the size of the addict population and their characteristics and (2) the ongoing methods and projects for treatment and rehabilitation, including size, staffing, services, person served, and other project elements.

Size and Priorities in the Resource
Commitment to Evaluation

The 1975 budget called for expenditures for drug control and prevention of $754 million. The proposed outlays looked to a larger rise in outlays for crime control than those for preventive activities. Indeed, the recommended levels of research and evaluation were lower in 1975 than what was estimated for 1974; $73.5 million in 1975 as compared with $77.9 million in 1974.

A total of $460.2 million in federal funds was for treatment and prevention. The federal government finances treatment for three-quarters of the drug abuser population. In 1975, while hard data are lacking, probably a sum 1.5 times the federal total or $690 million would be spent by federal, state, and local agencies.

The estimates are not differentiated by type of drug. We found earlier it was not possible from existing data to answer the question: What is being spent on control and prevention of "hard" drugs.[7]

The president, in his 1975 budget message, placed much emphasis on managing for program results with a focus on accomplishments and not just actions. The cut-offs of drug education programs reflects a response to the concern about equating resource commitments and accomplishments.

Expenditures that are available for drug prevention are made by many federal agencies. The principal agencies are DHEW and its constituent National Institute of Mental Health, the Veterans Administration, the Department of Defense, and the Department of Justice.

In an earlier study made for the National Commission on Marihuana and Drug Abuse, we identified some 30 grant programs through which support goes forward for drug control and prevention from the national government to the states and localities. Among the aids that may be applied to aid drug prevention efforts are grants for vocational rehabilitation and for juvenile delinquency prevention, the proposed community development grants to be administered by the Department of Housing and Urban Development. Also, more general types of federal assistance could be used for services to drug abusers or training of

personnel and management staffs. Among these are the public employment program, the Intergovernmental Personnel Act, Title IV-A of the Social Security
Act, and the manpower grants administered by the Department of Labor.

Nature and Problems in Drug Prevention
Evaluations

Evaluation studies cover differing aspects of drug abuse prevention—including follow-up studies, use of data systems (such as CODAP) for evaluation,
staffing of clinics, and analysis of criteria for measuring project "success." Perhaps the largest effort is the evaluation that is being done independently by two
different research groups—the School of Hygiene and Public Health at Johns
Hopkins University and the Planning Research Corporation. Much was expected
from this major evaluation. It was expected to fill a void, because up to the
time of the Johns Hopkins assessment evaluation efforts had been largely ad hoc
attempts at evaluating individual programs with little or no comparability or
agreement on definition of criteria. By facilitating the development and standardization of a set of criteria, SAODAP intended to assist evaluators in estimating
the effectiveness of drug abuse treatment and rehabilitation. Since all treatment
and rehabilitation modalities are essentially experimental, a single comprehensive evaluation system is needed to make the comparative analysis of various programs with similar objectives not only easier and more productive, but realistically possible for the first time.
    In spite of the emphasis on evaluation in drug abuse prevention programs,
efforts at the project level and on comparative data among projects for program
design purposes are frustrated by many factors. Some of the factors are characteristic of project evaluations generally, some are specific to the characteristics
of drug abuse.
    As with many other social program evaluations, methodology is inadequate.
The shortcomings indicate the need for more research on methods suitable for
evaluation. What has been happening is that an existing research methodology—
experiments, longitudinal survey, factor analysis, regressions—has come to be
applied to policy and program issues without first considering what specific
method would lend itself to analysis for political decision making.

    Autonomy of Evaluation Efforts: There exists in the field of drug abuse
education, prevention, control, treatment, and rehabilitation activities, a legion
of highly skilled, knowledgeable, well-intentioned, and deeply committed people.
Each of these persons has focused his efforts on one particular program or one
particular aspect of the drug abuse problem—generally to the exclusion of all
others. The vested interests, biases, prejudices, short-sightedness, and honest
convictions of those closely associated with programs may reduce objectivity of

monitoring or evaluation. It has been observed that the professional person who initiates a program has a deep interest in evaluating the program, only if he is relatively certain that the program is a success. This involvement in the program gives evidence of his enthusiasm and without that enthusiasm much of what is attained could not be. Yet, at the same time, this very involvement stands in the way of objectivity.

Compliance Control: Evaluation, like all other human activities, must face the constraints of limited fiscal resources. It must depend partly—often largely—on those persons working within the project to provide essential information and perspective. Given the incentives for persons working in particular programs or projects to bias or block evaluation efforts, the agency charged with evaluation must have the legislative authority to obtain information. Compulsory compliance forced upon project administrators and staff will probably not yield useful results in terms of subsequent action. Half-hearted or counterproductive efforts forced out of program or project staff is not the goal of compliance control. The goal of the evaluating agency should be a cooperative effort with a substantial and fair hearing of the ideas and opinions of those within the program. The knowledge that deliberate lack of a cooperative effort may result in an evaluation report biased against the program should be incentive for program personnel to provide necessary data. This all suggests that the structure of the evaluation function must be hierarchical, involving persons from the project level on up with adequate shares of program data accessibility and evaluation objectivity.

Dynamic Character: The drug abuse evaluation is a process in research experimentation and program development. Development is a dynamic process and to attempt to analyze it with static assumptions or definitions would be patently unproductive. While structuring a system to study and define output measures for current programs, it is important to build into that structure the capability for change. As more becomes known about the nature of the drug problem, new program goals and objectives will be defined and old ones abandoned. Changes may not come in large quantum jumps, but rather in small realignments, resulting from new knowledge, new perceptions, and a broader understanding of the problem and its potential solutions. For example, the trend in the way society at large views the drug abuse problem seems to indicate a measure of decriminalization over time. This will certainly affect goals and objectives in law enforcement programs. Additionally, the debate as to what constitutes rehabilitation of the addict is far from settled and, if there is ever any consensus, it will have an enormous effect on the output criteria applied to treatment and rehabilitation programs.

Data and Staff Resources: Trained evaluators are in short supply. The lack of knowledge and expertise on the part of program managers makes it difficult to carry out good evaluative studies. One consequence of lack of trained personnel is the change in the nature of the "treatments" that are being evaluated so that the conditions under assessment are changing.

Further lack of relevant data poses a general yet critical problem in evaluation. Data components required to match criteria are frequently hard to define and when defined may point to new data gathering efforts.

In the case of drug abuse evaluation is made far more difficult by:

1. The deep commitment of project directors to the work that is ongoing
2. The lack of record keeping or carelessness in such record keeping
3. The gaps between statement and performance
4. The difficulties of defining treatment modalities in a consistent way
5. The characteristic lying and deception of the drug abuser that impacts on methods of prevention and project administration
6. The illicit trading by project staff that is encouraged by market prices
7. The lack of laboratory controls, for example, in urinalysis

To carry out a technical assistance role, trained staff is needed that can aid the states and localities in designing and carrying out programs. Technical assistance required is both programmatic and managerial. Three solutions are offered as methods optional to providing technical assistance: (a) formation of another agency or office entity for the purpose; (b) in-house agency training to pass on information directly from federal agencies to states; (c) use of private consulting firms. In any case, shortages of trained staff need to be overcome by new recruitment and by staff training. Various organizations to carry out training are feasible and should be explored, including special training programs designed by the Civil Service Commission for this purpose, and use of specially designed programs of training.

Important Division in Responsibility Among Governments: Only a small beginning has been made at evaluation of program performance targeted at the process of division of responsibility between levels of government—federal, state, local.

The effectiveness of efforts by state and local governments and by the federal government to control and treat drug abuse in the United States has been hampered by a lack of coordination among the states, between states and localities, among the federal government, states, and localities and throughout the federal establishment.[8]

Present intergovernmental relations are characterized by fragmentation that gives rise to problems that may be outlined somewhat as follows:

1. Multiple Price Incentives: The 30-odd programs that finance drug abuse activities carry different price tags. SAODAP has authority to set a single non-federal share but the authority has not been used.

2. High Information Costs: When a state or local government decides to act on drug abuse, it faces a series of choices about what to do, how to do it, how to finance it, how to approach the problem of securing funds, and initially, of course, how to inquire about getting federal aid.

Costs of investigation rise as the number of federal grant programs tangentially related to drug abuse increase. Drug abuse prevention is a conglomeration of many policies and activities. Service provisions such as medical care, education, vocational rehabilitation, manpower training, and employment exchanges, as well as facility support, manpower training aids for professional and paraprofessional and governmental employees are part of drug abuse control activities—especially where intergovernmental programs are involved. Costs of obtaining information about these programs include: (a) the cost of search for aid support; (b) the cost of applying for eligible projects; (c) the cost of counsel for negotiation regarding compliance with requests for revisions, and review by state and local officials; and (d) costs of information relevant to project design, that is, the understanding of what works for whom, under what conditions, and with what certainty.

The search for funds has led to new institutional arrangements. Federal-state grant coordinators, men-in-Washington, and independent consultants have emerged to assist state and local governments in applying for federal assistance.

3. Multiple Grant Criteria: SAODAP was given broad authority far exceeding that of other granting agencies, including responsibility for promulgating uniform criteria, procedures, and forms for grant or contract application. When the director so determined, technical grant or contract requirements could be waived if there were inconsistencies among the requirements of federal agencies.

A detailed examination and costing of search and application procedures would greatly contribute to an understanding of present problems and perhaps point the way to their remedy. Federal resolution of the cost issue is complicated by the special needs and institutional arrangements in the community or state. Service packaging to meet particular community needs can best be done locally when the technical assistance from the national government is available to answer questions about experience elsewhere, on alternative program designs, both in terms of cost and effectiveness. Fund authority combinations and grant packaging are most efficiently accomplished by the federal government.

4. Administrative Cost Overhang: High administrative costs are one byproduct of the fragmentation of multiple grant-in-aid provisions. Application costs alone are so high that one wonders how many grants are made in amounts totaling less than the economic costs of obtaining the grant in the first place. In many instances, costs are also high for the federal agencies in reviewing the grant applications. Under existing grant-in-aid provisions, small sums often are paid in small amounts to many governments and other community organizations. These aids sometimes number in the hundreds for a single grant authority. Of the various programs, the one resulting in the largest number of separate projects was the Drug Education Program administered by the Office of Education of DHEW. Under that program 800 minigrants were awarded in fiscal year 1972; the legislation permits minigrants to be made in amounts under $5,000. The average grant under this program amounts to about $2,500 per school district.

In summary, evaluation, in the case of drug abuse, must contend with multilevels of government and with both private and public participation in carrying out the program. The legislation that set up SAODAP authorized a multiplicity and flexibility in aid from the national government to the state and local governments. (Much of the authority is that sought by other federal programs, including joint funding and packaging of aids). By and large, however, this authority has not been used. But, in its use lies the means of strengthening programs and providing ready access to evaluation findings for those who would be responsive to those findings.

There is much thought that the incremental use of heroin is on the down turn; that the peak has been reached. However, the problem of providing relief for those still addicted remains. Dickens had a way of posing the problem: national prosperity was the issue. ". . . isn't this a prosperous nation," Mr. M'Choakumchild asked, and a student replied, "I thought I couldn't know whether it was a prosperous nation or not, unless I knew who had got the money, and whether any of it was mine." And pressing the point, ". . . I thought," the student said, "it must be just as hard upon those who were starved, whether the others were a million or a million million."[9]

Notes

1. Mushkin, Selma J. "Evaluations: Use with Caution." *Evaluation*, 1 (2): 31-36, 1973.
2. Coleman, J.S. et al. *Equality of Educational Opportunity*. Washington, D.C.: U.S. Government Printing Office, 1966.
3. Mosteller, F. and Moynihan, D.P. (Eds.) *On Equality of Educational Opportunity*. New York: Vintage Books, 1972.
4. National Science Foundation. Program Announcement. Research Applied to National Needs. NSF 73-4, 1973; Averch, H.A. et al. *How Effective is Schooling? A Critical Review and Synthesis of Research Findings*. Santa Monica, California: The Rand Corporation, 1972.

5. Jencks, C. *Inequality: Reassessment of the Effect of Family and School-ing in America*. Scranton, Pennsylvania: Basic Books, 1972.

6. Salasin, S. "Experimentation Revisited: A Conversation with Donald T. Campbell." *Evaluation*, 1 (3): 7–13, 1973.

7. Mushkin, S.J.; Surmeier, J.; Kane, J. and Detling, D. "Federal Funding and Intergovernmental Coordination for Drug Addiction Programs." *Drug Use in America: Problem in Perspective*. Washington, D.C.: U.S. Government Printing Office, 1973. Appendix to Volume II.

8. Drug Abuse Office and Treatment Act of 1972, Public Law 92-255, Sec. 101 (7).

9. Dickens, Charles. *Hard Times*. London: Chapman and Hall, (undated).

14

Process and Outcome Measurement Using Goal Attainment Scaling

Thomas J. Kiresuk and Sander H. Lund

In a 1973 *Evaluation* monograph[1] describing the origin and nature of "goal attainment scaling," the similarity of management and evaluation systems to scientific theory building was explored. It was proposed that, in an organizational sense, "management by objectives" is an informal analogue to theory construction, since the ultimate dedications of management and the basic postulates of science both represent self-evident truths to which all subsequent statements must relate. Moreover, both approaches require empirical, objective, and (in the case of management science) pragmatic indicators to confirm a given set of propositions. This means that appropriate outcome measures can form an empirical base for validation of the "theory" of each particular organization. The coincidental development of management by objectives, along with pressure for empirical verification of both treatment effectiveness and particular explanations of mental illness, strongly influenced the general nature of outcome measurement in Hennepin County.

Over the years Hennepin County Mental Health Service had been moving toward an evaluation system that would provide a rational, coherent, and logically consistent explanatory and descriptive network of narrative and quantitative statements—statements that would take into account the definitions and dedications of the organization and serve as criteria for the effectiveness and efficiency of its activities. The evaluation mechanism itself involved using management and clinical data to influence subsequent goal setting and goal attainment in a continuous feedback cycle. Of this total system, the topic

The content of this chapter is drawn from a program evaluation system developed at Hennepin County Mental Health Service, Minneapolis, Minnesota. The system is the product of a collaboration between the Mental Health Service and the Program Evaluation Project (funded by the National Institute of Mental Health's Mental Health Services Development Branch, Howard Davis, Ph.D., director), and has benefitted from the work of many outstanding individuals. Particularly valuable have been the contributions of Dean Beaulieu, Ph.D., of the Outpatient Unit, and Zigfrids Stelmachers, Ph.D., of the Crisis Intervention Center. The evaluation mechanism itself is the result of 14 years of effort and is embedded in a management information system developed under the direction of Robert Sherman, Ph.D., with recent innovations by James Baxter. William Jepson, M.D., program director of the Mental Health Service, has described this system in his recent paper "Operational Statistics" presented at a Workshop on Management Information Systems sponsored by the Boston Regional Office of DHEW, Manchester, N.H., March 15, 1974. Dr. Jepson, together with Robert Reinkober, Hospital Administrator, has also made central contributions in the area of planning, programming, and budgeting systems (PPBS) and in providing the support necessary to maintain the evaluation.

of this chapter is restricted to process measurement. Actual working documents from the Mental Health Service are used to illustrate the nature, use, and probable future of process measurement in the system.

The definition of "process" used in this chapter should be clarified. In psychotherapy *process* is often taken to mean a systematic recording of all psycho-dynamically significant events that occur during the therapy hour. The term is also used to indicate an enumeration of all activities performed in order to achieve an outcome or result. Examples of the later usage would be "number of visits" and "number of unduplicated patient counts." A. Donabedian and J. Zusman[2] have defined process to indicate activities that have relevance to quality of care. Using this definition a variable such as "number of patient visits" would have to be related to some other qualifier ("number of psychoanalytic visits per patient," for example) to be properly considered a form of process measurement. The key to this definition is the presumed or established relationship of the process variable to the outcome of treatment.

Donabedian's[3] definition places process within an analysis of causality, "an unbroken chain of antecedent means followed by intermediate ends which are themselves the means to still further ends." His definition includes such considerations as "appropriateness of treatment," "justification of diagnosis and treatment," "technical competence," and so forth.

The thesis of this chapter is that the inclusion of process content into the goal attainment method of measurement, as used by the Hennepin County Mental Health Service Outpatient Unit, is compatible with this definition. The goal attainment method was conceived originally as a means of making mental health therapy subject to measurement. Since the process activities of the organization were already well documented, the main emphasis of the technique was focused on outcome determination. However, by including such indicators as "number of visits" within the scales of a program level follow-up guide, process variables were transformed into outcome goals and the cycle between process and outcome became complete. While this linkage brings about conceptual closure, we believe its ultimate and lasting value may be in a potential to use process information in determination of standards in the quality of services delivered.

The Hennepin County Mental Health Service is located in a downtown public general hospital, less than one mile from a state university. When the evaluation project began, the mental health service consisted of approximately 100 staff, who served about 5,000 patients and other clients per year. The service had these subunits: inpatient, outpatient, day hospital, child care, medication maintenance, social rehabilitation, and consultation and education. Since then a crisis intervention unit has been added. The treatment staff included psychiatrists, psychologists, social workers, allied health specialists, and students of all disciplines. Treatment philosophies and corresponding definitions of mental health varied accordingly. The patients were of all ages and all diagnostic categories, of both sexes, and from both middle and lower socioeconomic levels.

Initially, the Mental Health Service implemented a basic data collection
system. This was followed, in sequence, by (1) a means of assessing treatment
outcomes, (2) a formal management information system, (3) a cost-finding and
rate-setting procedure, and (4) a more detailed and meaningful data definition
system. All of this has been linked with the planning, programming, and
budgeting system required by county administration. In addition, random
clinical trials comparing various treatments and therapists have been permanent-
ly incorporated into the administration of the outpatient unit.

Table 14-1 shows a *goal attainment follow-up guide* selected from the
clinical evaluation system at Hennepin County. It was intended to provide a
basis for evaluating the services provided a client of the Mental Health Service's
crisis intervention unit.

Five problem areas were important for the client, and a brief description of
each was used as the heading for an individual scale. The outcome levels for the
scales were then written to indicate how each problem would be affected by
treatment. Some scales were written with the patient's involvement; others were
selected by the clinician alone. The expected level on the first scale, "education," was derived for this patient and indicates that some practical steps would
be taken by the patient, but would be taken with some ambivalence. The
range of outcomes on either side of the expected outcome were also developed
with the client's particular problem in mind. The reasoning behind the outcome selection went as follows: Given this patient, with her background, environment, abilities, liabilities, and hopes for the future, and given the capabilities
of our treatment staff to handle such cases (as well as the current state of knowledge), what can we expect her to be doing, to be like, at the time of follow-up.

Because the scales were weighted relative to one another, any set of values
could be used. The check marks indicate the clinician's estimate of the client's
status at the time the follow-up guide was constructed. The astericks indicate
the scoring by the follow-up worker. Using the formula developed by R. Sherman,[4] a summary goal attainment score was produced for the patient. Also,
comparing the intake with the follow-up score provided an estimate of the
change that took place during treatment.

The *goal attainment score* is basically an average of the outcome levels ad-
justed for (1) the number of scales, (2) the weight of the scales, and (3) the
intercorrelation of the scales. A modified formula has been developed by
Sherman to accommodate sets of outcome scores, an application particularly
relevant to summaries of process measures.[5]

Figure 14-1 shows a distribution of goal attainment scores calculated for
the first 402 patients followed up at Hennepin County Mental Health Service.
As can be seen, the distribution is symmetrical, with a mean of 51.90
and a standard deviation of about 10.00. The "X's" along the bottom
are the scores of a particular therapist. From this smaller distribution
one can discern the stabilization of a mean of his performace. If the sample of patients is randomly allocated, Figure 14-2 presents the therapist

Table 14-1
Goal Attainment Follow-up Guide

Sample Clinical Guide: Crisis Intervention Center
Program Evaluation Project

Check whether or not the scale has been mutually negotiated between patient and CIC interviewer.

Scale Attainment Levels	Scale Headings and Scale Weights				
	Scale 1: Education Yes X No ___ (w₁=20)	Scale 2: Suicide Yes ___ No X (w₂=30)	Scale 3: Manipulation Yes ___ No X (w₃=25)	Scale 4: Drug Abuse Yes X No ___ (w₄=30)	Scale 5: Dependency on CIC Yes X No ___ (w₅=10)
a. Most unfavorable treatment outcome thought likely (-2)	Patient has made no attempt to enroll in high school.	Patient has committed suicide.	Patient makes rounds of community service agencies demanding medication, and refuses other forms of treatment.	Patient reports addiction to "hard narcotics" (heroin, morphine).	Patient has contacted CIC by telephone or in person at least seven times since his first visit.
b. Less than expected success with treatment (-1)	Patient has enrolled in high school, but at time of follow-up has dropped out. √	Patient has acted on at least one suicidal impulse since her first contact with the CIC, but has not succeeded.	Patient no longer visits CIC with demands for medication but continues with other community agencies and still refuses other forms of treatment.	Patient has used "hard narcotics," but is not addicted, and/or uses hallucinogens (LSD, pot) more than four times a month. √	Patient has contacted CIC 5-6 times since intake.
c. Expected level of treatment success (0)	Patient has enrolled, and is in school at follow-up, but is attending class sporadically (misses an average of more than a third of her classes during a week). *	Patient reports she has had at least four suicidal impulses since her first contact with the CIC but has not acted on any of them. √	Patient no longer attempts to manipulate for drugs at community service agencies, but will not accept another form of treatment. *	Patient has not used "hard narcotics" during follow-up period, and uses hallucinogens between 1-4 times a month. *	Patient has contacted CIC 3-4 times since intake. √
d. More than expected success with treatment (+1)	Patient has enrolled, is in school at follow-up, and is attending classes consistently, but has no vocational goals.	Patient reports she had no suicidal impulses since her first contact with the CIC. *	Patient accepts nonmedication treatment at some community agency.	Patient uses hallucinogens less than once a month.	
e. Best anticipated success with treatment (+2)	Patient has enrolled, is in school at follow-up, is attending classes consistently, and has some vocational goal.	Patient reports she has had no suicidal impulses since her first contact with the CIC.	Patient accepts nonmedication treatment, and by own report shows signs of improvement.	At time of follow-up, patient is not using any illegal drugs.	Patient has not contacted CIC since intake. *

Level at intake: √
Level at Follow-up: *
Level at Intake: 29.4
Goal Attainment Score (Level at Follow-up):   62.2
Goal Attainment Change Score: +32.8

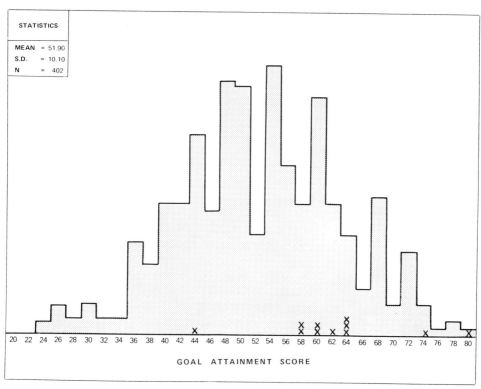

STATISTICS

MEAN = 51.90
S.D. = 10.10
N = 402

GOAL ATTAINMENT SCORE

The "X's" indicate the distribution of one therapist's Goal Attainment Scores.

Figure 14-1. Distribution of Goal Attainment Scores for the First 402 Patients Followed Up

with a comparison of his performance relative to that of the balance of the treatment staff.

One method of assessing the relevancy, appropriateness, and completeness of a follow-up guide is to subject its content to systematic audit. Such an audit could be performed by review committees, other professionals, or consumer advocates. At Hennepin County a procedure has been established to determine the degree of agreement between the intake worker who constructed the follow-up guide and the therapist who ultimately accepted the client for treatment. The questions asked were: (1) Are the scales relevant? (2) Are the scales realistic? (3) Would you modify the scale weights? (4) Would you modify the scale levels? and (5) Would you add any scales? This form of quality control helps to insure that the criteria used to assess an individual patient's success in therapy is professionally valid and meaningful.

Validity, in the sense that the term is used here, is determined by the self-evident nature of the content of a follow-up guide, and can be compared to the validity of service contracts generally. To the extent that contracting parties agree as to the nature, timing, and other conditions of the contract, its content is considered "valid." Sherman, coining the term "contract fullfillment analysis," developed this form of goal attainment scaling in collaboration with J. Lambillo, and it is probably this form of the technique that is most readily adaptable to quality audit or utilization review.[6]

The validity of goal attainment scaling in the traditional psychometric sense had been developed at length by G. Garwick,[7] who illustrates a number of relationships between goal attainment scaling and associated measures of treatment outcome. Sherman's declaration of the special appropriateness of the operational definition of content validity for goal attainment scaling is described in his paper, "Content Validity Argument for Goal Attainment Scaling."[8] An essential form of this aspect of validity is that it is especially dependent upon the reliability of the technique. In both the technical psychometric meaning of reliability, and in the less formal usage indicated in the previous paragraph, agreement by the contracters and by the follow-up scorers is a critically important criterion. Whether the content is clinical or administrative, process or outcome, agreement among the involved parties is essential.

In the clinical applications of goal attainment scaling, there have been many ways in which we have sought to display the content of the follow-up guides. G. Garwick and S. Lampman[9] have completed an omnibus content analysis of 1,000 Mental Health Service goal attainment follow-up guides, and have identified the 20 most frequently mentioned goal categories. They are:

1. Aggression
2. Alcohol use
3. Anxiety
4. Psychopathogical symptoms
5. Decisions
6. Depression
7. Drug use
8. Education
9. Family or marital concerns
10. Finances
11. Interpersonal or social activities
12. Legal problems
13. Living arrangements
14. Physical or medical problems
15. Self references
16. Sexuality
17. Suicide

18. Treatment
19. Work
20. Miscellaneous

Such classifications are the beginning of another possible process measure. That is, it could be stipulated in a system that quality of care is at least partially reflected in the number or variety of particular goal area references, based upon standards derived from a review of the history and current findings. Also, if these standards include a statement of the typical expectations associated with a goal area, a means would exist to assess the accuracy of prognosis.

Since the evaluation design at the Mental Health Service separates intake from therapy, it is possible to independently examine the influence of each upon the outcome of treatment. Figure 14-2 shows the mean goal attainment scores on the follow-up guides constructed by 15 Mental Health Service clinicians. As can be seen, while the scores vary, most are within a reasonable distance of the expected mean of 50. Information of this sort could be used as an adjunct to the process measure described in the preceding paragraph, functioning as an additional means of monitoring, and perhaps improving, accuracy of prognosis.

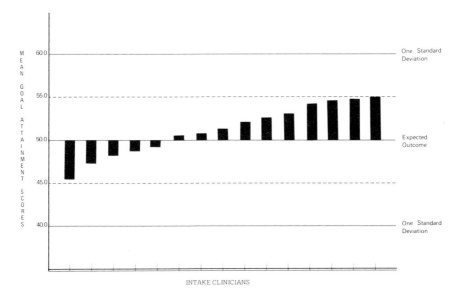

Figure 14-2. Distribution of Intake Clinican Goal Attainment Score Average Deviations from Expected Outcome Level (Clinicians Shown in This Figure had a Minimum of Ten Cases Followed Up)

Figure 14-3 shows the same sample of goal attainment scores, only this time they are analyzed according to the client's therapist. This application permits determination of the extent to which therapy is on course. In one setting, for example, the content of the follow-up guides direct the intermediate stages of treatment. In another setting they are used to help determine when a client is ready for discharge. In yet a third setting check marks on a follow-up guide replace chart notes, and if additional notes are required the guide is expanded to include the new content.

Although originally conceived solely as a clinical measure of treatment effectiveness, goal attainment scaling has been integrated into Hennepin County's planning, programming, and budgeting system to assess program-level goal attainment. Figure 14-4 shows the goal structure of the Adult Outpatient Unit of Hennepin County Mental Health Service. As can be seen, the format follows the traditional management by objectives style, beginning with a statement of the unit's overarching dedication (the mission statement) and continuing with increasingly detailed and specific goals, objectives, and subobjectives. In the "Direct Clinical Component" of the unit there are two kinds of objectives:

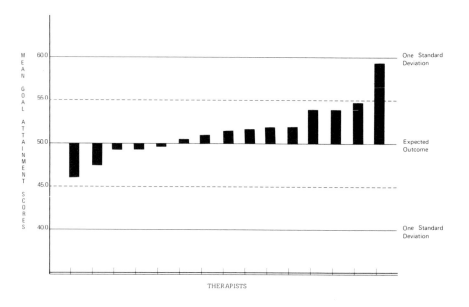

Figure 14-3. Distribution of Therapist Goal Attainment Score Deviations from Expected Outcome Level (Clinicians Shown in This Figure had a Minimum of Ten Cases Followed Up)

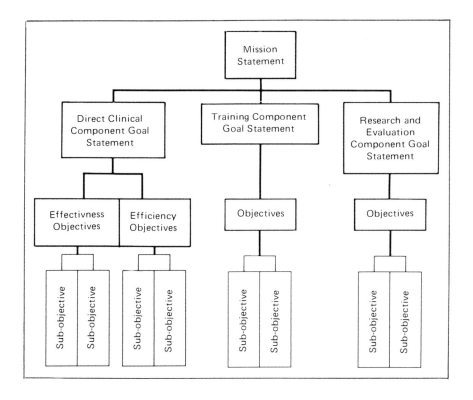

Figure 14-4. Hierarchical Relationship Among Mission, Goal, Objective, and Subobjective Statements, Which is the Logical Framework Utilized in the Applied Model

effectiveness objectives, relating to quality of services, and *efficiency objectives*, relating to the speed with which services are provided and the quantity of appropriate clients served.

Table 14-2 shows the content of the Adult Outpatient Department effectiveness subobjective relating to success of referral. Two things should be pointed out. First, the subobjective is developed using the five-point goal attainment scaling framework. The scale headings of the individual patient applications have now been converted to titles of objectives, elaborated so that the rationale can be more easily understood, and the attainment levels now contain expectations related to various efficiency and effectiveness measures. Second, the content of the scale is stated such that attainment of the subobjective can be assessed periodically. This facilitates development of a continuous feedback loop, and provides a criteria against which subsequent goal attainment can be assessed.

Table 14-2
Hennepin County Mental Health Service—Adult OPD Evaluation

Objective Type/Objective: Effectiveness/to insure that clients utilize appropriate community resources.

Evaluation Concern: To insure that clients who are referred from the Intake Unit to another agency, practitioner, etc., complete the referral (i.e., arrive at).

Scale Attainment Levels	Month of Follow-up Evaluation (1973)												Outcome Score
	Jan.	Feb.	Mar.	Apr.	May	Jun.	July	Aug.	Sep.	Oct.	Nov.	Dec.	
−2 Less than 15 percent of clients followed up during the month have completed the referral.													
−1 Between 16 and 44 percent of clients followed up during the month complete referral.													
Target Optimum Between 45 and 60 percent of clients followed up during the month complete referral.	--	--	--	--	--	--							
+1 Between 61 and 84 percent of clients followed up during the month complete referral.							*	*					This month's Index is 60. Cummulative Index is 60.
+2 Over 84 percent of clients followed up during the month complete referral.													

Measurement Method: Follow-up call to the agency, practitioner, etc. approximately 30 days after notification (Intake Committee) of the referral.

Reviewing the repeated follow-ups of the same guide, it can be seen how expectations and efforts to meet them begin to stabilize over time. This permits the derivation of local standards of care and also allows monitoring and manipulation of system activities. Accumulation of these standards from various outpatient settings could provide a tangible set of performance standards.

The organization of the Adult Outpatient Unit's evaluation system bears a close resemblance to the recommendations of Donabedian and Zusman. As D. Beaulieu and J. Baxter, the developers of the system, suggest, "Both process and outcome information are necessary for program evaluation. . . . Knowledge of the interaction of process and outcome variables . . . provide the best possible information for evaluative decision making."[10] A description of Beaulieu and Baxter's theoretical model is presented below:

> The theoretical evaluation model is based upon the assumption that the interaction between process and outcome and the interaction among program components can be observed. For example, if we attempt to increase utilization of clinical time for screening interviews by abbreviating the Officer of the Day (telephone) contacts, but then note a decline in the rate of successful referrals accomplished during these contacts, we will construe such a contingency as a possible interaction. That is, objectives can be established, the level of attainment of each can be monitored, and the degree to which accomplishing one affects the others can be recognized.

Table 14-3 presents evidence for the existence of the interaction between process and outcome described by Beaulieu. The data are taken from a study conducted at the Mental Health Service by C. Scheier, G. Wahlstrom, and J. Baxter[11] to determine the comparative value of group and individual intake. The data suggest that how a patient is processed through a system makes a difference in his ultimate outcome. Specifically, at the Mental Health Service, it appears that if a client can tolerate (or chose) group intake, he will have a significantly better likelihood of better than expected treatment outcome if he also receives group therapy. The same is true for patients who prefer individual therapy.

Another study at the Mental Health Service, conducted by R. Walker and J. Baxter,[12] has demonstrated that feedback to therapists on the outcome scores and consumer satisfaction ratings of their clients will influence subsequent treatment. The results of the study are presented in Table 14-4. Here, again, an administrative or management information process objective, feedback, appears to influence outcome measures.

G. Garwick and S. Jones[13] have conducted a third study at the Mental Health Service that suggests that goal setting itself may be a treatment facilitator. Fourteen cases were randomly assigned to two modes. In Mode A the goal

Table 14-3

Goal Attainment Follow-up Scores by Experimental Group

	Treatment Mode		
Intake Type	Individual	Group	Total
Individual			
Mean	54.6	50.9	53.0
Std. Dev.	10.2	13.8	11.9
Cases	23	18	41
Group			
Mean	50.5	57.7	53.7
Std. Dev.	10.4	9.2	10.4
Cases	19	16	35
Total			
Mean	52.7	54.0	53.3
Std. Dev.	10.4	12.2	11.2
Cases	42	34	76

Data Summary from: *Group Intake: An Alternative Mode of Clinical Assessment* (publication pending). A significant interaction effect was found between the mode of intake and treatment for randomly assigned cases ($p < 0.05$).

Table 14-4

Effect of Feedback of Goal Attainment Scores to Clinical Staff

Prefeedback			"Unbiased Sample"		
N	=	470	N	=	38
Mean	=	50.80	Mean	=	55.02
S.D.	=	11.04	S.D.	=	13.77
Variance	=	121.97	Variance	=	189.54

$t = 2.15$ $p < 0.02$ (one-tailed.)

attainment follow-up guide was made by an intake interviewer and a second goal attainment follow-up guide was made by a client (utilizing *guide* to goals), thus involving client in goal setting for himself. In Mode B the goal attainment follow-up guide was made by the intake interviewer only. As can be seen in Table 14-5, patients who constructed clinical follow-up guides for themselves did better in treatment than patients who did not. In this case an input procedure, the self-administration of a goal attainment follow-up guide, which might ordinarily be tallied as a process variable, has positive implications for the actual conduct of therapy.

Table 14-5

Goal Attainment Follow-up Guides from Both Modes Scored by Follow-up Interviewer Three Months After Beginning of Treatment

Mode	N	$\bar{x}$	S.D.
Mode A: (Goal attainment score based on intake interviewer follow-up guide)	7	71.24	6.57
Mode B: (Goal attainment score based on intake interviewer follow-up guide)	7	59.24	9.88
Total	14	65.24	

The difference in means is significant at the $p < 0.015$ level for 12 degrees of freedom.

Figure 14-5 represents a summary of one component of the Outpatient Unit: the Direct Clinical Services component. The steps used in calculating the index score are: The original GAS formula[a] is applied to the subobjective or lowest objective level that yields a subobjective attainment score. The subobjective attainment scores are aggregated using the *modified* GAS formula[b] yielding an objective index score. The index scores at the objective level are aggregated using the modified GAS formula yielding effectiveness and efficiency index scores. The effectiveness and efficiency index scores are again aggregated using the modified GAS formula yielding the program performance index score for the Direct Clinical Services Component. The various effectiveness and efficiency scores have been entered into a revised goal attainment formula to produce summary scores for effectiveness and efficiency. These are then combined to form a total "direct services index score."

---

[a]Original goal attainment score formula:

$$T_j = 50 + \frac{10\Sigma w_j x_j}{\sqrt{(1 - \rho) \Sigma w_j^2 + \rho(\Sigma w_j)^2}}$$

where it is recommended that ρ be taken as about 0.30.

[b]Modified goal attainment formula:

$$T' = 50 + \frac{\Sigma w_j (T_j - 50)}{\sqrt{(1 - \rho) \Sigma w_j^2 + \rho (\Sigma w_j)^2}}$$

where it may be necessary to select a value for ρ commensurate with the intercorrelations of the subobjective scores, T_j

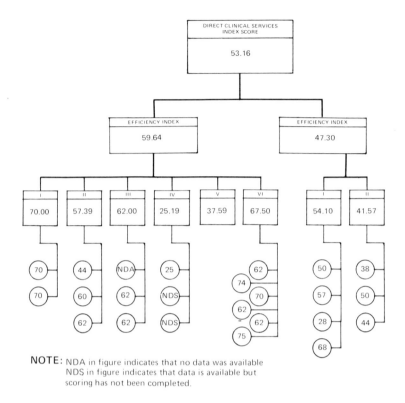

NOTE: NDA in figure indicates that no data was available
NDS in figure indicates that data is available but
scoring has not been completed.

Figure 14-5. Overview of Program Performance Index Score Generation
Process Using Cumulative Data from the First Year of the Redesign

At a given moment, using the system described herein, a cross-sectional review of staff effort is available, the content representing major areas of concern.
The outcome scores indicate the adequacy of prediction, as well as achievement. Here, as in most management reporting, the two effects are not separated
by research design and hence are indistinguishable.

While the diagram may give the impression of a static analysis, it should be
remembered that weekly, monthly, and quarterly feedback reports require a
great deal of deliberation, conflict resolution, and modification of clinical and
administrative practice. At this point the unit appears to be becoming increasingly more open to formal operations research. This trend will probably continue if the method is applied to staff, as it has been to graduate students in a
few studies.

Recalling Donabedian and Zusman's research regarding the relationship between process measures and treatment outcome, an exciting prospect now is the capacity of these measures to be open for review by community groups, professional societies, funders, and clients. The content and achievement of expected clinical and administrative outcomes can serve as a point of reference against which assessment can be made of program activities. The appropriateness, relevance, and "quality" of the program can be reviewed by community representatives and program directors in order to arrive jointly at a set of objectives that are realistic, professionally responsible, and consonant with the values of the community.

The strength and weakness of goal attainment scaling is its relativistic nature. However, through the process outlined above, local standards can be established and shared, without loss of relevance, with comparable settings. This process is at work in a number of human service agencies throughout the nation. Judging from the ingenuity and industry seen through our consultation and correspondence with 2,500 administrators, academicians, clinicians, and evaluators, our solution is soon to be superceded.

Notes

1. Kiresuk, T. "Goal Attainment Scaling at a County Mental Health Service," *Evaluation*, 1:2, 1973.
2. Donabedian, A. "Evaluating the Quality of Medical Care," *Milbank Memorial Fund Quarterly*, 44:166-203, 1966; Zusman, J. and Rose, E. "Evaluation of the Quality of Mental Health Services," *Archives of General Psychiatry*, 20:352-357, 1967; Zusman, J. and Slawson, M. "Service Quality Profile," *Archives of General Psychiatry*, 27: 692-698, 1972.
3. Donabedian, A. "Evaluating the Quality."
4. Sherman, R. "Contract Fulfillment Analysis," unpublished report, Program Evaluation Project, 1969.
5. Kiresuk, T. and Sherman R. "Goal Attainment Scaling: A General Method of Evaluating Comprehensive Community Mental Health Programs," *Community Mental Health Journal*, 1:4, 1968.
6. Lombillo, J.; Kiresuk, T.; and Sherman R. "Evaluation of the Effectiveness of a Community Mental Health Program," presented at the World Congress of Psychiatry, Mexico City, Dec. 1971.
7. Garwick, G. "A construct Validity Overview of Goal Attainment Scaling," *P.E.P Report 1969-1970*, Chapter 5, 1974.
8. Sherman, R. "Content Validity Argument for Goal Attainment Scaling," unpublished report, Program Evaluation Project, 1975.
9. Garwick, G. and Lampman, S. "Typical Problems in Bringing Patients to a Community Mental Health Center," *Community Mental Health Journal*, 8:4, 1972.

10. Beaulieu, D. and Baxter, J. "Evaluation of the Adult Outpatient Program, Hennepin County Mental Health Service," *P.E.P. Report 1969-1973*, Chapter 9, 1974.

11. Scheier, C.; Whalstrom, G.; and Baxter, J. "Group Intake: An Alternative Mode of Clinical Assessment (publication pending), Program Evaluation Project, 1972.

12. Walker, R. and Baxter, J. "Effects of Clinical Feedback," unpublished report, Program Evaluation Project, 1972.

13. Garwick, G. and Jones, S. "Guide to Goals," unpublished report, Program Evaluation Project, 1973.

Part IV

Crucial Issues in Evaluation

15

Responsibilities and Rights of the Evaluator in the Evaluation of Alcohol, Drug Abuse, and Mental Health Programs

Elmer A. Gardner

Program evaluation in the mental health field is in a period of transition. We are on the threshold of utilizing scientific methods more systematically in the evaluation of programs in the human service fields. This optimism arises from several developments: We have increasingly sophisticated evaluative technology to adopt from industry and the physical sciences; our resources have become more limited and, thus, allocation decisions can no longer be made solely on the basis of crises or special interest pressures; the human service fields are approaching a new level of maturity in which quantification and accountability will be more than a part of the rhetoric.

However, this optimism is tempered by a growing recognition by the public that scientific endeavor will not necessarily provide all the answers and may carry more risk than benefit—thus, a climate of some distrust of science has developed. Further, there is increasing realization among the scientific community that its role in society must be examined and monitored continuously in order to minimize the abuses and distorted communication that can occur with even the best of intentions. We see a beginning acceptance and utilization of program evaluation in the human service fields, accompanied as with most scientific endeavor, by a need to define more clearly the role of the evaluator and the evaluator's relationship with others engaged in program development and operation. Thus, discussion of responsibilities and rights of the evaluator can now assume more meaning.

The rights and responsibilities of the evaluator, as reflected in these trends, rest on a broad conceptualization of program evaluation. *Program evaluation* is generically a composite of those processes that relate to the necessary short- and long-range objective assessment of the worth of a human services organization or system and those processes relevant to the planning for, and implementation of, changes in response to that assessment. This conceptualization assumes the utilization of scientific methods and techniques although obviously this is not always feasible in actual practice. It includes evaluation of structure and process in addition to outcome and encompasses other definitions used in the field of scientific management: cost benefit analysis, systems analysis, the utilization and quality audit, plannning-programming budgeting systems (PPBS), and operations research (OR).

Considerable ambiguity exists about these definitions and their respective distinctions. Many would disagree with such an all-encompassing definition for program evaluation and would limit the term to outcome measurement;

231

these persons would probably view themselves as disinterested, impartial scientists, divorced from management. In actual practice, though, most evaluators do become concerned with cost benefit ratios, do become involved with planning, implementation, and problem solving in the organization, and do not function consistently as disinterested, impartial social scientists in the usual sense. Thus, in a discussion of rights and responsibilities, this generic, integrative conceptualization provides more meaningful material for role definitions.

Given this broad perspective on program evaluation, the evaluator is viewed as one participant in a social network, whether it be a small limited organization or a system of services. Such a network involves several groups or aggregates: the general public and/or a special interest group representing the public, one or more sources of funding, a sample of subjects who receive service or serve as controls during the course of a formal assessment, and the program personnel. These then are the major groups with whom the evaluator is essentially involved during the evaluative process. It should be emphasized that the evaluator is seen as an active and vital participant in all phases, each of which suggests specific or overlapping functions, rights, and responsibilities for the evaluator. That process includes four major phases:

1. The formulation of program goals, defining as precisely as possible the values and priority scheme for the service program
2. Selection of the criteria to be used in determining success—the development of the standards for measuring quantity and quality of service, the benefits of service, and the indexes for relating cost to benefit
3. The design and conduct of the studies necessary for the program evaluation
4. Interpreting or explaining the findings of the assessment to the appropriate groups; recommending further program activities and actions that may be needed to improve or sustain the degree of success, or recommending termination of the program

Phase 1 and Phase 2

In both the formulation of program objectives and in the selection of criteria the evaluator has four major responsibilities that define complementary rights and can be viewed in terms of specific role functions. For the sake of brevity this discussion is concerned only with the formulation of program objectives.

First, the evaluator should serve as an educator or counselor to the program personnel and the public in delineating the boundaries of the system for evaluation. For example, if a methadone treatment program in an urban area is the focus of evaluation, is it necessary to consider the mental health center that houses the program or the other drug abuse services in the area that may serve some of the same population? Should the evaluation be limited to the population who enter treatment of should it include all those referred to the program?

Obviously, the boundaries of the system to be evaluated will be dependent upon the goals one wishes to achieve and the latter depends, in turn, upon the values and priorities of the participant groups. Although the evaluator should not have sole responsibility for assuring the input of all participant groups in the elaboration of program goals, he or she should insist that all relevant groups are represented. The usual practice of guessing the intentions of the program administrator or obtaining loosely stated global objectives from the funding sources and/or program administrator accounts in large part for the irrelevancy or inappropriateness of many evaluative efforts. Using the same example of a methadone treatment program, participant groups could include representatives of the community served by the program, the known addict or high-risk populations, local and federal governmental agencies, and the program administrator, plus a variety of program personnel.

But identification and selection of participants for this phase of formulating program goals and the subsequent selection of criteria, though difficult and time consuming processes, are only first steps in the involvement of these groups. Several issues require clarification if participant groups are to make informed contributions to the formulation of actual program goals. A variety of issues must be understood and utilized by all: the difference between system or total program goals versus component goals; the levels of objectives—intermediate or ultimate; the evaluation of effort, performance, efficiency, and achievement. The articulation of goals within the boundaries of constraints such as budgetary limitations, would be another part of this educational interaction between the evaluator and the other participants.

In addition to this educational role, the evaluator has another responsibility: to be an advocate, a proponent for the ultimate selection and precise definition of goals that are most susceptible to objective scrutiny and are most easily measureable. In the human services systems, and particularly in mental health or drug abuse programs where there is frequently considerable emotional attachment to therapeutic proposals and where our technology has lacked precision, this type of advocacy may be controversial though vital to evaluation. For example, in a drug abuse program, program personnel and representatives of the population to be served may believe a major goal of the service is the development of a more ethical and loving individual and that this is vital to the elimination of the addictive tendency in the program's clients. However, such a goal may not be amenable to unbiased or measurable assessment. Thus, the evaluator has both the right and responsibility to advocate for a balance between goals that are too global for assessment and those that are precise but of too little value to be socially meaningful.

These complementary rights and responsibilities in the formulation of

program objectives imply an active role for the evaluator and relationships with
a variety of participant groups in what might be frequently a lengthy, difficult
negotiation. In this sense, the evaluator has two other responsibilities: to serve
as an arbiter and an "integrator" of multiple views, and to avoid interjecting
his or her own value system to the exclusion of others in the formulation of
program objectives.

In essence, the evaluator must have contact with all relevant groups in the
formulation of program objectives, must play a role in conceptualizing the
system to be evaluated, and has the right to be a significant voice in specifying
which goals are to be evaluated and how these goals are to be stated.

In the view I have presented the program evaluator has a role somewhat
analogous to that of a judge or a therapist: to provide an unbiased assessment,
to be an impartial observer and yet be involved sufficiently to define the type
of evidence needed and the limits within which that evidence is to be presented. Once the limits and type of evidence have been defined, the evaluator
uses the tools of the scientific method for obtaining and interpreting this
evidence.

Phase 3

Basically, the evaluator has the responsibility of selecting and utilizing most
effectively the methods that will assure an unbiased assessment, in determining
the degree of success for achieving the agreed upon program goals. This responsibility obviously impinges upon the rights of other program participants, the
clients, the program personnel, and management, and suggests some more
specific responsibilities.

First, the evaluator has a responsibility for balancing the societal or group
rights with the rights of the individual in the evaluative investigation. Obviously,
in the mental health and substance abuse fields, the issues subsumed by this
responsibility are crucial in any research effort and can not receive too much
attention. For any program providing a new service approach society has the
right to knowledge about the effectiveness and generalizability of this approach.
Does a mental health center reduce the mental hospital admission rate among
its catchment population? If so, at what cost to the patient or the family or
community?

Similarly, the population served by a program, and particularly the high-
risk subpopulation, has a right to know about the effectiveness of the particular
service and the degree of success to be expected. That is, is it worth the cost in
time, money, or discomfort? For example, how effective is a residential treatment program for drug abusers—for what population and at what cost? How
would it compare with a methadone treatment program? Are controlled studies
needed to provide an adequate assessment? If so, what type of controls are

required? Do these questions require long-range studies and how much personal data must be obtained to provide appropriate standards for measuring quality of improvement? The answers to all or most of these questions involve some infringement upon individual rights; the type of evaluative method required may infringe upon privacy, confidentiality, or the right to treatment and each of these issues deserves special attention.

Privacy—the right of an individual to retain information about himself from others and to protect himself from intrusion by society—must be compromised to some degree in an adequate evaluation of almost any new mental health or drug abuse program. While recognizing the sensitivity of mental health services and data, I believe the issue of privacy is frequently used as a smokescreen by overzealous proponents of a new approach or by program personnel in order to avoid adequate assessment. In achieving a proper balance between protection of individual privacy and society's right to appropriate program evaluation, the evaluator must again act as an educator. He or she must involve all participant groups, and must serve as an advocate for objective assessment. Acting in isolation or in collaboration with only a program administrator may lead to an insensitivity toward individual privacy or to a misunderstanding on the part of others about the need for certain data. Informed consent may permit an individual to refuse participation in a study and may assure the population served that no individual's privacy will be invaded anymore than that to which he agrees. But I believe this is less adequate than an intensive effort at educating the appropriate groups about the requirements of an evaluative effort—the method and the type of data needed. This, in turn, will force the evaluator and others to give careful consideration a priori to privacy versus the benefits of the study.

The issue of confidentiality presents other considerations. The evaluator obviously has the responsibility of guarding against the disclosure of information for which there has been an agreement restricting such disclosure. Whenever possible, data required for evaluative purposes should be drawn from that collected for service needs, thus avoiding the collection of additional data. But this should be understood by all participant groups; the use of such service data by the evaluation personnel, however innocent it may appear, should be agreed upon. Under this kind of arrangement, evaluation personnel must be involved in the specifications of data to be collected routinely and have easy access to the data required for evaluative analysis.

In the balance between the needs of society and the individual the evaluator has a second major responsibility: to assure the utilization of appropriate scientific methods without undue interference in the provision of service and appropriate care to the program's clients.

Should an individual be denied service or the choice of a particular type of service to provide control or matched samples in an evaluative study? This is a difficult decision and again one that I believe has been used as a smokescreen to cover the fear that a new approach may prove ineffective or to cover the resistance of program personnel to the burdens and rigor of evaluative research.

Here, too, the evaluator must be sufficiently involved to be sensitive to the needs and reasonable resistance of the program personnel and clients but should not easily compromise the scientific rigor of the evaluation. Both as program administrator and as evaluator I have witnessed the easy acceptance of uncontrolled research or the assessment of structure or effort rather than achievement in the evaluation of state hospital admissions, a day hospital, a crises center program, home treatment service, methadone treatment program, and the entire concept of a community mental health center, all under the rationale of providing service to the individual when the value of the service has been largely unknown.

In the evaluation of mental health programs, the avoidance of undue interference with the provision of service also requires consideration of the milieu in which the service is provided and the attitudes of the care givers. I can only urge that the evaluator give sufficient thought about these aspects of the service in the judgments regarding proper study methodology. Similarly, in mental health program evaluation where psychological instruments are often required, the evaluator must balance the study requirements with proper provision of service in deciding upon appropriate data collection.

Phase 4

The evaluator should be responsible for providing a comprehensible interpretation of the assessment to all relevant groups: program personnel, funding sources, clients, and the appropriate community or the general public. The publication of journal articles, books, or the distribution of reports is not adequate. The evaluative findings must be disseminated in a manner that assures the attention of the appropriate groups and must be understood by all parties. This too assumes an active educative role for the evaluator. The failure of most program evaluators to assume this responsibility for diffusion of research findings has been a major deterrent to realization of the potential influence of evaluative research. The dissemination of evaluation findings overlaps with the translation of the assessment into recommendations for program change. As an active participant in the organization or system I would only note that the evaluator also should be responsible for translating the assessment into recommendations for necessary program change.

I have not commented much upon the rights of the evaluator but assume that the responsibilities I have delineated in all phases of program evaluation suggest complementary rights; further, that the evaluator has the right to major input into all program decisions and to insist that the objectivity of assessment be compromised only when it is absolutely necessary. The evaluator also has the right to insist upon proper dissemination of the assessment findings in an unbiased presentation and that evaluation lead to appropriate program change; only with the greatest reluctance should this not be the case.

In conclusion, I believe that the vital importance of adequate program evaluation of human service systems is finally being recognized. In order for this recognition to be reflected routinely in policy and management decisions, it will be necessary for evaluators to understand the uniqueness of their scientist role and to accept the responsibilities mandated by this unique role.

Bibliography

Carstairs, G.M., "Problems in Evaluative Research." In *Community Mental Health*, edited by Williams, R.H. and Ozarin, L.D. New York: Jossey-Bass, 1968.

Donabedian, A., *Evaluating the Quality of Medical Care*. Milbank Memorial Fund Quarterly, 44, 3. New York, 1966.

Gardner, E.A., "Evaluation of Mental Health Services." In *Psychiatric Epidemiology*, edited by Hare, E.H. and Wing, J.K. London: Oxford University Press, 1970.

Gruenberg, E.M., "Can the Reorganization of Psychiatric Services Prevent Some Cases of Social Breakdown?" In *Psychiatry in Transition*, edited by Stokes, A.B. Toronto: University of Toronto Press, 1967.

MacMahon, B.; Pugh, T.F.; and Hutchison, G.B., "Principles in the Evaluation of Community Mental Health Programs." *American Journal of Public Health*, 51, 7: 963, 1961.

Suchman, E.A., *Evaluative Research: Principles and Practice in Public Service and Social Action Programs*. New York: Russell Sage Foundation, 1967.

Zusman, J. and Ross, E., "Evaluation of the Quality of Mental Health Services." *Archives of General Psychiatry*, 20, 3: 352, 1969.

16

Evaluation in Relation to Policy and Administration

Carol H. Weiss

Evaluation can contribute to policy making; it can contribute to the administration of programs, and it can provide evidence for program accountability to constituents and publics. All of these are significant functions, and those of use in the business of evaluation have a tendency to tout them all and justify our efforts on multiple grounds. Evaluation, after all, provides evidence, if it is done well—objective, dispassionate, persuasive evidence that can be used as the basis for a variety of decisions. But the history of evaluation experience demonstrates that all-purpose evaluation is a rarity, and that we had better know at the outset which set of purposes it is to serve. Then we can begin to develop an evaluation model, system, or study that serves the purposes of policy, or of administration and management, or of program practice, or of accountability.

What kinds of decisions are we facing in the fields of alcoholism, drug abuse, and mental health? Certainly there are policy questions: Which new initiatives should be undertaken? Which existing programs should be expanded, institutionalized, modified, or terminated? How should we allocate resources among such components as treatment, prevention, education, follow-up, and research, and how should we allocate resources across institutions and agencies?

The administrative questions are equally compelling. What strategies of program operation shall be selected? What techniques shall be emphasized, which staffing patterns, organizational structures, management and planning tools, and reward systems? How can we improve the effectiveness of the agency's operation day to day, month to month?

There is a further set of questions that evaluation can contribute evidence for: questions about clients' expectations and goals, and how well these are being met. Just as we can press evaluation into the service of accountability to Office of Management and Budget (OMB) and the Congress, to the Department of Health, Education, and Welfare (HEW) and Alcohol, Drug Abuse and Mental Health Administration (ADAMHA), to community groups and taxpayers, so can we use evaluation to provide a consumer's eye view of program effectiveness. Evaluation can serve as a mechanism of accountability for a variety of constituents.

The primary purpose of evaluation is utilitarian. It can serve other functions as well, such as testing theory, but its basic function is to provide evidence about program effectiveness so that wise decisions can be made about the program in the future. But which decisions are we attending to? If we tackle a

239

policy question (for example, are particular types of drug abuse programs effective), we need a certain type of evaluation design, data, and analysis. We need to know the effects of the program on persons exposed to the program and randomly assigned controls not exposed; we need outcome data on the extent of drug use among both groups over appropriate intervals of time, and (if for any reason our randomized experimental design is compromised in execution), we need to introduce further procedures to insure that observed effects are attributable to the *program* and not to extraneous conditions. With this type of evaluation we can give sound information to policy makers on the extent to which the program is successful in reducing drug abuse and (depending upon some value criteria about how much success is "enough") we can contribute to decisions about whether to extend, modify, or cut back the program.

But what can we tell the administrator? Let us assume that the evaluation shows a modest level of success. The program administrator runs a particular operation. He wants to know how he can improve the services he manages; which particular techniques worked well; which methods should be emphasized and which should be changed or dropped. On which kinds of people were different techniques more or less successful: did males react differently from females, were older people different from younger, were there differences if people had higher educational levels or received continuity of service from the same worker? What facilities, equipment, discussion methods, staff attitudes, made a difference on outcomes? An evaluation dedicated to administrative and practical ends has to have something to say about issues like these.

It is obviously possible for evaluations to be designed to answer both orders of question. Research procedures to tackle them simultaneously are well known and in fact, most evaluation studies and evaluation systems tend to undertake all of this—and more. But in trying to be all things to all men, they almost inevitably run into problems. First, the overall policy question involves big decisions and the expenditure of large sums. Therefore, decisions should be based on the best and most valid data to be had. Is the program working? Is it better than no program at all or better than the kinds of programs traditionally available? Is success or no success attributable to the program itself or to outside or transient conditions? To get valid answers to these questions, experimental design with random assignment is required. But under the conditions that fit administrative operations, random assignment is often sacrificed on the altar of operational practicability.

A second serious problem in trying to combine the policy and the administrative evaluation is that for policy purposes, the program should be explicitly defined and firmly controlled. The policy maker should know precisely what it is that works or does not work. If the program proves good, he should know specifically what to fund and set up and have people trained to do. He should be able to define which ingredients of the total package are essential for success. But again under most field conditions, when administrators are seeking practical answers to practical questions, the program stimulus is imprecise. It depends on the inevitable vagaries of staffing, organization, structure, the time and the place, the clientele, and the shifts and haphazard changes that occur as outside conditions alter. If the evaluation shows that the program had little success, should the policy maker conclude that programs of this like should be abandoned, or is the absence of effect a consequence of specific (and alterable) current conditions?

A third problem concerns the scale of evaluation: its scope and cost. Policy makers, particularly at federal levels but at state levels, too, want generalizations: Program A has this much effect across a range of conditions and Program B has that much effect. They need evaluative data across time and place, evaluative evidence that washes out the influence of idiosyncratic personalities and events. On the other hand, the local administrator is concerned about *his* program, here and now, and the people it serves. He is not necessarily agog with pleasure at collecting data comparable with that of 30 other programs when the data do not seem germane to the issues at hand. He wants to take into account those very local idiosyncrasies that seem distorting and misleading to the high-level policy maker.

These are important differences in perspective. The solution, it seems to me, is to gear evaluation designs specifically to the *decisions* that are going to be made. What decisions are pending? If they are policy decisions, for example, whether to extend a pilot program to other sites, or if they are administrative decisions, whether to reduce case loads or use paraprofessionals, the evaluator should select the appropriate questions, criteria, study design, data, and priorities. Only when he knows what the key decisions are can he plan evaluation to yield maximum payoff.

The ideal conditions for evaluation for policy purposes are not easy to attain. We have suggested what the ideal requirements would be: experimental design, an explicit and stable program, and sufficient sites for generalizability. These research conditions will yield valid conclusions about program outcomes, and when policy makers are considering in the tens and hundreds of millions of dollars, they should be able to base them on thoroughly credible, valid information. But ongoing programs are not usually hospitable to such research requirements. The imperatives of *service*—helping people—tend to get in the way.

The closest that researchers have come to ideal policy evaluation is through recent "social experiments." Researchers have undertaken a set of studies geared to developing future programs, such as the negative income tax, housing allowances, and health insurance experiments.

These social experiments are a way of planning rationally for the future. Unlike the backward stance of most evaluative efforts that survey the success of past programming, social experiments involve launching and testing prototypes of new ventures. Their function is to inform the policy maker of the viability and effectiveness of innovations before he commits large amounts of money, time, and effort to a major national undertaking. Certainly the last decade has demonstrated that many program ideas that sound persuasive and even unimpeachable in principle, given our present state of knowledge, flounder in operation. If policy makers can look at the consequences of a test run of a program before expanding on a nationwide basis, they have the opportunity to reject the ineffective, improve the marginally effective, and mitigate the counter-productive side effects of new programs. It is for this type of major new policy decision that social experimentation is designed.

Social experiments are research. Their goal is to test. They are true experiments, with random assignment of participants to program and control conditions, and with before and after measurement; and the program is explicitly defined and firmly controlled, with the evaluation researchers responsible for insuring that the program "stimulus" adheres to the prescribed principles and modes of operation. Social experiments tend to be run in several sites with different external environments so that outcomes can be generalized over a range of conditions. Furthermore, if several variants of the basic program are run simultaneously, it is possible to gauge the effects of variations in treatment.

Some social experiments have been run specifically to test possible *adverse* effects that critics of the proposal have raised. The negative income tax experiment, for example, paid a lot of attention to the question of whether people earning just a notch above the guaranteed income would drop out of the labor force. This is a real concern. If there is a substantial drop in work, and many more people become eligible for benefits, the program would be much more expensive than advocates claim. So experimentation can collect evidence about negative counterclaims as well as hypothesized benefits of new social programs.

So long as social experiments were more a dream of beleaguered evaluators than a practical reality, there was a tendency to emphasize the advantages and ignore possible limitations. The advantages, if all goes well, are delightful. With this kind of design, evaluation researchers can draw firm conclusions about the merit of a program. Among other things, when the program adheres to well-defined principles and procedures, there is little uncertainty about whether the program had had a fair test or whether its failings are the result of faulty administration or operation. It is probably no accident that most of the new social experiments—the negative income tax, housing allowances, and health insurance experiments—all involve direct payment of money. Money is easier to control than are services, and they are not subject to the varieties and whimsicalities of human differences.

The recent experience has also highlighted some of the difficulties. Social experiments are costly, because a prototype *program* has to be administered as completely as a sophisticated research study. Usually it is possible to sample only a few sites, with a sacrifice in generalizability to other places and conditions. When the effects on small scattered groups of recipients are studied, the data may not be representative of outcomes that would have ensued if the program had saturated the areas. Furthermore, even when the researchers are in charge, program operations are not always well-handled, external conditions do change, there are ethical problems in giving benefits to an experimental group (and not to controls) and then taking them away after the study is over. Long periods can elapse before the results become available for decisional purposes, and the reformist impetus that launched the experiment may have run out of steam.

Another limitation may be a dearth of plausible new programs to test. Before a social experiment is launched, the hard rational analysis that leads to the development of a new program has to be done: the nature of the social problem analyzed, its dynamics explored, the causal linkages hypothesized (or better yet, understood), effective points of intervention identified, the likelihood of successful intervention plausibly established, the political context for supporting and sustaining the intervention examined and found appropriate, and the likely benefits and the distribution of those benefits deemed sufficient to warrant the social cost. Social experimentation is useful for policy making only when such analysis has generated a program or policy that is *worth* the testing. When a new social initiative has been developed and has sufficient credibility to be considered by policy makers, social experimentation provides an elegant data base for decision making. The kinds of information that it produces can prevent costly national failures and lead to better informed and more successful choices at the policy level.

Social experiments look toward future plans. But what about policy decisions regarding existing programs? How can we design evaluations that give good measures of the impact of ongoing programs so that policy decisions can be made about expansion, modification, or termination? If good social experimentation is hard when researchers are in control, how can we hope to get valid measures of outcome within the turbulent conditions, conflictive interests, and political pressures of a working program?

It seems to me that there are two answers. One is when major policy questions are valid, when authentic allocation decisions will hinge on evaluative evidence, the evaluators have to be given the conditions and the control to do the best possible research. Otherwise, they run the danger of producing inadequate or misleading evidence that contributes little to decisional rationality. This will mean shifting the locus of authority over certain program decisions to the evaluation team.

The second solution is to recognize that go/no-go kinds of policy decisions are relatively rare. On only a few occasions do policy makers truly consider terminating a program—and even then it is not usually on the grounds of effectiveness or ineffectiveness. Most programs build up layers of alliances among legislators, bureaucrats, professional guilds, constituents, and publics that protect them from drastic dismemberment. Even in the last few years, when the administration has proposed eliminating a number of major programs, the rationale has been less the matter of *ineffectiveness* than of differences in political philosophy. Evaluations of some programs, such as federal grants to low-income college students, found highly successful outcomes and the programs were still scheduled for the axe because the administration favored loans and work rather than outright subsidies to students.

The policy questions are often more circumscribed than they are posed. Policy makers may ask, "Is this program worth continuing?" but even if results should show out-and-out failure, the usual reaction is to patch it up and try again. And most results are not unremittingly bleak. Evaluations often come up with mixed results—some good, some qualified, some poor outcomes—and the appropriate action is to look for modifications in strategy and practice. Thus, what started out as evaluation for policy purposes comes pretty close to evaluation for administrative purposes.

For administrative purposes, traditional evaluation methods—well executed— have considerable potential. By "traditional evaluation," I mean before/after (or before/during/after) evaluation of the effects of ongoing programs under conditions that are usually less than the research ideal. For administrative decisions, even compromise designs can make significant contributions. Usually the service imperatives of ongoing programs preclude randomized assignment to experimental and control groups, and an approximation, such as "contrast groups," is resorted to. Further, the program is not under the evaluator's con- trol so that the stimulus wobbles around in response to internal and external opportunities and constraints.

Traditional evaluation, if it is conducted with rigor and sophistication (and some luck), can give good estimates of overall program effectiveness. But given the constraints under which it often operates, it is better suited for comparing the worth of alternative program strategies. Comparative study of the effects of different program components with different populations can yield evidence of what strategies work best with what groups. Variations in mode of operation and intensity of service can also be tested. When administrators and managers face decisions about whether to emphasize one set of methods or another, to scrap one technique and adopt a different one, the findings of traditional evaluation provide relevant information. By comparing the outcomes of variant approaches and program components within the context of the programs about which decisions will be made, evaluation demonstrates their relative worth in the operating context and helps the decision maker choose wisely. Since evalua- tion takes time and money, this approach is not likely to be worthwhile for assessing minor program features, but when choices of some magnitude are contemplated, it can make a significant contribution to the rationality of decision making.

A further development that can have important impact deserves mention. One of the pervasive problems with many past evaluations has been that they have been one-shot affairs. The evaluators come in, do a study of more or less elegance, and after their work is over, depart. But what about the rest of the time? Decisions still have to be made on a regular basis on all kinds of matters—intake criteria, staffing, hours of service, and so on. To meet continuing decisional needs, evaluative data can be built into an ongoing information system.

Most programs collect data, in fact often vast quantities of data, on clients, staff, finances, process, and plans. With the available computer technology, what used to be file cards in file boxes and file folders are now more likely to be computer files. Within the past decade much effort has gone into turning the scattered bits and pieces of information, originally collected for a variety of different reasons, into comprehensive data systems for management use. But not many of the systems have included evaluative data, data on client outcomes, as part of the array. Sometimes this is not very hard to add. Even without the paraphernalia of computers, relatively simple measures of program success can be devised (for example, job placement, maintenance of one's own home) and follow-up data collected on a systematic basis. With this input the information system has the capability for analyzing a wide range of program conditions (for example, length of service, referral flow, unit costs) against the types of client outcomes that ensued. If the data are selected and arranged with due care, such information can provide enormously useful guidance for decision making on a regular basis.

However, one thing we have learned is that program managers are likely to need some training in how to make best use of such information, both at the input and the output end. At the input end they have to be involved in defining what data go into the system, which data are important. One cause for neglect of even sophisticated information systems is data overload. Too much information is spewed out, more than decision makers want, need, or can digest, and much of it is marginal to their concerns. The first essential, then, is that at the outset, we need to know the values and priorities of the intended user audience: What program objectives do they most value? On what basis will they judge the merit of the program? Are they concerned only with the achievement of the official goals of the program, or are they also interested in some of the political and symbolic functions that programs serve—degree of effort, style of service, visibility, consumer representation. By finding out in advance the needs and priorities of the intended users of the data, the information system starts out with two advantages: (1) It knows what information is valued and therefore likely to be used; and (2) instead of adding more data on top, it can winnow out the unnecessary in advance and concentrate on priorities.

A system like this can be expanded to serve an accountability function. A program is responsible to different publics—to the funders, whether public or private, who provide the money; to its clients who are entitled to effective service; to other organizations, that refer clients, provide collateral services, receive its departing successes or failures; to citizen groups. If information on *their* image of program goals and priorites is collected, too, we can add their concerns into the system.

Once the relevant audiences are identified, and their criteria of program effectiveness understood, the evaluator can develop *measures* of these criteria and input them into the system. Then at regular intervals, data are produced that display the success of the program on these measures. Since different user audiences are likely to have different programmatic values and priorities, the information system can become multidimensional and collect data that show "success" on the range of different criteria that are being applied. It may be that there are trade-offs among different criteria, that for example one group's criterion of success is inconsistent with a criterion of another group: For example, increased coverage of the target population may be inversely related to client satisfaction with services. Data, particularly the trend data over time that such a system produces, highlight such issues and may help lead to their resolution.

With the outcome data defined by the relevant user groups, the account-ability system allows periodic reporting to each group of how well the pro-gram is doing in *their* own terms.

The key characteristic of the system is that it provides the information that the audience has defined as relevant to their goals and their needs. It enables them to make decisions and take actions on the basis of the kind of information that they value.

It is important to keep the basic system as simple as possible so that the data clearly show what each audience wants to know. Furthermore, most users will need help in interpreting the data and understanding the implications of the data for action. This kind of educational and interpretive input is an impor-tant part of any information system.

There should also be incentives and rewards for putting evaluation findings to use. This is a big subject in itself and deserves more than passing mention. But here, let me note, it is possible that one way to motivate decision makers to pay attention to evaluation data is to report findings to an array of actors—administrators, practitioners, clients, program planners, funders—and to trust in a legal kind of adversary proceeding to provide incentives for action. Each user group is encouraged to work for changes that will improve performance on the criteria that they have set, and each user group has a way of checking on the progress that is made.

One of the things an evaluator always asks of a program before undertaking a study is, "What are the goals?" It is a question we less often ask about evalua-tion itself. But certainly if we had to answer the question, the primary answer would be that evaluation should make for better human services and wiser allo-cation of resources among and within programs. Our record has not been spec-tacular so far. Only as we design evaluations to fit the needs of decision makers—the issues they face, the information that will clarify the issues, and the salience to them of different kinds of information—do we stand a better change of reaching this goal.

17

Training for Evaluators
Paul McCullough

The title of this chapter has changed several times since it was first decided to include an overview of training. The original title was "evaluation training" suggesting a concern about developing evaluation or evaluators as a distinct professional discipline. One could imagine establishing a series of university programs that would produce mental health or human service evaluators armed with all the appropriate methodological skills to measure social programs. These individuals would then be hired by mental health, social welfare, corrections, or drug abuse agencies and would evaluate programs. This approach would produce a discipline known as "evaluators," perhaps similar to those people known as a "statistician" or "biostatistician."

As I thought further about the issue a second title emerged—"training for evaluation." This implied there was a body of evaluation methods and techniques to which an individual could be exposed and he/she would then apply them to a content area of interest. The techniques would be taught in a series of appropriately labeled courses in graduate schools, in short summer sessions, or by other appropriate methods. The students would be drawn from the disciplines already at work in the fields of health, mental health, or drug abuse. They would already be familiar with the content area. A major decision would be what to teach them, when, and where.

The current title, "training for evaluators," is a compromise between the other two. While the changing title is a minor point, it may be illustrative of the fact that the issues involved in both training and evaluation keep slipping past each other. Once can easily debate the relative merits of training versus education, research versus evaluation, the need for knowledge of methods versus knowledge of content. I do not propose to resolve these issues, but rather to attempt an overview of the current situation and make some suggestions for the future. That is, this presentation is more a statement of a problem rather than a statement of a solution. It is the *individual* who does evaluation, who is responsible for evaluation, and who utilizes the results of evaluation. One of the consequences of this view is that each professional (professional is used here in a broad sense to indicate all service providers or delivery system personnel) has the task of asking questions similar to the following: "Am I doing any good?" "Is this program working?" "Is the agency having the desired effect on the social problems it was created to deal with?"

My opinion is that evaluation is not a separate discipline, but an integral part of each discipline. While evaluation may be a subspecialty within each profession, an "evaluation ethic" should be built into every educational program. This is an "ethic" that encourages the individual to ask himself and his colleagues the appropriate questions about the effects of their intervention and allows him to anticipate being asked those same questions by his colleagues.

In some ways this is already done in human service agencies, in clinical case supervision, in tissue pathology checks, in the elaborate hierarchy of nurse, charge nurse, head nurse, supervisor nurse in hospitals and so forth. Most professional education programs include exposure to some research techniques and establish some standards of professional performance. In addition standards for service are becoming increasingly important in relation to national health insurance and program accreditation in contract for service situations.

However, the kind of evaluation with which we are concerned is different than this. It is not just concerned with whether one has performed a certain action appropriately or in a standard fashion. It is concerned with whether the action has had the desired consequences for the individual client, or with whether an entire intervention program is working, or with whether the agency is generating the desired product, or with whether there might be a more effective or efficient way to do any of the above.

The individual professions need to continue their efforts to pass along ethical and performance standards and to teach laboratory research techniques. But, they also need to lay the groundwork in their students for judging the effects of programs and of judging their impact on social problems.

It is unreasonable to tell students they must do program evaluation or to exhort working professionals to do the same without giving them *some* information about what to do and how to do it. That is, training in techniques and methods is needed but a major issue is still that it is the individual who is responsible for not only maintaining professional standards but also for evaluating his efforts and for utilizing the results. It is that interest and/or motivation that professional education should build into its students.

Some individuals have an interest in doing evaluation, some are more interested in the results of evaluation. In my experience at the local level the interested persons are either those with a pocketful of evaluation methods that "should work" or persons suddenly faced with questions they cannot answer. The latter group frequently have titles like administrator, director, or supervisor. They are usually clinicians who have been recently promoted and suddenly have responsibilities that their individual professional educational programs did not prepare them for, for example, how to budget, how to plan, how to choose between alternative courses of action, how to evaluate. This is not meant as a put-down for administrators, but rather is meant to call attention to the observation that many program directors or administrators suddenly become interested in evaluation when they have to deal with a set of questions with which they are unfamiliar. It is a common complaint that mental health professionals lack management skills, including the effective use of data to help make decisions, and that this is a major problem in community mental health services.

Clearly one of the issues in considering training for evaluators is to decide what is meant by *evaluation*. The word is used here to mean the systematic collection of information about programs in order to provide data about their operation, effectiveness, and efficiency. The information should be useful in decision making and program development. In this context evaluation is a management and organizational tool, not simply a research activity. It is what Carol Weiss refers to (in chapter 16) as "administrative evaluation as opposed to social policy analysis."

I have begun to talk about this type of activity as "program analysis" rather than evaluation, because of the threatening overtones of the latter term and the implication that it is something only a research person does.

Therefore, having decided by prejudice that evaluation is *not* a separate discipline or profession, three questions come to mind: (1) What are the evaluation tasks to be done? (2) How are current evaluators trained? (3) How should evaluators be trained?

What are the Tasks to be Done?

In an effort to obtain an up-to-date picture of what a mental health evaluator would be asked to do, the Division of Community Psychiatry (SUNY/ Buffalo)[a] conducted a survey of a sample of mental health facilities in February of 1974. The data to be reported are from the 225 initial returns out of 882 questionnaires. This is approximately a 25 percent return and there is a potentially large nonresponse bias in the results. Because of this potential bias and because the data have not been analyzed fully, they are presented with some trepidation and a great deal of faith that they reflect the real world. I do not know what type of scale the data represent or even if the items form a scale. One purpose in doing the survey was to see if a scale could be developed that would measure the status of evaluation in an agency.

In order to provide a framework for devising the questionnaire, an idea was adopted from the Program Evaluation Project, University of California, San Francisco.[1] As reported previously in this book (chapter 11), project staff proposed a conceptual model for use by evaluators and program managers

[a]The author wishes to thank Robert Joss, acting director, Operations Research Unit, Department of Psychiatry, State University of New York at Buffalo, for his able assistance in collecting and tabulating the survey information. The conclusions presented here are the author's.

in assessing their own capability to do evaluation. Their conceptualization grew out of site visits to more than 60 Community Mental Health Centers. The model focused on *three* dimensions of the evaluation process in the *context* of management decision making. The three dimensions are: (1) levels of evaluation activity, (2) levels of information capability, and (3) roles of the evaluator. They proposed four levels of sophistication or foci of activities in each dimension that would allow an observer to "describe" a mental health agency in terms of its ability to support certain evaluation processes.

In developing the questionnaire I modified their terminology and attempted to generate questions that would "measure" the status of each respondent along each dimension. The model is represented in Figure 17-1.

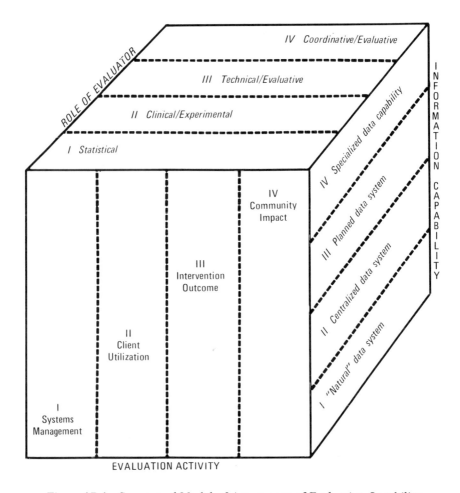

Figure 17-1. Conceptual Model of Assessment of Evaluation Capability

The surveyed agencies were asked to respond to each of 36 questions in three different ways. First, was the activity described currently being done (yes-no)? Second, was the activity described important to management whether being done or not (high-low)? Third, was there a need for training relative to that activity (high-low)?

As indicated earlier, each dimension was divided into four levels (indicated by Roman numerals) and three questions generated for each level. Therefore there were 12 questions per dimension or 36 questions in all. In the survey the questions were not ordered according to level but were mixed randomly. In the following tables the questions have been ordered according to level and the responses are presented in terms of percentage of agencies responding "yes" or "high." A few quick observations on the findings follow.

Level of Evaluation Activity

There is a decrease in the number of centers "doing" an activity as one moves from Level I to Level IV. This suggests an increasing level of sophistication as difficulty exists in the survey items. All items are judged to be important for management with the exception of "data on the social functioning of client." This seems peculiar given that "social functioning" is frequently cited as a major outcome of impact dimension for evaluating treatment and programs. The need for training does not appear to have an easily recognized pattern of response. A "high" training need is reported to exist in a significant number (27 percent to 67 percent) of agencies for all items. This suggests that different training packages are required depending on the stage of development of the individual agency. (See Table 17-1.)

Level of Information Capability

Again, there is a general decrease in the number of centers doing an activity as the level of sophistication increases. There is clear increase in the number of persons judging an item important to management as the level increases. The capability to do cost-effectiveness studies was judged most important and may represent the increasing demands for such data by funding agencies. Again, there does not appear to be a clear pattern relative to training except for training in cost-effectiveness and community studies. The respondents indicate some need for training on all items. (See Table 17-2.)

Role of the Evaluator

The "currently done" question indicates that evaluators are operating in all

Table 17-1
Level of Evaluation Activity

Questionnaire Item	Currently Done	Highly Important	High Training Need
Demographic characteristics of clients served	77%	75%	27%
Routine statistical reports of consultation-education activities	72	74	36
Data regarding client problem/symptom status at admission	83	87	38
Distribution of staff time among various activities	80	83	27
Data regarding continuity of care	60	89	49
Utilization rates for catchment area population groups	58	76	30
Data on client satisfaction	44	82	54
Data on patient change or goal attainment	48	90	67
Data on efficiency of services	43	88	64
Data on prevalence or incidence of mental illness for area served	36	74	49
Data on the social functioning of client (e.g., employment, interpersonal relations) after service	45	56	52
Data from other social agencies regarding your service to them	33	72	39

four roles included on this dimension. The largest percentage of "yes" responses appear in Level III. This suggests that while the evaluator is used by the agency manager, he is not consistently part of management. However, the importance of the activity specified generally increases as the level increases. Again, there is no single item judged to have an exceptionally high training need. (See Table 17-3.)

Table 17-2
Information System Capability

Questionnaire Item	Currently Done	Highly Important	High Training Need
Individual service providers keep personal appointment books or activity logs	80%	66%	23%
Program data retrieved through personal contact and knowledge	80	71	31
Demographic data only available in patient charts	29	42	23
Data collected in standardized categories for federal/state reports	84	67	25
Data collected and stored at central location in facility	76	81	32
Use standardized admission/termination forms	92	81	22
Data collection part of routine activities of individual service providers	82	82	35
Data collection forms combined and designed to reduce redundancy	62	86	44
All data categories operationally defined	52	77	44
Data can be quickly retrieved and analyzed to answer unanticipated questions	33	81	58
Data can be used to study community need and/or impact	52	83	62
Agency can do cost-effectiveness analyses	51	90	67

Summary

Of the three dimensions of the model, the dimension regarding the evaluator's role appears most diffuse. While this result may be due to some lack of precision in the questionnaire items, it is apparently also due to an uncertain

Table 17-3
Role of Evaluator

Questionnaire Item	Currently Done	Highly Important	High Training Need
Data compiled by "statistical" clerk	73%	68%	37%
"Statistical" clerk responsible for coordination of all data collection	31	50	34
"Statistical" clerk reports to agency director	43	44	23
Data collected by "evaluator" for individual research interest	46	41	40
Research projects are specifically relevant to management concerns	48	66	44
Research reports are timely for administration	56	80	44
Data collected by "evaluator" are used for monitoring agency functions	71	82	49
Data collected by "evaluator" utilized in agency decision making	72	84	53
Data collected by "evaluator" used in budget justification	66	78	49
"Evaluator" participates in management decisions	60	75	47
"Evaluator" plans data collection in context of agency issues	40	78	52
Manager and "evaluator" jointly plan data system	57	75	51

idea of what the evaluator is supposed to do, and at what level of activity or technical sophistication. The respondents' judgments about training needs also has an uncertain pattern. The largest percent (11 percent to 16 percent) of nonresponses were generated in this area. This suggests that the respondents did not know if training would do any good or what training would be useful. However, the highest training needs are found at Levels III and IV. Also, there are some tasks that are considered important but are *not* training problems, for example, using standardized admission/termination forms. These items are usually at Levels I and II. They appear to be problems of implementation or problems of deciding that the activity should be done or of convincing the staff it should be done. That is, the successful completion of an evaluation task is not necessarily a training problem. There are some things we know how to do but do not do them for other reasons.

How are Evaluators Trained?

Given the tentative conclusion that the questionnaire items do represent in some way the reality of the evaluation tasks to be done, the next question is, "Is there anyone doing them?" If the answer is yes, what kind of people are they?

In 1972 NIMH conducted a survey of research activities in federally funded centers.[2] Tabulations of 189 out of 325 community mental health centers queried indicated that 60 percent of the centers reported that they had a person whose primary responsibility was research and evaluation. This included persons who spent part time or full time in this endeavor. The current survey indicates that 70 percent of the 225 agencies responding had designated a person with primary responsibility for evaluation. Tables 17-4 and 17-5 give some information regarding the characteristics of these persons. For example: There are still a relatively large group of facilities (30 percent) without a person responsible for evaluation activities. The largest single group of evaluators are trained as psychologists. As I do not know of any psychologists who were trained as evaluators per se, I assume they (and others) learned about evaluation on the job rather than in their professional education.

The areas of training in Table 17-5 do not correspond one to one with the tasks to be done as defined by the survey items. Experimental design and statistics, along with training in evaluation itself, are judged most important for a person responsible for evaluation activities. These are also the areas in which most existing evaluators had training. This suggests a concern with obtaining general statistical and experimental skills in the evaluator role. It is noted that the responses in the survey relative to the role of the evaluator indicated that most were operating at the technical/evaluative level.

Although training in management was judged important, few existing evaluators had training in this area. Such training or expertise would indeed seem important if evaluators are to be incorporated into management. It is to be noted that a large percentage of the respondents would not or could not judge the importance of the skills listed relative to evaluation.

In general there appears to be no *overwhelmingly* appropriate technical skill existing or considered to be important in evaluation. A little of everything seems appropriate. When I am looking for help with an evaluation problem,

Table 17-4
Information on Persons in Evaluator Role

Facilities with someone on staff with primary responsibility for evaluation activities.

Yes, full time or greater than full time	37.8%
Yes, part time	32.4%
None or unknown	29.7%

Discipline in which the person in the evaluator role was trained.

Psychology	40.0%
Sociology	8.8%
Psychiatry	5.8%
Social work	5.3%
Other	9.3%
None or unknown	30.7%

Highest degree obtained by person in evaluator role.

Ph.D.	34.8%
M.D.	4.0%
M.A.	7.6%
M.S.W.	4.5%
M.S.	3.1%
B.S.	3.1%
Other	10.7%
None or unknown	32.1%

Table 17-5
Training of Persons with Primary Responsibility for Evaluation

	Had Training		Considered Important for Evaluation	
	Yes	*No +* *No Response*	*Yes*	*No +* *Do Not Know +* *No Response*
Biostatistics	27%	73%	26%	74%
Computer programming	36	64	48	52
Demography	31	69	44	66
Epidemiology	25	75	28	72
Evaluation	56	44	62	38
Experimental design/methodology	62	38	57	43
Management or administration systems/techniques	36	64	53	47
Probability and statistics	64	36	59	41

I do not look for someone by discipline but for someone with experience in either the skill area or content area with which I am concerned. This person generally turns out to have statistical or research design skills. It is surprising that training in biostatistics or epidemiology was not judged to be more important than they were. Skills in these areas seem relevant to measuring intervention outcome and community impact. As university-based degree programs in these areas (public health statistics, biostatistics, epidemiology) have existed for some time, the experiences of these programs *might* offer some insights into problems and issues relevant to training for evaluators. A review of the articles published in the *American Statistician* and *American Journal of Public Health* reveals a relatively large number dealing with training of statisticians, particularly public health statisticians. These are summarized briefly in order to emphasize some additional points.

In 1963 an APHA Subcommittee on Educational Qualifications of Public Health Statisticians published their deliberations on the functions and classifications of public health statisticians.[3]

They saw the statisticians as called upon to perform the following tasks:

1. Design of studies
2. Data collection
3. Compilation and tabulation of data
4. Analysis
5. Communication or presentation of findings
6. Consultation to others
7. Independent investigation of problems of own choosing

They also proposed four levels of "statistician" that attempted to take into account differing levels of responsibility and differing primary concerns. The major distinction in concerns was between statisticians interested in "operations" (ongoing data collection and analysis activities) and those interested in "methodology" (statistical theory).

The four levels of statistician proposed were:

1. Entry and training level (e.g., routine compiling and tabulating of data)
2. Operations (e.g., development of data collection and handling procedures); methodology (e.g., determination of appropriate statistics)
3. Operations (e.g., supervising statistical staff); methodology (e.g., statistical theory, research in statistics)
4. Pose and define research questions (e.g., initiate complex epidemiological investigations)

It was recommended that the level 2 statistician be a Masters graduate and that levels 3 and 4 statisticians hold Ph.D. degrees.

They called attention to two points relevant here: (1) "In the small health agency, and at many echelons in the large agency, there will continue to be a need for the *general practitioner* statistician" (p. 91); and (2) "Experience with the data in a given field is *essential* in order to avoid the perils of statistically valid but substantively meaningless analysis" (p. 92).

The "operations" statistician was most likely to be found in state and local health departments. The "methodology" statistician was most likely to be found in schools of public health and research institutes. The description of the "operations" type of statistician (levels 2 and 3) seem appropriate for a mental health evaluator, if the skills described are in fact appropriate.

At about the same time B. Greenberg[4] was making the case for the necessity of field training for biostatisticians enrolled in schools of public health. His concern was that statistics not be learned or taught in isolation from the problems the graduates would be asked to deal with on the job. Almost concurrently another author[5] was arguing that biostatisticians were being downgraded because of the absence of any relationship between academic training and function. Greenberg made the point that an important consideration is that the field training "be part of the university program and under its supervision" (p. 21). While it is reasonable that the university control its own educational program, it is equally reasonable that the agency controls what it is willing to buy — more about this point later.

In 1966 W. Taylor[6] reported on biometry training programs for the American Statistical Association. In his discussion he calls attention to the complaints of public health workers regarding the theoretical statistician's failure to communicate clearly with people in the field and his lack of familiarity with the subject matter of operating agencies. To be fair he also comments on the subject matter specialist who regards himself as a statistician and of the foolish things he can do. Taylor appears to conclude that we need persons with statistical know-how *plus*, with the *plus* hard to define but concerned with subject matter involvement. He also recommends that teachers of statistics take some training in teaching. I would like to extend this comment to include evaluators who should also take some training in training so that they can educate their colleagues and constituencies more effectively.

In 1968 the Social Science Research Council[7] underlined the need for a variety of statistical training courses, ranging from statistical clerks to managers and policy makers. A major point of their recommendations was that the field of *data collection* was a specialty that called for development in the future.

In 1968 Anita Bahn[8] identified five major groups of persons engaged in both statistics and public health. She wished to outline the training needs of each group in order to stimulate the training programs of universities to produce more appropriate statisticians. These five groups were:

1.   Mathematical statisticians

2. Epidemiologists
3. Other health professionals
4. Public health and mental health program statisticians
5. Health program planners and system analysts

She felt the largest unmet need was for the "practical statistician" experienced in the "*art* of collecting, processing, and interpreting . . . data for planning, monitoring, and evaluating health programs" (p. 19). This person must know about medical records, data collection systems, questionnaire construction, computer principles, and report writing. The practical statistician must understand program goals, be able to translate them into questions, provide quick answers for the administrator, and have *judgement* as to whether differences found are large enough to be important.

While this is only a partial list of the characteristics of a practical statistician, these characteristics are relevant to those needed for the mental health evaluator as well.

Public health statistical training programs have also responded to these various statements of need. In 1970 the Statistics Section of the APHA published a report on the *Education and Training of Statisticians for Health Agencies.*[9]

They surveyed both health agencies and teaching institutions during 1968. A few of the findings were:

1. There were 973 funded statistical positions in 102 state/local/federal health agencies; 187 of these positions were in state mental health departments.
2. There were 186 vacancies in the 973 positions.
3. A major need was for statisticians at the "operations" level in public health.
4. Operating agencies complained that the university training programs were too theoretical, did not orient graduates toward agency work, and were not graduating enough students.
5. The 18 schools offering training programs in public health statistics produced about 37 public health statisticians per year. These same schools had a capacity of 166 students per year.
6. The Biostatistics Departments of schools of public health indicated that they had graduated 330 persons between 1960 and 1968; 36 had gone to work in local/state/federal health agencies (20 percent); 154 had stayed in universities (47 percent).
7. Part of the committee's conclusions were that the traditional university training programs were apt to train the student out of public health and into academia; statisticians needed to demonstrate the usefulness of their skills to the top administration of operating agencies; schools of public health need to reestablish working relationships with health agencies, and the "too

theoretical" nature of their graduates was probably due to the selective
recruitment of mathematical/research oriented students.

At the 1973 APHA annual meeting an additional report was delivered to the
Statistics Section on the same general subject.[10] At this time the committee reported that health agencies desired more "program planning" and "evaluation"
in the curricula of health statisticians. They wished that statisticians had a better
appreciation of public health and medical care and more knowledge of data
collection, storage, retrieval and reduction of data, all of which are apparently
not part of the traditional educational curricula of statisticians.

This brief survey of the literature regarding statistical training programs
results in the following conclusions:

1. The type of technical skills useful in mental health evaluation are those
    described as for the "operations" statistician or "practical" statistician. We
    need a general practitioner evaluator. We also need the technical skills with
    a plus as suggested by W. Taylor.
2. The literature review suggests that the field of public health statistics has
    struggled with the "how to train" and "who to train" issues for ten years
    without clear resolution.
3. The typical degree-oriented, university-based statistics program is difficult
    to change, tends to be too theoretical, and does not provide enough grad-
    uates to fill the needs of the public health field much less the mental health
    field.
4. Knowledge of statistical techniques and experimental methods is useful but
    not sufficient training for evaluators.
5. *If* we are going to train evaluators in university-based programs a different
    type of educational delivery system is needed.

In fact there are several "different" training programs that have developed
in response to some of the issues raised above. One major characteristic of
these programs has been to provide field experiences for the university student.
A few of them are listed below as illustrations and one briefly described.

Faculty of Medicine, McMaster University in Hamilton, Canada, offers a
masters degree in either clinical epidemiology or health care research. One curriculum is designed to provide health professionals who have direct care responsibilities with a knowledge of epidemiology and biometry methods for clinical
research. The other curriculum concentrates on epidemiology, biostatistics,
health economics, and operations research for B.A. graduates in social service.
Each requires a year of university residence with emphasis on field experience.

School of Community Service and Public Affairs, University of Oregon,
has a program for undergraduates in program evaluation and development. The

basic objective is to develop student competencies necessary for evaluators at job entry level. The basic course format is field placement with intensive supervision from agency and university faculty.

Department of Educational Psychology, New Mexico State University, offers a three-year program leading to a Ph.D. with emphasis on mental health evaluation and research. The curriculum includes an emphasis on computer programming, biometry, sampling procedures, and field experiences.

School of Public Health, UCLA, offers a graduate training program in evaluation and social analysis. It is my understanding that the program is geared for persons at the graduate and post graduate level of education. The course content emphasizes the merging of sociology research methods with health and mental health concerns.

These programs range from undergraduate to post graduate levels. In addition there has been some planning and curriculum development relative to including statistical and program analysis skills in the proliferating A.A. degree programs for human service workers in community colleges.

While these are descriptions of programs that are "different" than the traditional statistical training programs, there is little information on how they have worked or how well the graduates have accomplished the tasks to be done in agencies where they are employed. It appears that the graduates are competent but few in number.

School of Public Health, University of North Carolina, operated a program designed to "upgrade the skills of existing mental health statisticians and to recruit new persons into the field and educate them to be mental health statisticians." The educational objective was to train persons at the masters level for the role of statistician or program analyst in mental health. It was a 12-month program with a field placement and additional opportunities for interaction with operating agencies. A final report of this project is available.[11] Some of its results are presented to emphasize a few additional points.

The authors report that 12 persons enrolled in the three academic years of operation; 9 of the 12 were already working as statisticians in mental health agencies of some sort when they enrolled; 10 of the 12 successfully graduated with M.S.P.H. degrees; and 7 of the 10 graduates took positions in mental health statistics, with the 3 others taking positons in public health statistics.

The authors of the report point out that the program was constantly *under-utilized* (i.e., more students could have been accepted); it was expensive when cost-benefit was measured by student stipends and faculty salaries versus the number of graduates. They also comment that is is difficult for persons to leave their employment for one to two years to return to school. This should come as no surprise. However, they feel it was feasible to train persons in a university-based degree program for positions in mental health statistics. Certainly, based on this single program, their success in returning their graduates to the field of mental health statistics was greater percentage-wise than the schools of public health reported on above.

While I do not know the cost of this particular program, I have had the opportunity to see two other training proposals for evaluators of similar nature. One averaged $45,000 per graduated student at a doctorate level; another averaged $16,000 per graduate with a mixture of both masters and doctorate degrees; a third averaged $30,000 per doctorate and produced eight graduates. These figures include tuition, fees, student stipends, and faculty salaries.

This is clearly expensive. In comparison, cost figures from several medium-sized universities show that it costs $6,248 to produce a B.A. psychologist plus an additional $10,716 to produce a Ph.D. psychologist.[12] These figures do *not* include student stipends. At approximately $17,000 per Ph.D. some of the average costs for evaluators do not seem out of line and some seem very expensive particularly if what is needed is the "general practitioner" evaluator.

As another comparison consider training costs for airline pilots. An official of the United Airlines[13] indicated that it cost about $15,000 to train a new pilot. This is postgraduate training as applicants already hold a "professional" degree as a commercial pilot. In addition, another $150,000 is spent in training each pilot during a full career with the company (30 years), about $5,000 per year for learning new skills, meeting recertification requirements, and proficiency testing. It clearly costs money to keep a staff up-to-date and trained to do new tasks.

In summary, while there is some essential conflict between the goal of the university—to give students the best education possible—and the goals of the agency—to solve their immediate and practical problems—some programs are developing and have been developed to relate the two more closely. However, it does not appear likely that university *degree* programs will fill the manpower or training needs of the mental health evaluation field because: (1) not enough graduates are produced, (2) most workers cannot return to school for a year or more, (3) the analysis needs of the agencies are heterogeneous *and* change quickly, and (4) agencies cannot wait two to five years for the super evaluator to be produced. However, since a great deal of the statistical and experimental design expertise needed for evaluation are to be found in the univeristy, we need to develop new ways of tapping it. While the university "system" may be frustrating to the operating agency, we must be careful not to throw out the baby with the bath water.

How Should Evaluators be Trained?

There is not one answer to this question or if there is I do not know it. As

D.R. Brogan and B.G. Greenberg point out in their report[14] there is a constant dilemma between providing education in an academic setting like a university or providing training in the field for those already working in the area. They comment that while short courses or special workshops for working personnel have a place in the total picture, they "cannot be substituted for the discipline and rigor of a full educational program" (p. 77). While this may be true, it is also valid to say that a full educational program cannot be substituted for a timely and problem-specific learning experience in the field.

This dilemma is not only faced by the field of evaluation or by statisticians but by the entire educational system in our country. It is rapidly becoming apparent that a basic professional education or educational degree of any nature is no longer sufficient to insure continued competence. The phenomena of Professional Standards Review Organizations, mandatory professional certification and recertification laws, the addition of "new careerists" to the traditional core of mental health professionals, and the rapidly changing treatment and delivery systems all imply a need to supply educational and training services to persons already working and in a way that is more accessible to those who will use it.

I believe a major way in which we will deliver such services in the future will be through the mode of continuing education for persons who have already received their basic institutional education. There needs to be greater emphasis on life-long or career-long learning as in the United Airlines illustration. The tactics used to train or educate adults are different (or should be) from those used to educate children. The adult learns best when he/she participates in establishing the goals of training and when the training is relevant to the tasks faced on the job. This is not news to most evaluators who discovered that they were not prepared fully for the job they were requested to do and had to learn as they went along. Conferences, short courses, special workshops, and individual technical assistance have been and will continue to be used to train persons in evaluation. These methods may be the only way to train to meet the *immediate* needs of the operating agencies. Both administrators and legislators need to become aware that all out-of-state meetings or conferences are not sight-seeing junkets but may serve the serious purposes of learning the state of the art, finding resources, and discussing common problems with colleagues.

The APHA Statistics Committee report already cited noted that one basic reason why statistics programs are research oriented is related to funding. Training grants were given to universities to train students for research positions. The current funding patterns and climate do not seem amenable to increased institutional training grants—particularly in professional graduate schools and in the social sciences where enrollments are predicted to decrease. *If* our training objective is to improve the quantity and quality of our current evaluation and evaluators, we will need to do it with a continuing education type of effort where the student defines the problem and has major input into the type of education program provided.

To paraphrase a comment by Anita Bahn in her 1968 article, the process of training evaluators "requires exposure to real problems, familiarity with the subject matter and with the quality of the data. It cannot be accomplished by seeking problems which illustrate a method, but by starting with important problems and then seeking the optimum method to answer them" (p. 21). As Tom Kiresuk notes in chapter 14, the staff of his agency began to use Goal Attainment Scaling because it fit their needs not because they were taught it.

If agencies or evaluators want training, they must be prepared to help fund it. If they fund it, it is reasonable to expect the agency will control (or provide heavy input into) the educational program. University faculty in statistics or in other fields can be major resources or contributors to these activities but the agency should supervise the training not the university.

In order to know how to ask the university faculty—or anyone else—to assist, agencies and evaluators must know better the tasks to be done and the kind of evaluation needed. Perhaps those tasks and types of evaluation outlined in the survey. In addition, it looks as though we have as many different levels of evaluators as we do statisticians. Some are concerned with operations, some with methods, some with theory, and some with management. Let us define the evaluator's roles more clearly. There are no super evaluators who will solve all the problems or a super training program that will provide all the skills.

Because agencies vary in their organization and in their developmental stage, the nature of the questions to be answered by agencies will also vary. Let us be more clear as to where we are and where we are going next. In a recent NIMH publication regarding minimum statistical systems in mental health centers, Myles Cooper[15] recommended that information systems be put together in progressive modules rather than installed all at once. Although we may not need to reinvent the evaluation wheel in each agency, we need to learn to drive the evaluation car. Training for evaluators may need to be progressively developed in the same way; that is, we need training for several levels of evaluators. Some agencies can use the statistical clerk and some the technical/evaluative person. This means we must think in terms of career-long education—university-based or otherwise.

In order to make the whole thing work, we cannot just train or educate methodologists or "operations" statisticians. We also need to train the administrators and directors of service programs. They need to know how to utilize the information produced by the evaluator and to learn the relevance of data to management. Without this understanding the "evaluator" will never assume the coordinative/educative role conceptualized in Figure 17-1. There is no essential reason why the administrator cannot also be trained in evaluation. It would probably be desirable, although he may not have time to do the evaluation work. If the administrator/director does not see the usefulness of data to management, he will not see the usefulness of providing training to his evaluation staff. Without his support, nothing happens. In the same way as evaluative data can be used as a stimulus for change in mental health services, training can easily be conceptualized as a vehicle for organizational change. A recent article on models of organizational change[16] specifically calls attention to the relation between research-training and such change. As the name of the game these days is program development and improvement, we need to utilize both evaluation and training in this effort.

Notes

1. McIntyre, M.; Attkisson, C.; and Keeler, T. "Components of Program Evaluation Capability in Community Mental Health Centers," in *Resource Materials for Community Mental Health Program Evaluation*, Part I, Elements of Program Evaluation, NIMH, 1974.
2. Personal communication, Charles Windle.
3. "Educational Qualifications of Statisticians in the Health Sciences," *Am. J. Pub. Health,* 53, pp. 88-96, 1963.
4. Greenberg, B. "Field Training for Biostatisticians," *Amer. Statistician*, pp. 19-22, 1964.
5. Tayback, M. "The Biostatistician and Health Administration," *Am. J. Pub. Health*, 54, pp. 603-608, 1964.
6. Taylor, W. "A Report of an Inventory of Biometry," *Am. Statistician*, pp. 16-20, 1966.
7. Tacuber, C.; Mastieler, F.; and Webbink, P. "Social Science Research Council Committee on Statistical Training," *Am. Statistician*, pp. 10-11, 1967.
8. Bahn, A. "Mathematical Preparation for Training Statisticians in Biomedical Science and Public Health," *Am. Statistician*, pp. 18-22, 1968.
9. "Education and Training of Statisticians for Health Agencies: A Report of the Committee of the Statistics Section," *Am. J. Pub. Health,* 60, pp. 1530-1545, 1970.
10. "Statistics Curricula in Schools of Public Health." A Committee Report of the Statistics Section 1973 Annual Meeting, A.P.H. Association, San Francisco.
11. Brogan, D.R., and Greenberg, B.G. "An Educational Program in Mental Health Statistics," *Comm. M. H. Journal*, 9, pp. 68-78, 1973.
12. The information reported was generated by the *National Center for Higher Education Management Systems at WICHE* from field tests of a cost data system conducted at: State University of New York at Plattsburg, June, 1973; University of Wisconsin/LaCrosse, November 1973; Shippensburg State College, Pennsylvania, October 1973; and Central Washington State College, November 1973.
13. Personal Communication, Flight Operations Training Center, United Airlines, Denver, Colorado, May 1974.

14. Brogan and Greenberg, "An Educational Program."
15. "Guidelines for a Minimum Statistical and Accounting System for Community Mental Health Centers." NIMH, Mental Health Statistics, Methodological Reports, Series C, No. 7, 1974.
16. Sashkin, M.; Morris, W.; and Harst, L. "A Comparison of Social and Organizational Change Models: Information Flow and Data Use Processes," *Psychol. Rev,* 80, pp. 510-526, 1973.

18

Evaluation in Alcohol, Drug Abuse, and Mental Health Programs: The Service Administrator's View

Eugene A. Hargrove

Evaluation has become a very important issue in the late sixties and early seventies. The sudden interest in evaluation of social programs and systems is no different from the demand emerging from the general public regarding conduct of banking, automobile industries, or labor. We in the health fields are being asked to account publicly for the product that our systems are designed to produce—more mentally healthy human beings. Program evaluation can be regarded as a question of accountability to the public and in terms the public can understand. The magnitude of the challenge is comparable to that facing any other organization and must be met with deliberation.

Evaluation cannot be conducted as an isolated activity. It is an integral part of management, one of the triad—planning, implementation, evaluation— that make up the total management package, and it is discussed in those terms from the vantage point of 15 years' personal experience in a state department of mental health.

We began our formal approach to the problem of evaluation in 1965 with a thorough and critical examination of the management technique currently in vogue, that is, embarking on a program and at some later date evaluating the results in light of what we had accomplished in the course of the program. We were not entirely satisfied with this inductive method and explored other approaches, finally adopting a deductive logical system of managment. It first establishes for us a picture of what we want our clients, program, and organization to look like and then we determine what we would do to bring this about. We then looked at the results in terms of predefined outcome. Refinement of this system and its sophisticated application resulted in a program quite different and we think more effective than the classic methodology.

Building on an approach first conceived by Dr. Irwin Jarett, called "key factor analysis,"[1] we adapted general systems theory to a formal sequential logic and implemented this on a statewide basis throughout the mental health systems. Systems theory has assumed great prominence in application for planning, for evaluation, and for a number of other functions related to social systems of this country within the last several years. Unfortunately, many of these applications have proved to be rather dismal failures and many people are somewhat disenchanted with the "systems approach." Much of this disenchantment is based on an automatic assumption that the systems approach requires prior identification of problems. In fact, the systems approach says no such thing; this is one of the errors made in dealing with general systems theory. Systems theory allows one to define a system in many alternative ways. Defining the problem first is simply one of these ways and unfortunately one of the least productive.

In traditional management approaches problems are defined piece-meal and usually tackled piece-meal. Planning divisions, evaluation divisions, statistical divisions, and divisions for implementing programs such as staff development and in-service training are set up as unrelated activities, added as needed to existing organizations, rather than after assessment of the entire system to see where modifications are necessary. This has led to a fragmentation of approach and discontinuity of effort that makes evaluation virtually impossible. Does this mean that by application of the systems theory we are trying to achieve standardization of our efforts? No, indeed. What we seek to do is to create a variety of efforts that are tailored to the needs of differing individuals, communities, and regions but at the same time maintain unity in the accomplishment.

Edmund Sinnott, writing in *Cell and Psyche*, expressed the idea thus: "It is not the character of the constituents or components which make up any living organisms system, but the relations between them which are the most significant."[2] We subscribe to this view and feel that the relationships between the several portions of the mental health program contribute more to the overall effectiveness of the system than the components themselves. How does one find the route to operational applications from such a complex theory? There are several operational approaches of general systems theory but as I mentioned earlier, the one we have found the most useful and suitable to us in a state program is key factor analysis. In its simplest statement *key factor analysis* is a logically ordered way of perceiving the world around us so as to provide rational answers to the problems that confront us in everyday life. It does this by shifting the focus of attention away from details to a perception of the system in which we live and operate. It does this so as to bring into bold relief previously undetected relationships between our organizations, our value systems, our wishes and desires for ourselves and others. Key factor analysis is a synthesis of a general systems theory, the behavioral sciences, and the business-oriented disciplines.

Using key factor analysis we are able to account in the strictest meaning of the word for the effectiveness, the efficiency, and the overall performance for any and all of the activities of the organization. The results are expressed in terms of benefits that accrue to our clients and the community within which we operate. Benefits are defined as the values assigned to output, whereas costs are the values assigned to input; that is, those resources utilized in order to produce benefits. Benefits are considered in light of changes in human behavior scored against the value system of the society in which the individual lives. It is in the area of benefits that we feel the more relevant measures of organizational effectiveness lie.

The process of evaluation can flourish only in an environment of interested,

accepting managers and personnel who are enthusiastic and interested in knowing the effect of their work. The behavior of an organization will differ depending upon which part of the system is used to control the organization. Also,
the behavior and motivation of the individuals within that organization will
differ. Certain aspects of the organization and the behavior of the people within it can be influenced to a significant degree, depending on whether we elect
to control input or output. An analysis of these differences utilizing the concept of "system-generated pressures" reveals that controls imposed on input
stifle initiative, lead to behavior that circumvents the formal system and places
the goals of the individuals within the system in conflict with that of the system
of which they are a part. Output controls, on the other hand, encourage
creativity, self-motivation, and self-fulfillment on the part of the individuals
who are a part of the system, and give them the perspective from which they
can identify their own contribution to the effectiveness of the system as a
whole. Concensus is fostered.

In considering the various steps that are involved in key factor analysis, it
should again be emphasized that planning, implementation, and evaluation
are a part of a holistic philosophy of management and cannot be separated one
from the other.

The first step is to define the purpose of the organization. Purpose here
has a very limited definition. It is simply to state what needs of what people
the organization intends to meet.

From the statement of purpose comes defintion of a set of objectives
stated in terms of the output expected. These are concise descriptions of the
end product sought, stated in terms of the value system of the community
within which the organization operates. They are not a list of the various
means by which these states might be achieved. Above all, they are quantified
statements that set target dates and levels of accomplishments.

The third step is to group the objectives together, using the single criterion
of concurrent accomplishment. This is the step at which the first tentative
resource allocations are made.

The fourth, fifth, and sixth steps all have to do with the building of information systems that allow us to know where we are in terms of these objectives.
They are, namely, the definition of key factors, key indicators, and the establishment of the data base, which will support these measures.

We now proceed to the next step where we introduce the term "goal." In
key factor analysis *goals* are defined as realistic statements that reflect the intentions and priorities of a group. They describe the change in an individual
or group that is sought as a result of a program. Goals must be measurable in
terms of dates and levels of accomplishment of the stated change to be brought
about. The degree to which the dates and levels are reached measures program
effectiveness.

In the beginning of our process most goals were activity-oriented rather than output-oriented. That is, goals concerned with what were the desired results or consequences for an activity, rather than a reflection of what was to be accomplished by the activity. A goal relating to changes in drinking patterns is a statement of outcome in contrast to a goal to provide group therapy, which is an activity statement. The former is more difficult to accomplish than the latter, which is self-fulfilling, that is, carrying out the activity satifies the goal, no matter what the consequences. We now find goals much more outcome-oriented as a contrast. It is one thing to say, "Our goal is to prevent alcoholism"; it is quite another to say, "One will reduce the incidence of alcoholism by 1980 by 25 percent for the entire population." The latter is more operational and provides a more objective standard for goal direction and evaluation. Goals should be as operational as possible but must not be confused with the methods devised to achieve these goals.

Key factor analysis is not all that we were doing in the area of program evaluation. We had need for research and evaluation studies from other approaches. We find such activities essential to the successful implementation of the planning/implementation/evaluation system. In addition to the management group, which used key factor analysis, we had a well-staffed evaluation section within our research division headed by an outstanding sociologist, Dr. Jean Thrasher. This division conducted evaluation studies primarily of two types: population studies and outcome studies. As you are aware, in population studies the concern and focus are with characteristics of defined populations and subpopulations with two basic goals. The first is to provide baseline data for program planning and subsequent evaluation. The second is to document change from a previous point in time. Epidemiologic studies as well as attitude survey and analyses of census material fall into this field.

Outcome studies are the types of activity most closely associated with program evaluation and are concerned with the results of forms of intervention or organizational arrangements. The usual procedure in this type of study is to get some information about the program itself, its goals and activities, and then collect information concerning the recipients of the service. Alternatively it is possible to assess the impact of a program by comparing populations or areas having a particular program with those that do not. In either event the concern is with outcomes of specific programs: program-population-outcome forming the parameters of the investigation.

It is very often useful, and sometimes necessary, to isolate and evaluate a particular set of activities designated as a program and to look at certain aspects of these activities apart from the context within which they are performed. This is, in effect, what we have been doing in the studies of program outcomes and this is by far the most frequent technique of evaluative research. While admittedly useful, such an approach is inevitably artificial. Organizations do not pursue one goal. They pursue multiple goals simultaneously and a given program or set of activities is necessarily influenced in important ways by other programs and other goals within the organization.

We agree with several prominent men in the field of program evaluation that it is often misleading to examine the achievement of program goals out of context since an accurate evaluation is possible only when each goal and program is seen in the context of multiple goals and the limited resources available for organizational effectiveness. We are thus broadening the scope of our evaluation efforts to place evaluation within the organizational context on which the programs being evaluated have their locus. We have selected four distinct, but clearly interdependent foci.

First is the *population to be served*. We would focus here upon the characteristics of the population to be served, the problems faced by the population, and the degree to which these problems are mental health related. We are also concerned with the goals of mental health programs as they relate to and with the identified problems and with the health manpower available to attack these problems. This information will also be in a form suitable for assessing change and monitoring program effectiveness.

The second focus is the *clientele*. Although the mental health of all citizens of the state is the concern of a department of mental health, only a portion of the citizens are recipients of direct or indirect services, that is, become identified as clients. Information concerning clients, in the context of the population generally, can tell us much about our programs and our effectiveness. The focus here is upon the characteristics of the client population as these compare with the characteristics of the population as a whole.

Our third focus is the *organization*. Of primary concern here is the need to document the actual allocation of resources among many goals and demands within the organization, and to investigate sources of satisfaction as well as points of strain. This focus involves the organization of the area, the institutions, the regions, and the central office. These data will, of course, be fed into the key factor process.

As a fourth focus we concentrate on *articulation*. Our purpose here is to look at the articulation or joining of the various components of the system to see how this articulation is accomplished to form an overall system of mental health care. We are also looking at the articulation of components of the mental health system to various elements of the organizational environment. A final focus would be upon points of strain.

The relationships between the evaluation section and the management group that is using key factor analysis is crucial. Each helps sustain the other. Each complements the other. They are not separate parallel processes.

I hope that in describing our work I have been able to convey to you something more than the essence of a philosophy of management. I hope you sense the enthusiasm I feel regarding the work that we have undertaken. A formal approach to planning-evaluation is not an effort to be taken lightly. It requires planning; it requires resources; and it requires commitment from all parts of the organization that is frankly difficult to maintain.

The structure that I have outlined is not necessarily the only one wherein program evaluation can take place. Others will approach it differently, depending upon the uniqueness and variability of their own programs. But in whatever ways we may implement it, program evaluation must begin to permeate the entire mental health system. Only through this process can we begin to respond to the mandate that we are being given to optimize our operations in behalf of the mentally ill, the alcoholic, and the mentally retarded, and to obtain desired sensitivity to the mental health needs of our communities.

Notes

1.   Jarett, Irwin. *Key Factor Analysis: A Handbook*, Raleigh, N.C.: Jarett, Rader and Longhurst, 1970.
2.   Sinnott, Edmund W., *Cell and Psyche: The Biology of Purpose*, Chapel Hill, N.C.: The University of North Carolina Press, 1950, p. 20.

Index

Abendberg Institute, 82, 86

Abstention, as goal for alcoholics, xviii, 196

Accountability, 72, 80, 131, 144, 146, 182, 231, 239, 245, 267

Administration, of evaluation, 95, 98

Administrative uses, of evaluation, 169, 181, 239, 244, 248

Admissions, as impact indicator, 97, 99, 110*t*, 122

"After only" measurement, 46

Aggression, 17

Alcohol abuse measures, 14, 39, 41-45, 53, 150, 195

Alcohol abuse programs, 36, 37, 163, 192

Alcohol, Drug Abuse and Mental Health Administration (ADAMHA), xv, 28, 32, 36-38, 39, 45-48

Alcoholism, 161, 191-200; assessment problems, 17; treatment studies, 30, 125-126, 191, 198-199

Algorithms, for data transformation, 74

Alienation, 89

Allen, Vernon, 15

American Indian Alcohol programs, 192

American Institutes for Research, 56

Analytic models, for assessing treatment effects, 75-76

Annals of the American Academy of Political and Social Sciences, 59

Antabuse, 28, 36

APHA Report on Education and Training for Statisticians, 259-260, 263

APHA Statistics Section, 260

APHA Subcommittee on Educational Qualifications of Public Health Statisticians, 257-258

Armor, David, 194

Army Neuropsychiatric Screening Adjunct, 15-16

Assessment, of needs, 177, 182, 184

Attkisson, C. Clifford, 181-190

Attrition, 13, 48

Audit function, of service programs, 61, 69

Bahn, Anita, 258-259, 264

Baker, Frank, 51, 57, 61

Bauer, Raymond A., 59

Baxter, James, 213, 223

Beaulieu, Dean, 213, 223

Bed needs, 111

"Before-and-after" measurement, 46-47, 102. *See also* Traditional evaluation

Behavioral change, 5-6, 17, 21, 42

Bergin, A.E., 50, 56, 144

Bissonnette, R., 89*n*

Blane, Howard, 194

Bloom, B.L., 162, 172

Bockoven, J.S., 80*n*

Brogan, D.R., 261, 263

Burden on family, 100, 104-105, 112-116

California Five-County Study, 131-134

California Test of Personality, 54

Campbell, Donald T., 55, 59, 205

Caro, F., 50, 56

Case-registers, 104, 128. *See also* Registers, psychiatric

Catchment areas, 38-39, 48, 161, 163

Categorization, of evaluation studies, xvi, 5

Census data, 37, 105, 162, 164, 171, 183, 271

Chichester and District Community Service, 96 passim

Children, 81, 113, 119, 171

Client data, 133, 167, 193-194, 271. *See also* Information systems

Client identification, 65, 73

Clinical judgement, 43

Clinical objectives, 104; irrelevance of to evaluation research, 11, 35, 121

Clinical outcomes, 106, 113*t*, 115*t*, 121, 123

Clinical trials, 48, 89*n*

Cochrane, A.L., 12

CODAP (Client Oriented Data Acquisition Process), 207

Coding, 73

Cohort design, 72

273

List of Contributors

C. Clifford Attkisson, Ph.D. is associated with the Langley Porter Neuropsychiatric Institute, San Francisco, California.

Daniel B. Fishman, Ph.D., is associate director of the Adams County Mental Health Center, Commerce City, Colorado.

Elmer A. Gardner, M.D., was formerly director of the Psychiatric Case Register and chairman of a committee that recently studied the reorganization of the Alcoholism, Drug Abuse, and Mental Health Administration. He is currently in the private practice of psychiatry.

Ellen B. Gold, M.A., is with the Department of Epidemiology, School of Public Health, Johns Hopkins University.

Marshall R. Hanson, Ph.D., is head of Evaluation Resources Branch, Department of Health, State of California, Sacramento, California.

William A. Hargreaves, Ph.D., is associate professor of psychology in residence at Langley Porter Institute, San Francisco, California.

Eugene A. Hargrove, M.D., is professor of psychiatry and behavioral sciences at The George Washington University, Washington, D.C.

Thomas J. Kiresuk, Ph.D., is director and principal investigator, Program Evaluation Project, Hennepin County Mental Health Center, Minneapolis, Minnesota.

Adeline Levine, Ph.D., is professor and chairman of the Department of Sociology at State University of New York, Buffalo, New York.

Murray Levine, Ph.D., is a professor of psychology at State University of New York, Buffalo, New York.

Sander H. Lund, is assistant director, Program Evaluation Project, Hennepin County Mental Health Center, Minneapolis, Minnesota.

Paul McCullough, Ph.D. is director of the Manpower Development for Program Analysis, Western Interstate Commission for Higher Education, Boulder, Colorado.

Margaret H. McIntyre, is associated with the Langley Porter Neuropsychiatric Institute, San Francisco, California.

David Mechanic, Ph.D., is John Bascomb Professor of the Department of Sociology, University of Wisconsin, Madison, Wisconsin.

B.J. Morrison, M.S.S.W., is program evaluation officer of the River Region Mental Health/Mental Retardation Board, Louisville, Kentucky.

Selma J. Mushkin, is director of the Public Service Laboratory at Georgetown University, Washington, D.C.

Donald G. Patterson, is program analyst, Office of Program Development and Analysis, NIAAA, Rockville, Maryland.

Peter Sainsbury, M.D., is director and consultant psychiatrist, Medical Research Council, Clinical Psychiatry Unit, Graylingwell Hospital, Chichester, Sussex, Great Britain.

S.B. Sells, Ph.D., is research professor and director of the Institute of Behavioral Research at Texas Christian University, Fort Worth, Texas.

Larry M. Siegel, is a research associate at Langley Porter Neuropsychiatric Institute, San Francisco, California.

William G. Smith, M.D., is Professor of Psychiatry, Rockford School of Medicine, University of Illinois, and Consultant to the Singer Zone Center, Rockford, Illinois.

Martin Sundel, Ph.D. is research director of the River Region Mental Health/ Mental Retardation Board, Louisville, Kentucky.

Carol H. Weiss, is with the Bureau of Applied Social Research at Columbia University, New York, New York.

Daniel M. Wilner, Ph.D., is professor of Public Health and Social and Preventive Medicine at UCLA Center for Health Sciences, Los Angeles, California.

About the Editors

Jack Zusman is Medical Director, Gateways Hospital, Los Angeles. He received the A.B. from Columbia College, the M.A. in psychology from Indiana University, the M.D. from Albert Einstein College of Medicine, and the M.P.H. from Columbia University School of Public Health. Dr. Zusman was a Postdoctoral Fellow in Law and Psychology at Stanford Law School. After eight years with the U.S. Public Health Service, he joined the faculty of School of Medicine, State University of New York at Buffalo. Until recently he was Professor of Psychiatry, Director of the Division of Community Psychiatry and Adjunct Professor of Law and Psychiatry there. Dr. Zusman has coauthored one book and edited three books in addition to this one.

Cecil R. Wurster is Chief, Statistical Program Development Branch, Division of Biometry, National Institute of Mental Health. He received the B.S. in Management at Louisiana State University, and the M.A. in Psychology from Louisiana State University. From 1952 to 1954 Mr. Wurster was a research psychologist with the U.S. Air Force. From 1954 to 1962 he was Chief, Division of Research, at Louisiana State Department of Hospitals. Mr. Wurster has also written numerous articles in professional journals.